BLOODSHOT

D0470191

SETTING
THE WORLD
ON FIRE

DUANE SWIERCZYNSKI | MANUEL GARCIA | ARTURO LOZZI

CONTENTS

Collection Cover Art: Arturo Lozzi

Assistant Editor: Josh Johns (#1-2)
Associate Editor: Jody LeHeup
Editor: Warren Simons

VALIANT.

Peter Cuneo
Chairman

Dinesh Shamdasani
CEO & Chief Creative Officer

Gavin Cuneo
Chief Operating Officer & CFO

Fred Pierce
Publisher

Warren Simons
VP Editor-in-Chief

Walter Black
VP Operations

Hunter Gorinson
Director of Marketing,
Communications & Digital Media

Atom! Freeman
Director of Sales

Matthew Klein
Andy Liegl
John Petrie
Sales Managers

Josh Johns
Associate Director of Digital Media and Development

Travis Escarfullery
Jeff Walker
Production & Design Managers

Tom Brennan
Editor

Kyle Andrukiewicz
Editor and Creative Executive

Peter Stern
Publishing & Operations Manager

Andrew Steinbeiser
Marketing & Communications Manager

Danny Khazem
Editorial Operations Manager

Ivan Cohen
Collection Editor

Steve Blackwell
Collection Designer

Lauren Hitzhusen
Editorial Assistant

Rian Hughes/Device
Trade Dress & Book Design

Russell Brown
President, Consumer Products,
Promotions and Ad Sales

Geeta Singh
Licensing Manager

DUANE SWIERCZYNSKI | MANUEL GARCIA | ARTURO LOZZI | STEFANO GAUDIANO

BLOODSHOT®

VALIANT

#1

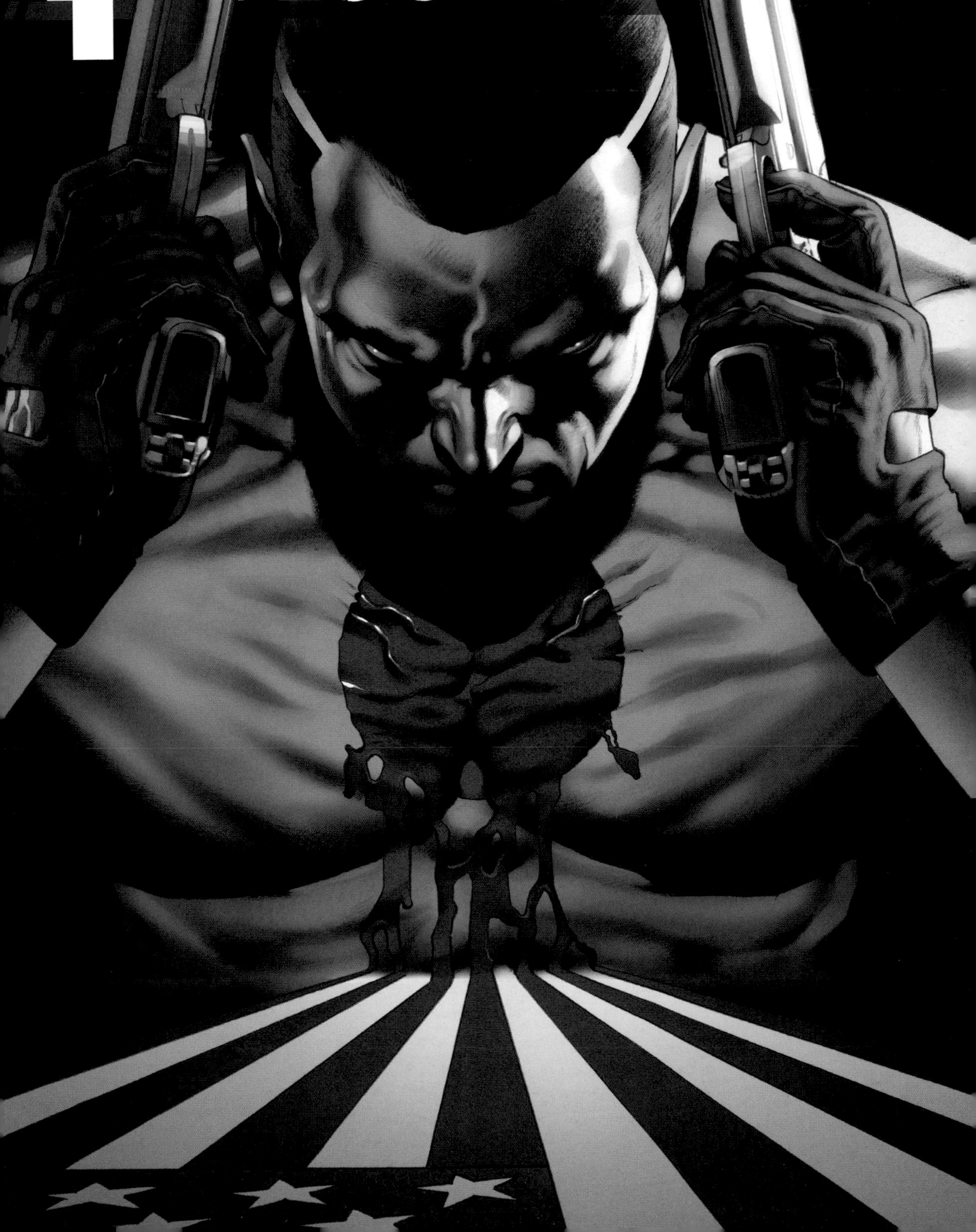

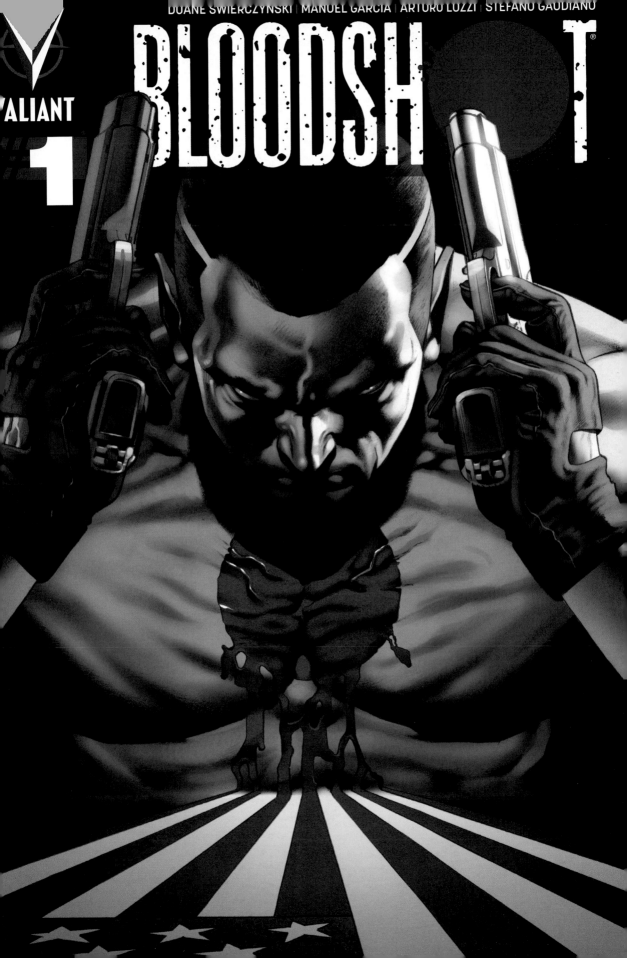

Project: BLOODSHOT

ADVANCED NANITE CAPABILITY OVERVIEW

Basic Information

- A nanite is a robot the size of a nanometer or smaller. A single human hair is 25,000 nanites wide.
- Bloodshot has billions of these microscopic machines coursing through his bloodstream. These nanites are programmed to assist Bloodshot with his various missions.
- Biomolecular nanotech motors enhance Bloodshot's strength, speed and reaction time beyond the limits of a normal human.
- Due to a nanite's ability to create, manipulate and destroy matter on a subatomic level, the true limits of Bloodshot's abilities are unknown.

Medical Applications

- Bloodshot's nanites possess the ability to reconnect torn skin, arteries, muscle tissue and nerve fibers; rebuild bone; and repair and reconstruct damaged organs to allow for rapid and complete recovery from extreme traumatic injury.
- Nano-manipulation of physiological responses allows Bloodshot to survive extended exposure to hostile and toxic environments, including extremes of heat and cold, high atmospheric pressure, low-oxygen environments and long-term lack of food and water.
- Sub-cellular repair capabilities restore and restart metabolic processes in terminally damaged tissue.

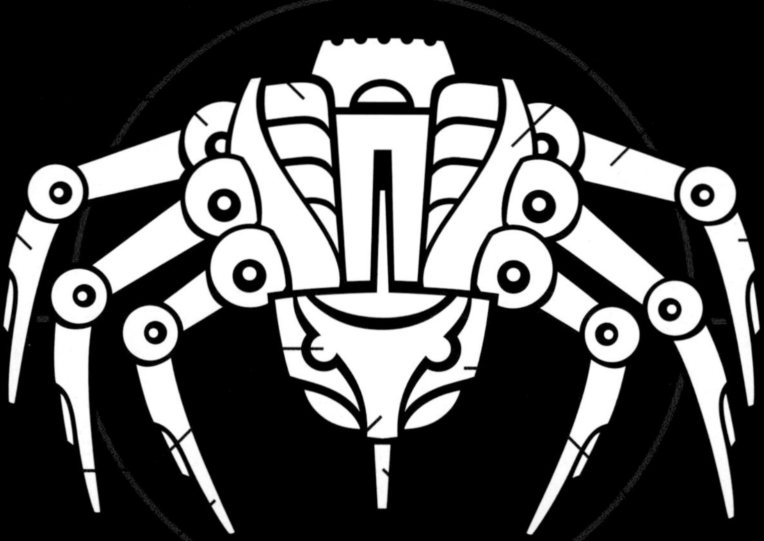

Military Applications

- Nanite implants expand the range of sensory function, extending hearing into the ultrasonic and sight into the infrared and ultraviolet ranges. Additionally, nanites can detect chemical weapons, explosives and radioactive emissions.
- The nanites' full control over cellular structures allows Bloodshot to shape-shift or "morph" for limited periods of time.
- Neuron-nanite quantum interface allows Bloodshot to receive, transmit, and manipulate electromagnetic wavelengths and frequencies and directly interface with and control electronic and computerized machinery.

Possible Dangers

- Although it is highly unlikely, hostile forces with their own nanotechnology could theoretically hack and reprogram the nanites inside of Bloodshot should he ever be captured by the enemy.
- Some scientists fear that molecular self-assembly could allow nanites to replicate uncontrollably. The effect this would have on Bloodshot is unknown.
- The aforementioned potential for nanites to self-replicate is also the basis for the apocalyptic "Grey Goo" theory. This is the idea that self-replicating nanites mass producing uncontrollably could form an ever-growing wave of "Grey Goo" that would devour all matter on Earth.

Design: Rian Hughes

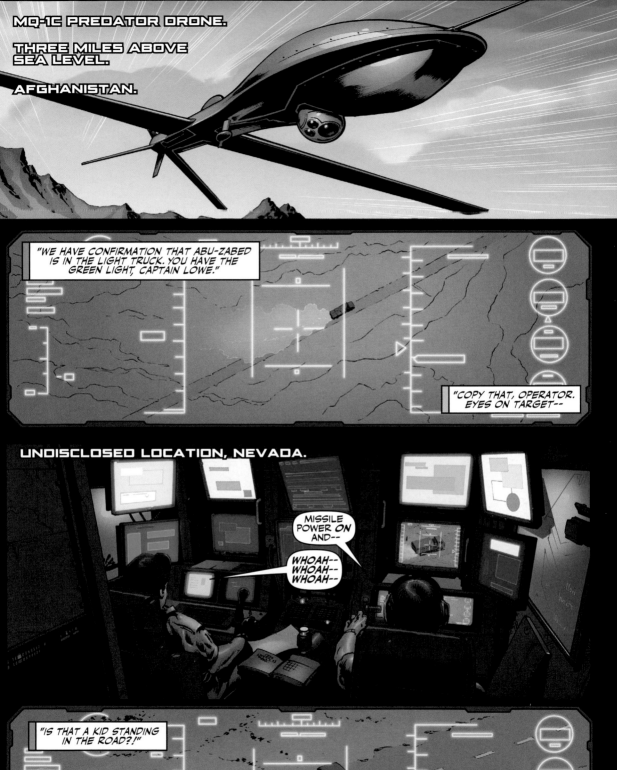

MQ-1C PREDATOR DRONE.

THREE MILES ABOVE
SEA LEVEL.

AFGHANISTAN.

"WE HAVE CONFIRMATION THAT ABU-ZABED IS IN THE LIGHT TRUCK. YOU HAVE THE GREEN LIGHT, CAPTAIN LOWE."

"COPY THAT, OPERATOR. EYES ON TARGET--

UNDISCLOSED LOCATION, NEVADA.

MISSILE POWER ON AND--

WHOAH-- WHOAH-- WHOAH--

"IS THAT A KID STANDING IN THE ROAD?!"

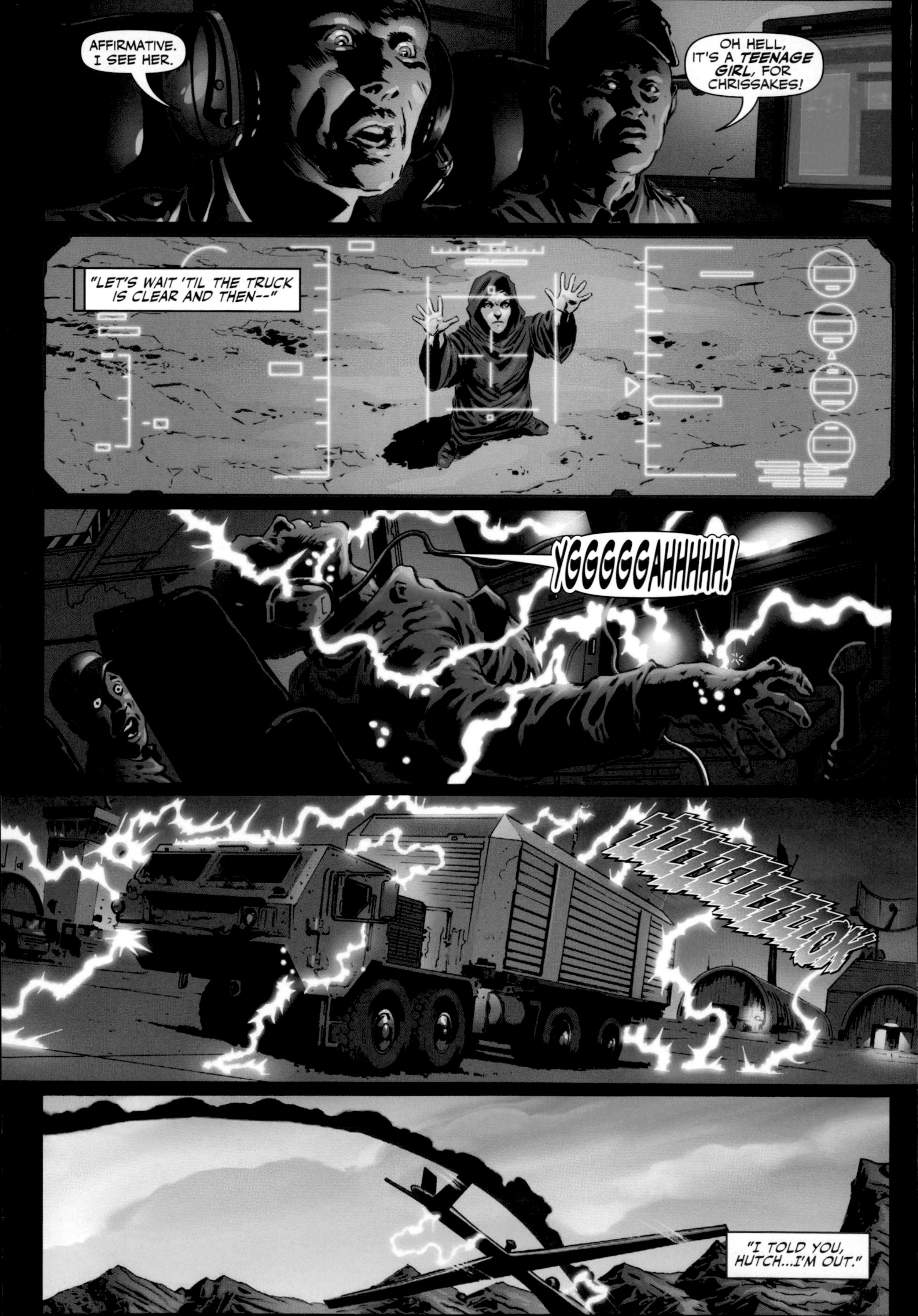
AFFIRMATIVE. I SEE HER.
OH HELL, IT'S A TEENAGE GIRL, FOR CHRISSAKES!
"LET'S WAIT 'TIL THE TRUCK IS CLEAR AND THEN--"
YGGGGGAHHHHH!
"I TOLD YOU, HUTCH...I'M OUT."

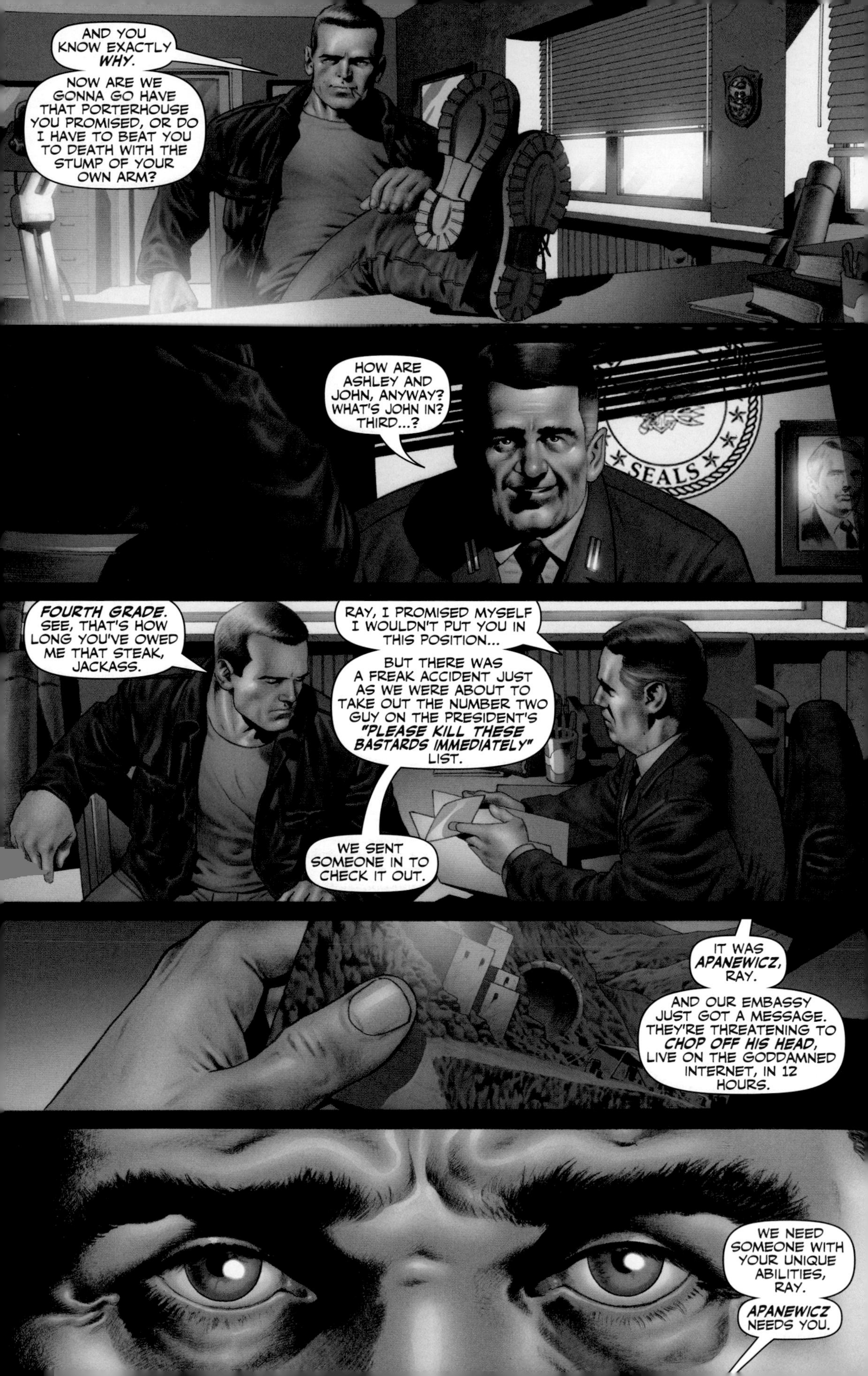
AND YOU KNOW EXACTLY WHY.
NOW ARE WE GONNA GO HAVE THAT PORTERHOUSE YOU PROMISED, OR DO I HAVE TO BEAT YOU TO DEATH WITH THE STUMP OF YOUR OWN ARM?
HOW ARE ASHLEY AND JOHN, ANYWAY? WHAT'S JOHN IN? THIRD...?
SEALS
FOURTH GRADE. SEE, THAT'S HOW LONG YOU'VE OWED ME THAT STEAK, JACKASS.
RAY, I PROMISED MYSELF I WOULDN'T PUT YOU IN THIS POSITION...
BUT THERE WAS A FREAK ACCIDENT JUST AS WE WERE ABOUT TO TAKE OUT THE NUMBER TWO GUY ON THE PRESIDENT'S "PLEASE KILL THESE BASTARDS IMMEDIATELY" LIST.
WE SENT SOMEONE IN TO CHECK IT OUT.
IT WAS APANEWICZ, RAY.
AND OUR EMBASSY JUST GOT A MESSAGE. THEY'RE THREATENING TO CHOP OFF HIS HEAD, LIVE ON THE GODDAMNED INTERNET, IN 12 HOURS.
WE NEED SOMEONE WITH YOUR UNIQUE ABILITIES, RAY.
APANEWICZ NEEDS YOU.

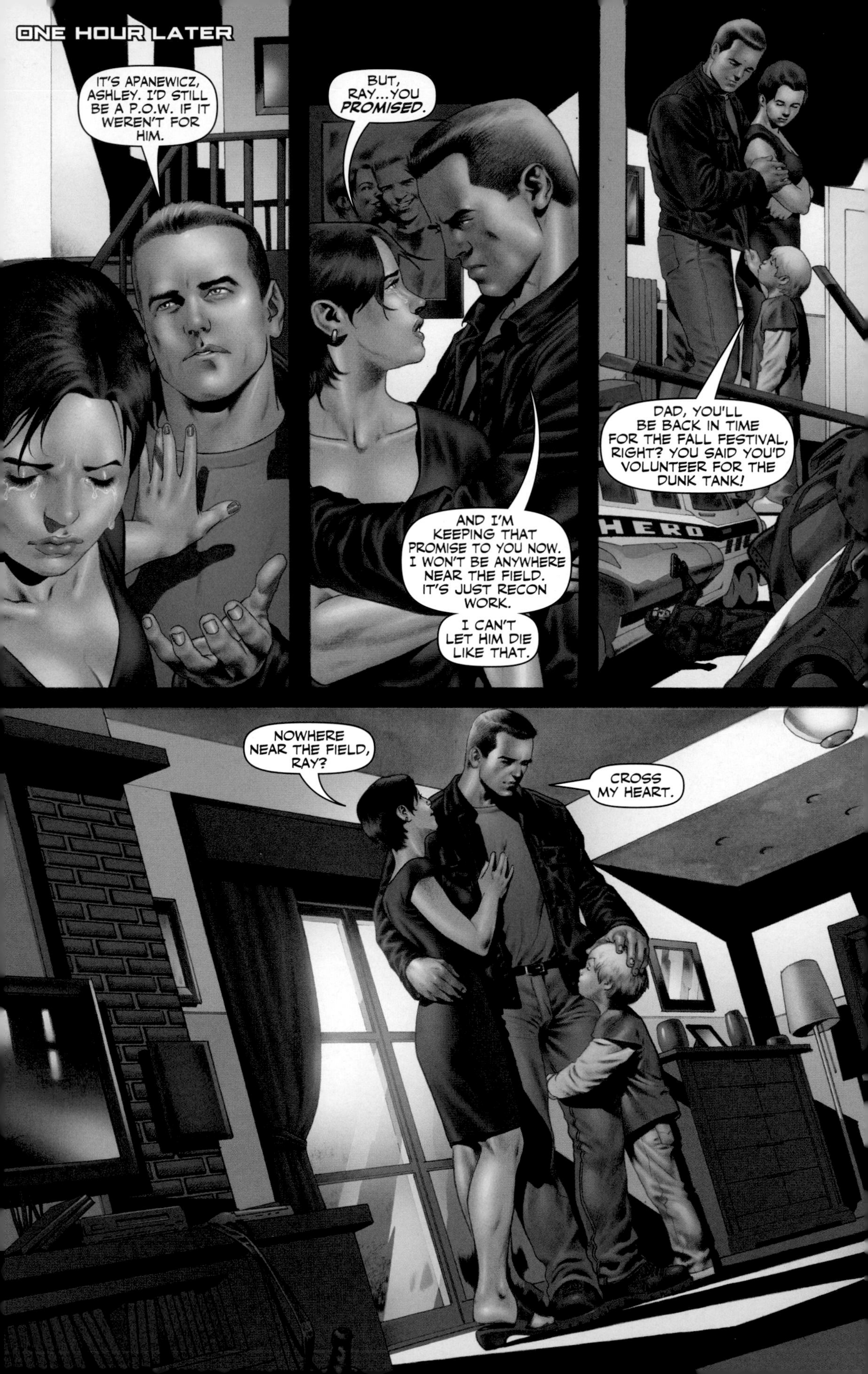
ONE HOUR LATER
IT'S APANEWICZ, ASHLEY. I'D STILL BE A P.O.W. IF IT WEREN'T FOR HIM.
BUT, RAY...YOU *PROMISED*.
AND I'M KEEPING THAT PROMISE TO YOU NOW. I WON'T BE ANYWHERE NEAR THE FIELD. IT'S JUST RECON WORK.
I CAN'T LET HIM DIE LIKE THAT.
DAD, YOU'LL BE BACK IN TIME FOR THE FALL FESTIVAL, RIGHT? YOU SAID YOU'D VOLUNTEER FOR THE DUNK TANK!
HERO
NOWHERE NEAR THE FIELD, RAY?
CROSS MY HEART.

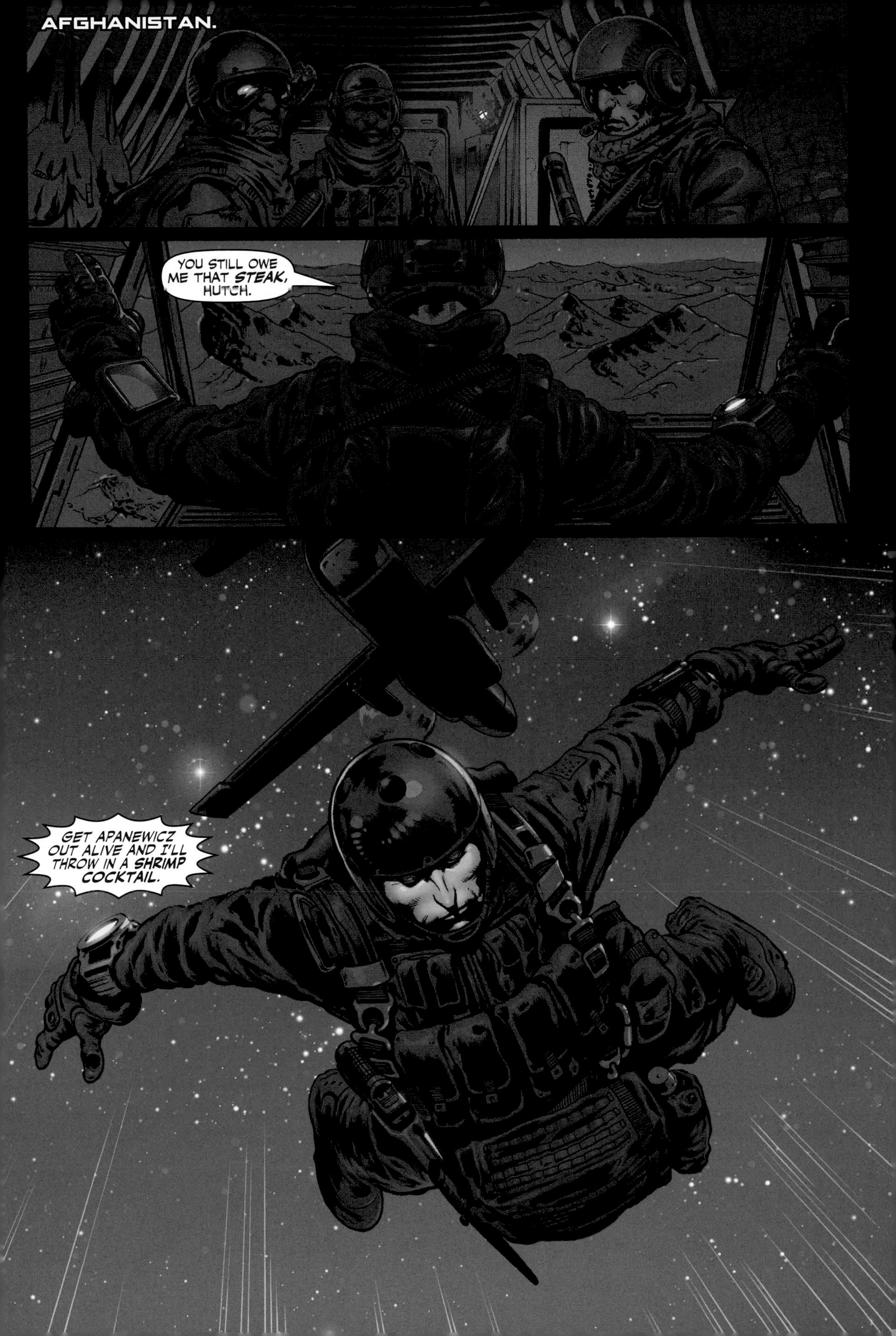
AFGHANISTAN.
YOU STILL OWE ME THAT STEAK, HUTCH.
GET APANEWICZ OUT ALIVE AND I'LL THROW IN A SHRIMP COCKTAIL.

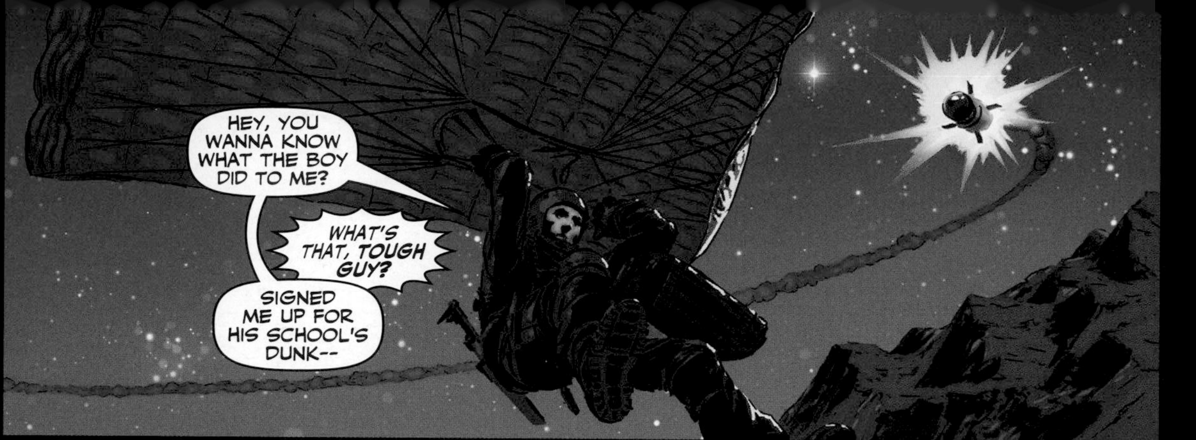

HEY, YOU WANNA KNOW WHAT THE BOY DID TO ME?
WHAT'S THAT, TOUGH GUY?
SIGNED ME UP FOR HIS SCHOOL'S DUNK--

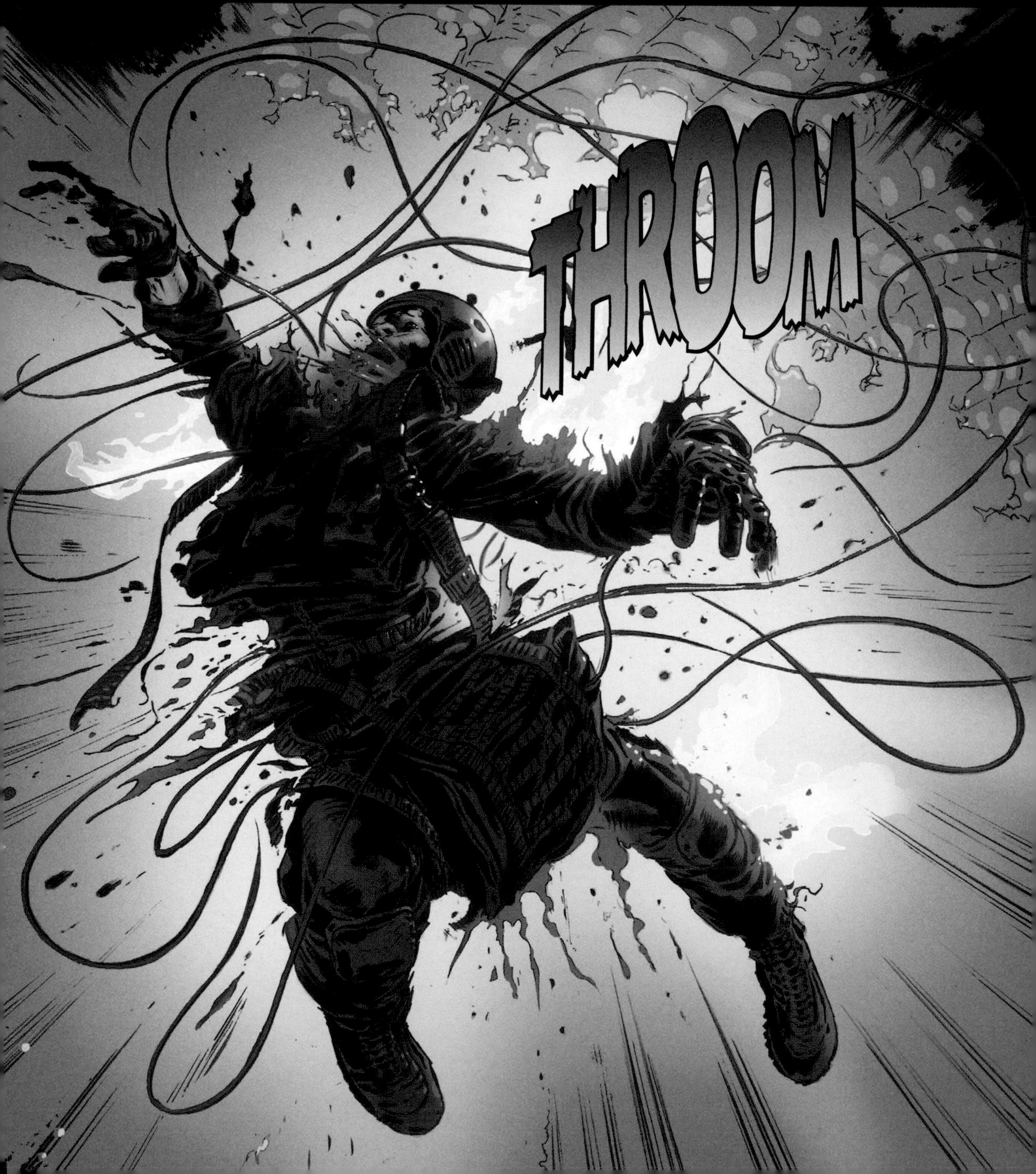

THROOM

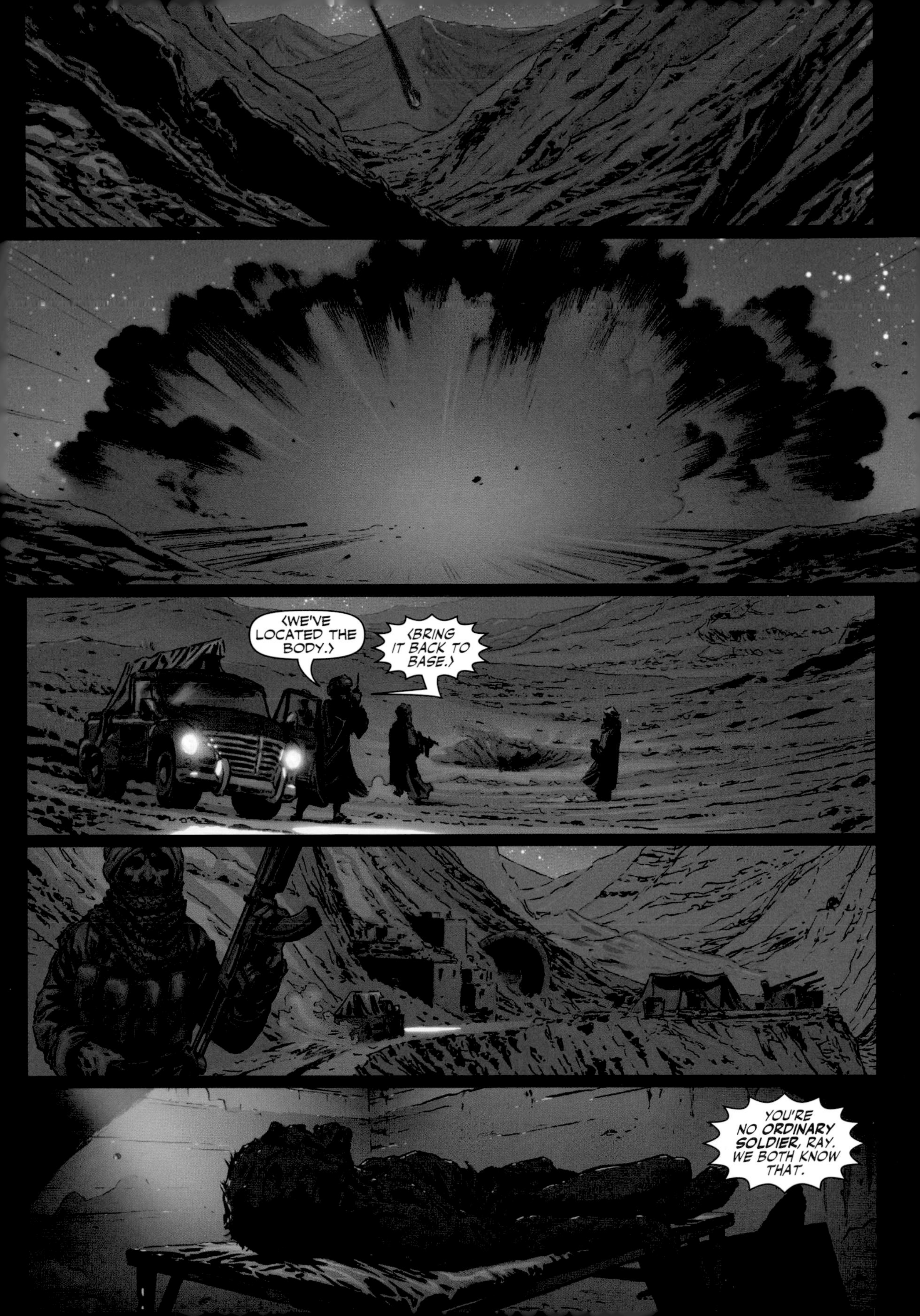
<WE'VE LOCATED THE BODY.>
<BRING IT BACK TO BASE.>
YOU'RE NO ORDINARY SOLDIER, RAY. WE BOTH KNOW THAT.

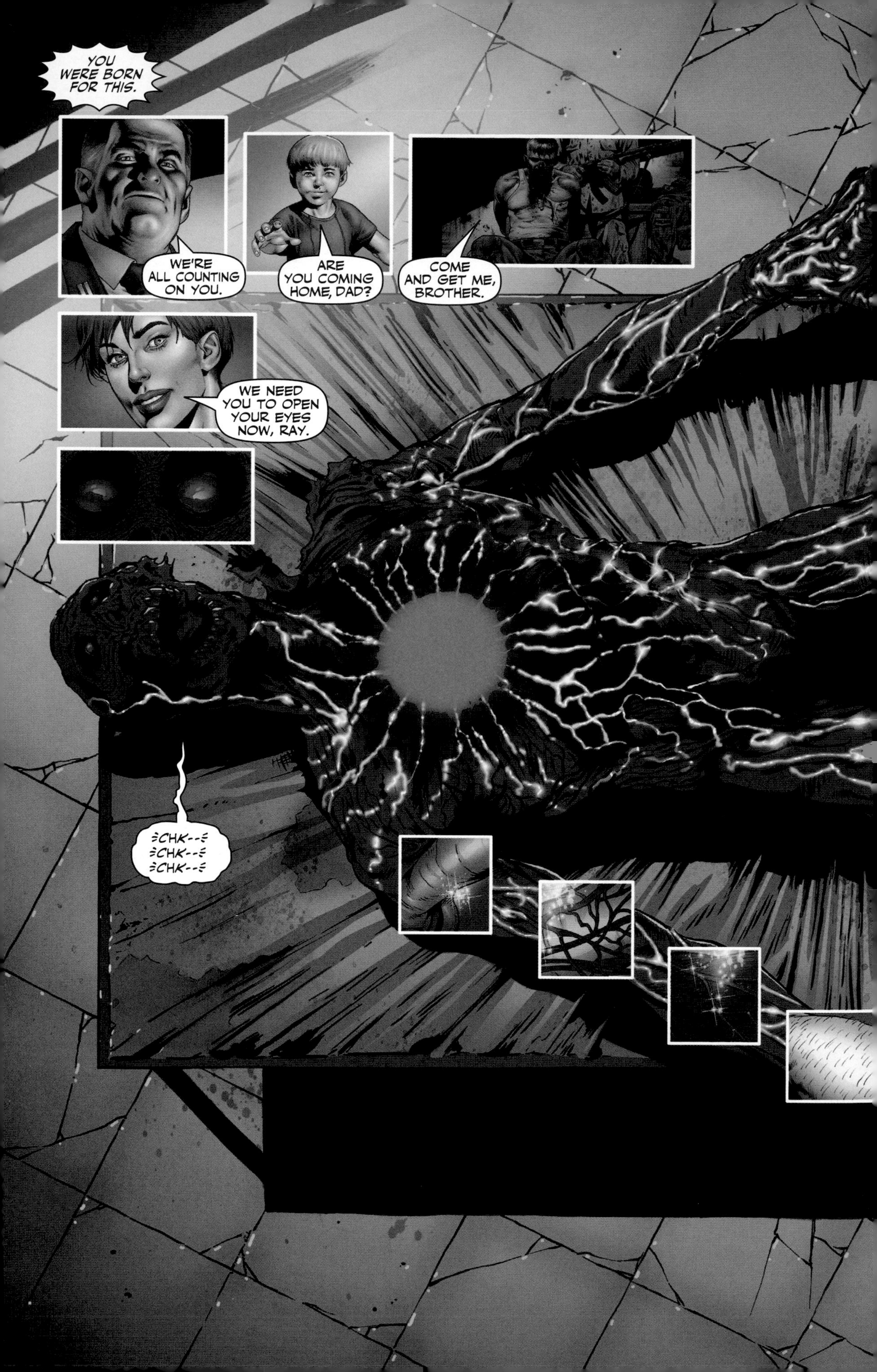
YOU WERE BORN FOR THIS.
WE'RE ALL COUNTING ON YOU.
ARE YOU COMING HOME, DAD?
COME AND GET ME, BROTHER.
WE NEED YOU TO OPEN YOUR EYES NOW, RAY.
CHK-- CHK-- CHK--

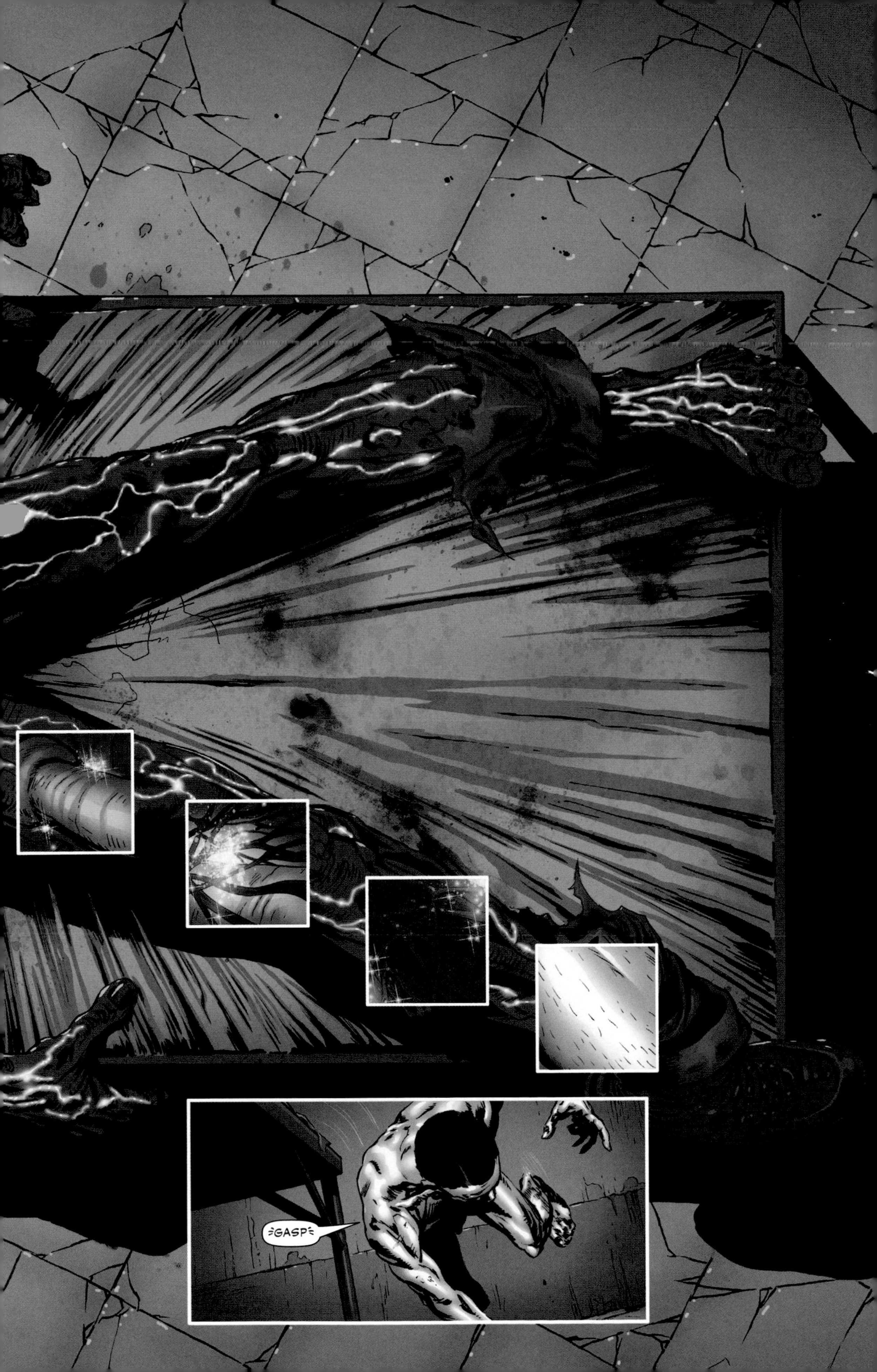
GASP

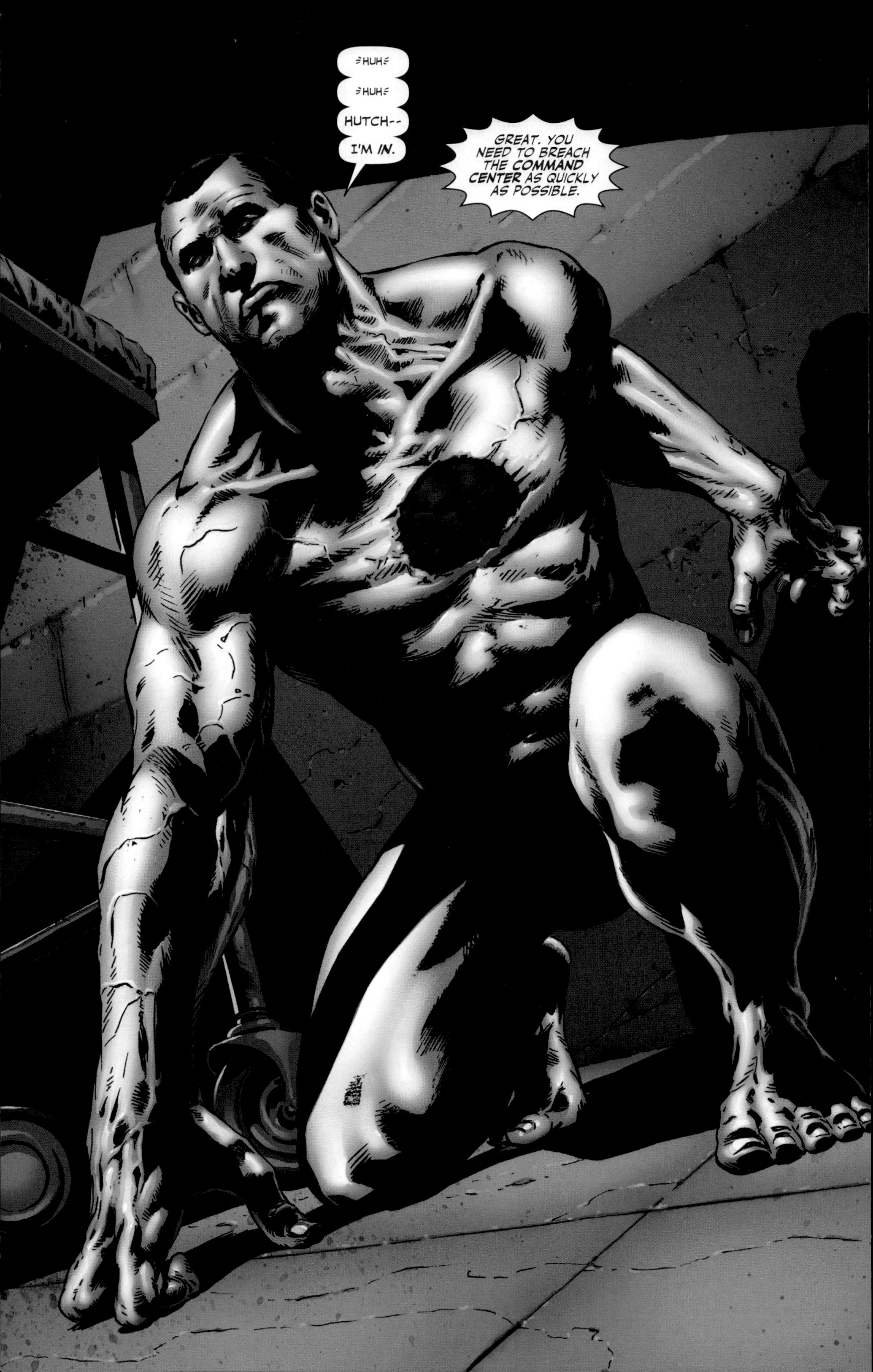

HUH
HUH
HUTCH--
I'M *IN*.
GREAT. YOU NEED TO BREACH THE **COMMAND CENTER** AS QUICKLY AS POSSIBLE.

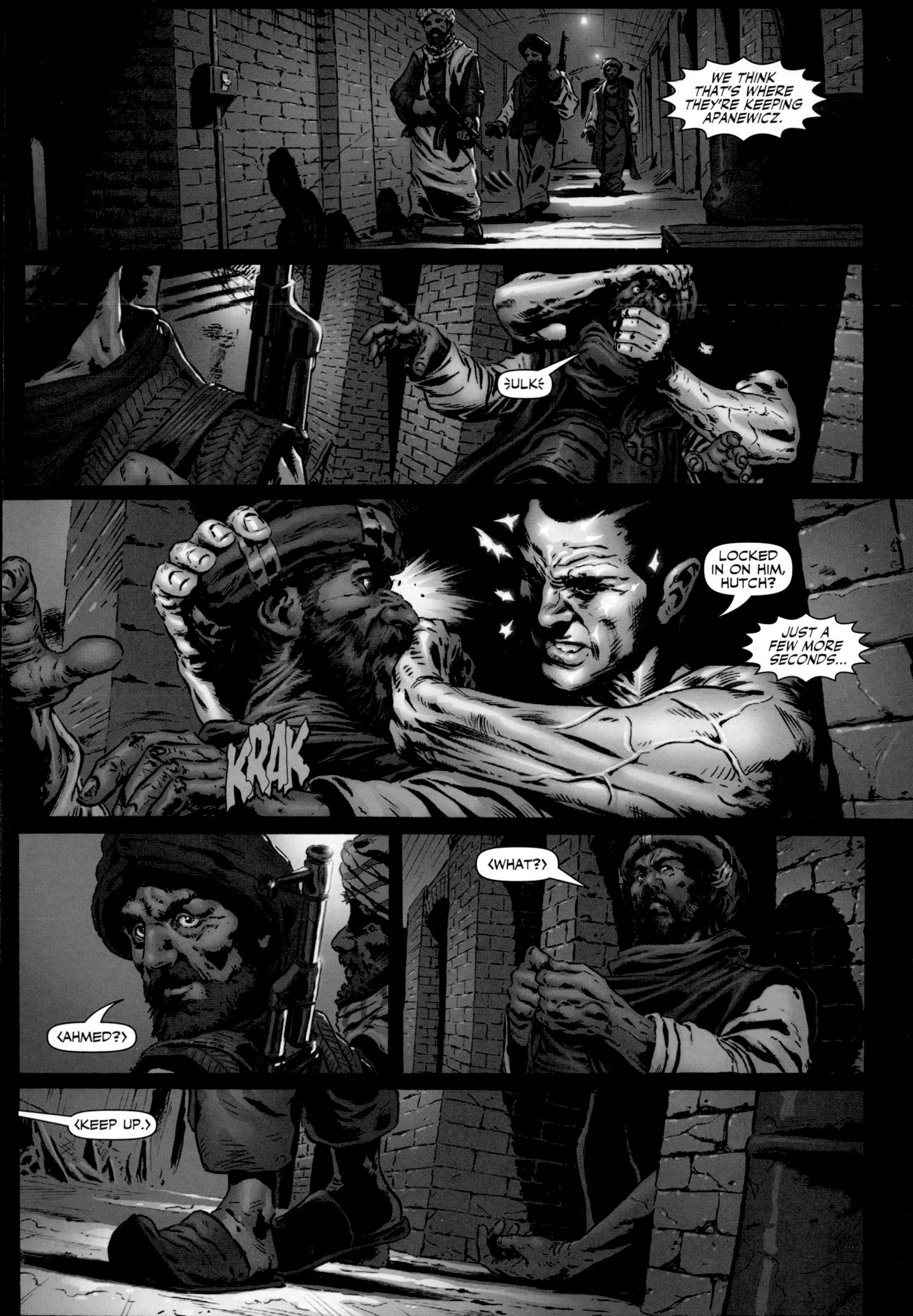
WE THINK THAT'S WHERE THEY'RE KEEPING APANEWICZ.
ULK
LOCKED IN ON HIM, HUTCH?
JUST A FEW MORE SECONDS...
KRAK
‹AHMED?›
‹WHAT?›
‹KEEP UP.›

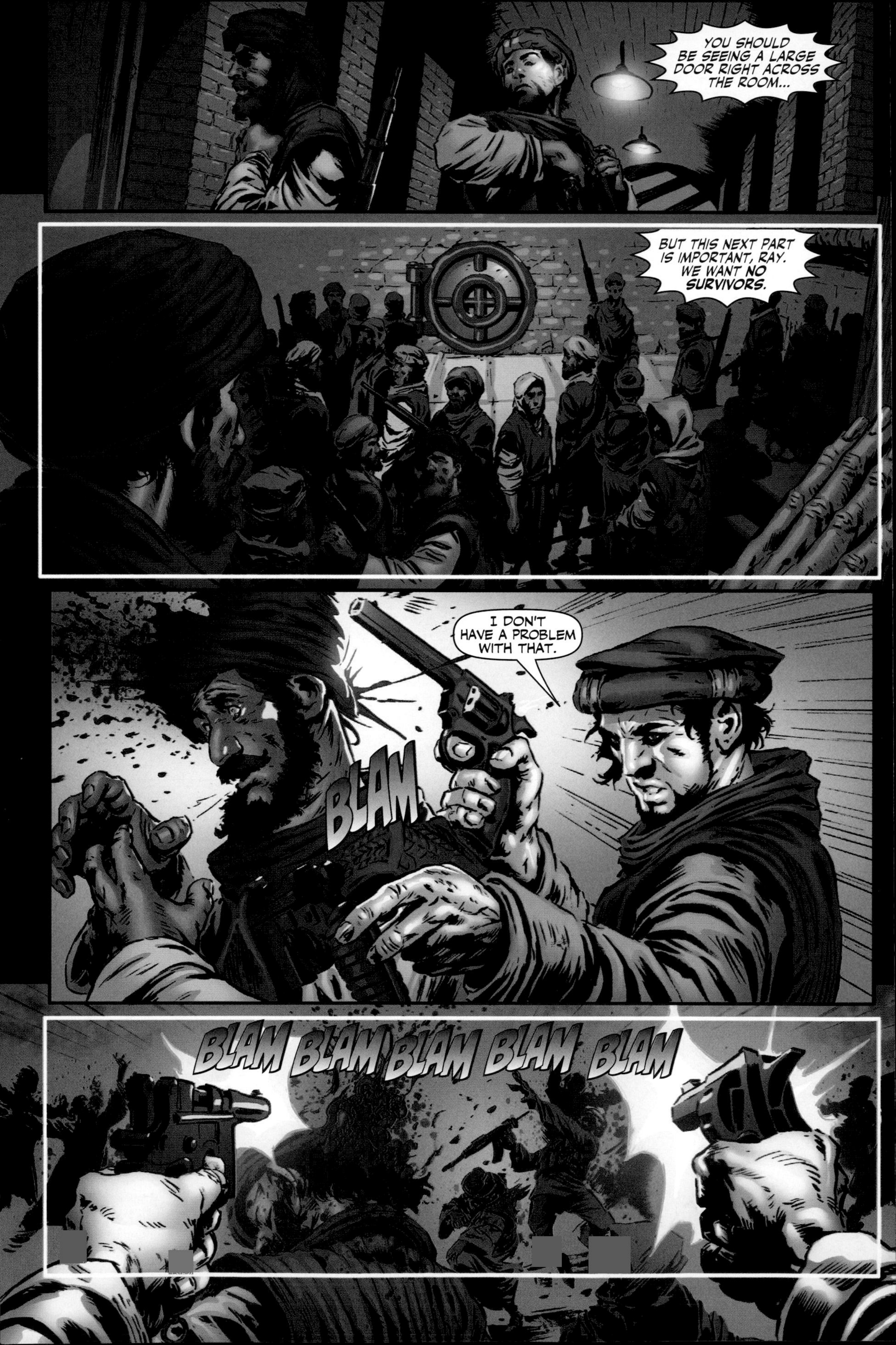
YOU SHOULD BE SEEING A LARGE DOOR RIGHT ACROSS THE ROOM...
BUT THIS NEXT PART IS IMPORTANT, RAY. WE WANT NO SURVIVORS.
I DON'T HAVE A PROBLEM WITH THAT.
BLAM
BLAM BLAM BLAM BLAM BLAM

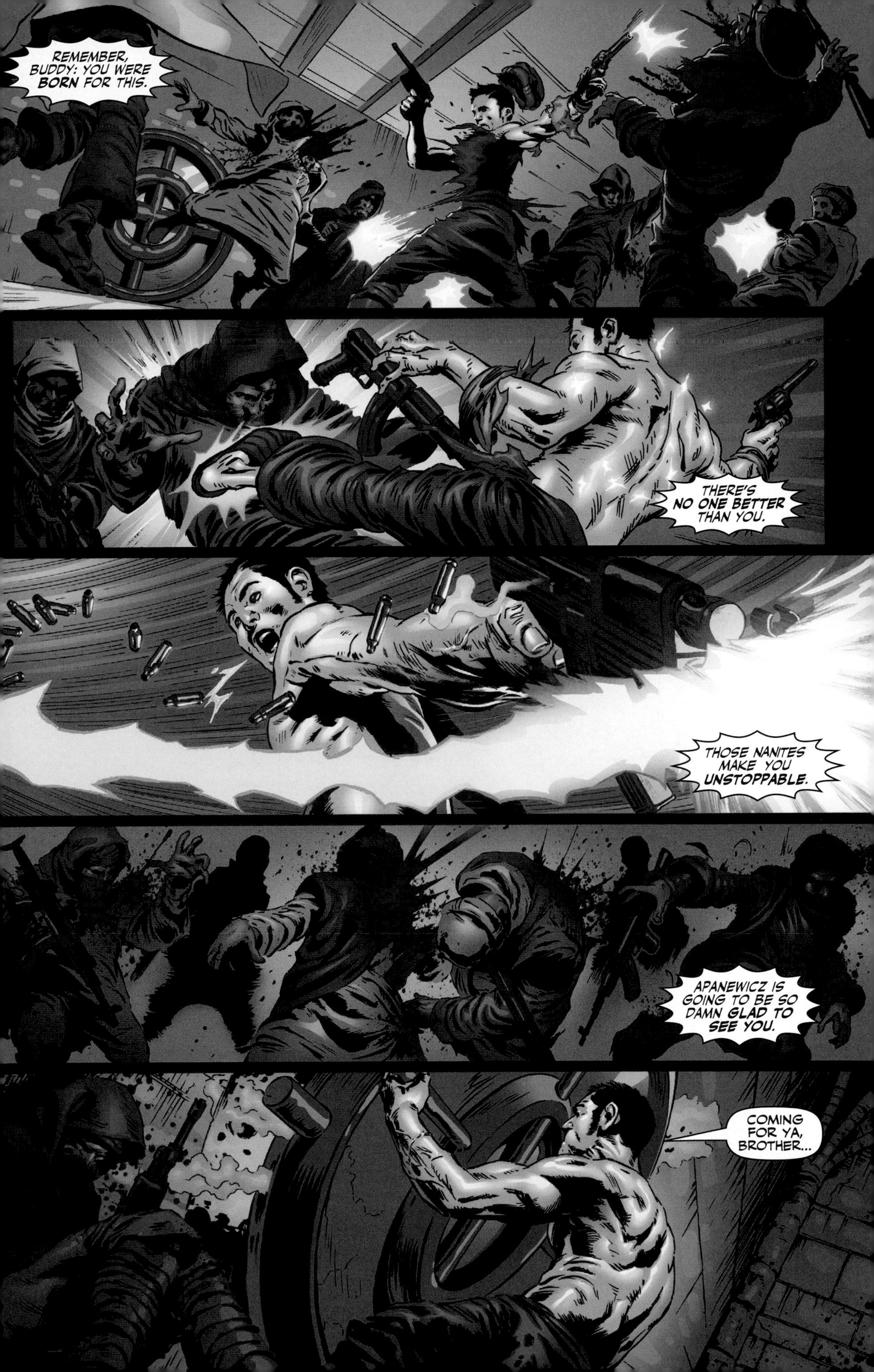
REMEMBER, BUDDY: YOU WERE BORN FOR THIS.
THERE'S NO ONE BETTER THAN YOU.
THOSE NANITES MAKE YOU UNSTOPPABLE.
APANEWICZ IS GOING TO BE SO DAMN GLAD TO SEE YOU.
COMING FOR YA, BROTHER...

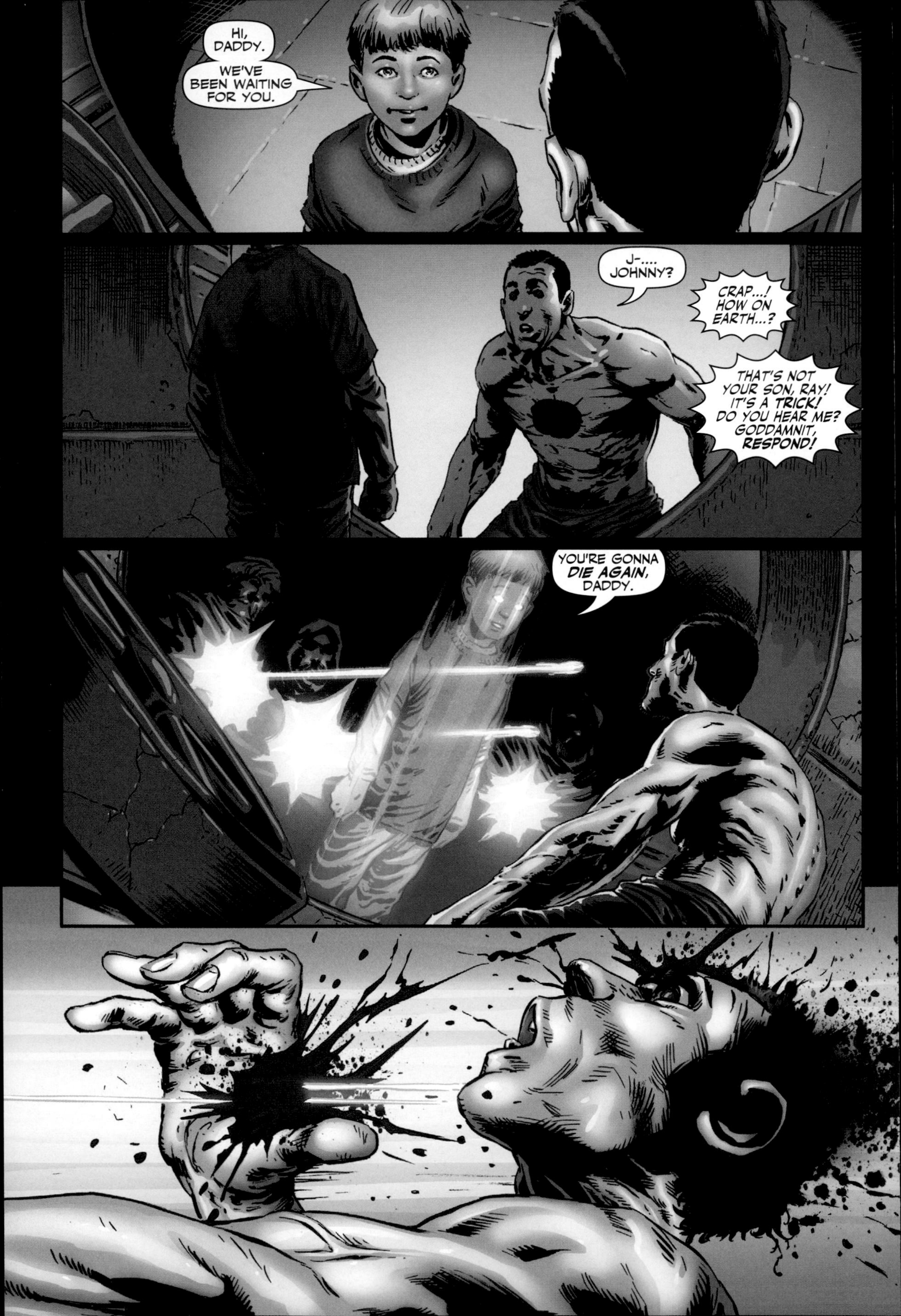
HI, DADDY.
WE'VE BEEN WAITING FOR YOU.
J-.... JOHNNY?
CRAP...! HOW ON EARTH...?
THAT'S NOT YOUR SON, RAY! IT'S A **TRICK!** DO YOU HEAR ME? GODDAMNIT, **RESPOND!**
YOU'RE GONNA ***DIE AGAIN,*** DADDY.

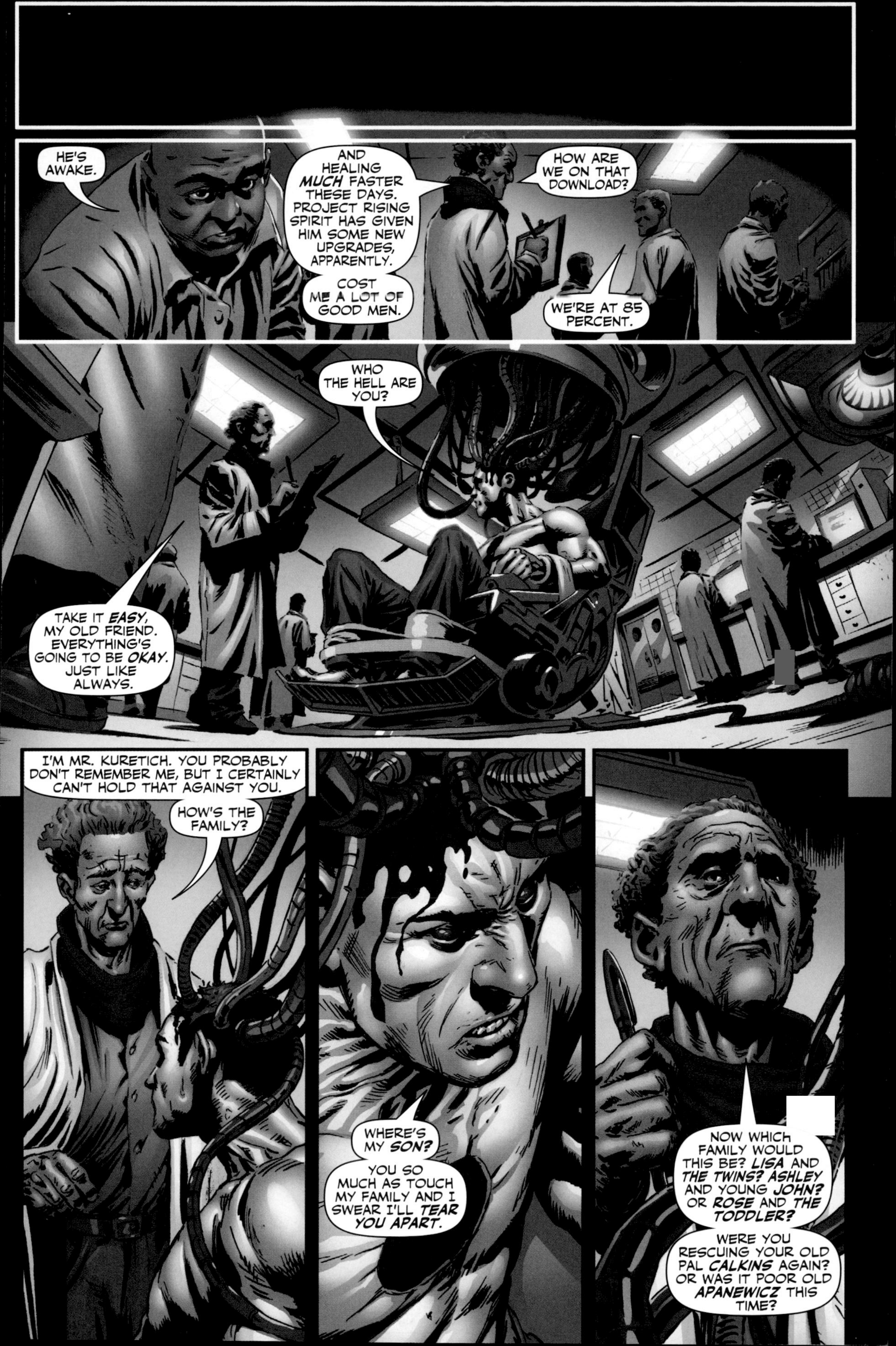
HE'S AWAKE.
AND HEALING *MUCH* FASTER THESE DAYS. PROJECT RISING SPIRIT HAS GIVEN HIM SOME NEW UPGRADES, APPARENTLY.
COST ME A LOT OF GOOD MEN.
HOW ARE WE ON THAT DOWNLOAD?
WE'RE AT 85 PERCENT.
WHO THE HELL ARE YOU?
TAKE IT *EASY*, MY OLD FRIEND. EVERYTHING'S GOING TO BE *OKAY*. JUST LIKE ALWAYS.
I'M MR. KURETICH. YOU PROBABLY DON'T REMEMBER ME, BUT I CERTAINLY CAN'T HOLD THAT AGAINST YOU.
HOW'S THE FAMILY?
WHERE'S MY *SON?*
YOU SO MUCH AS TOUCH MY FAMILY AND I SWEAR I'LL *TEAR YOU APART*.
NOW WHICH FAMILY WOULD THIS BE? *LISA* AND *THE TWINS? ASHLEY* AND YOUNG *JOHN?* OR *ROSE* AND *THE TODDLER?*
WERE YOU RESCUING YOUR OLD PAL *CALKINS* AGAIN? OR WAS IT POOR OLD *APANEWICZ* THIS TIME?

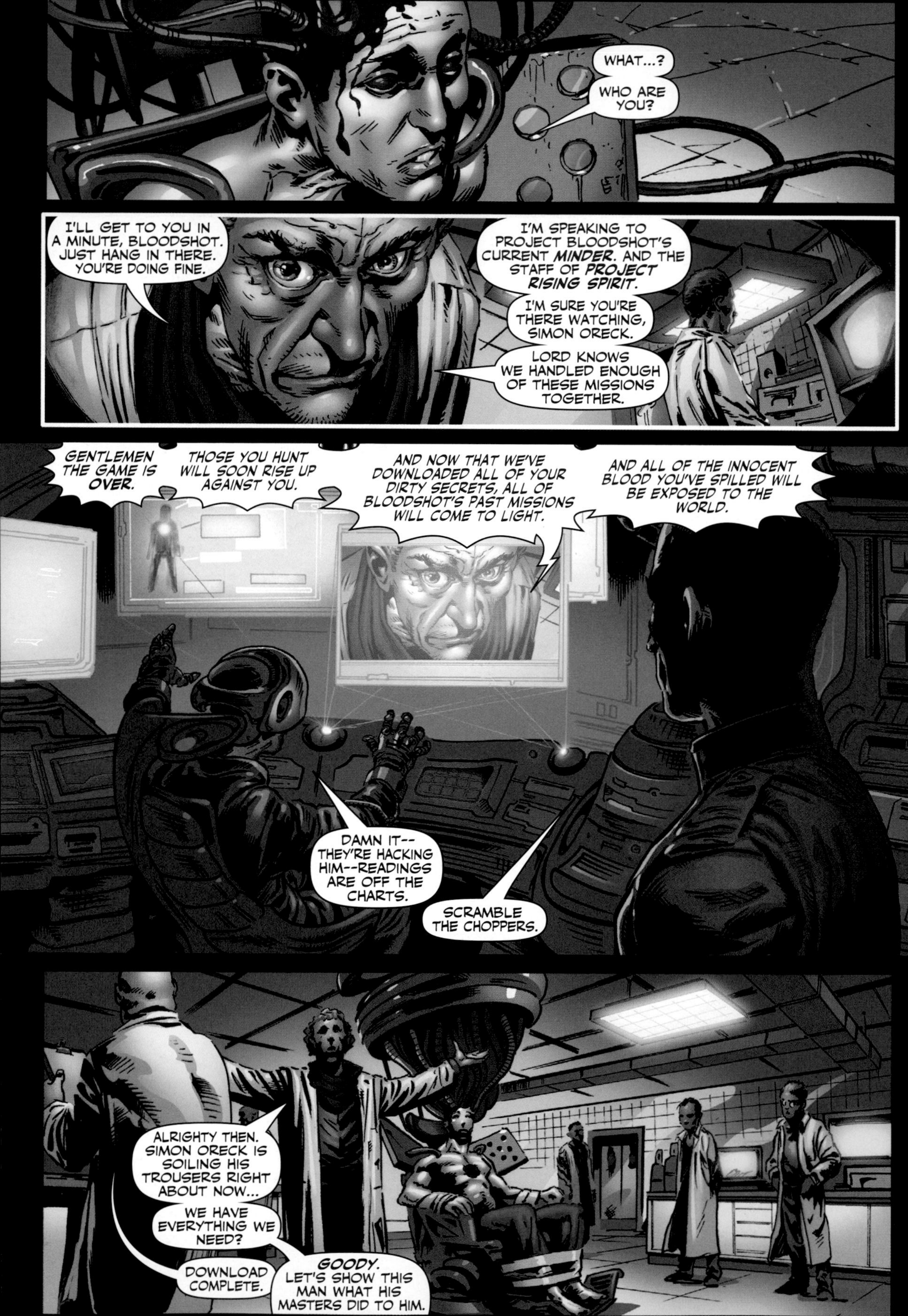
WHAT...?
WHO ARE YOU?
I'LL GET TO YOU IN A MINUTE, BLOODSHOT. JUST HANG IN THERE. YOU'RE DOING FINE.
I'M SPEAKING TO PROJECT BLOODSHOT'S CURRENT *MINDER*. AND THE STAFF OF *PROJECT RISING SPIRIT*.
I'M SURE YOU'RE THERE WATCHING, SIMON ORECK.
LORD KNOWS WE HANDLED ENOUGH OF THESE MISSIONS TOGETHER.
GENTLEMEN THE GAME IS **OVER**.
THOSE YOU HUNT WILL SOON RISE UP AGAINST YOU.
AND NOW THAT WE'VE DOWNLOADED ALL OF YOUR DIRTY SECRETS, ALL OF BLOODSHOT'S PAST MISSIONS WILL COME TO LIGHT.
AND ALL OF THE INNOCENT BLOOD YOU'VE SPILLED WILL BE EXPOSED TO THE WORLD.
DAMN IT-- THEY'RE HACKING HIM--READINGS ARE OFF THE CHARTS.
SCRAMBLE THE CHOPPERS.
ALRIGHTY THEN. SIMON ORECK IS SOILING HIS TROUSERS RIGHT ABOUT NOW...
WE HAVE EVERYTHING WE NEED?
DOWNLOAD COMPLETE.
GOODY. LET'S SHOW THIS MAN WHAT HIS MASTERS DID TO HIM.

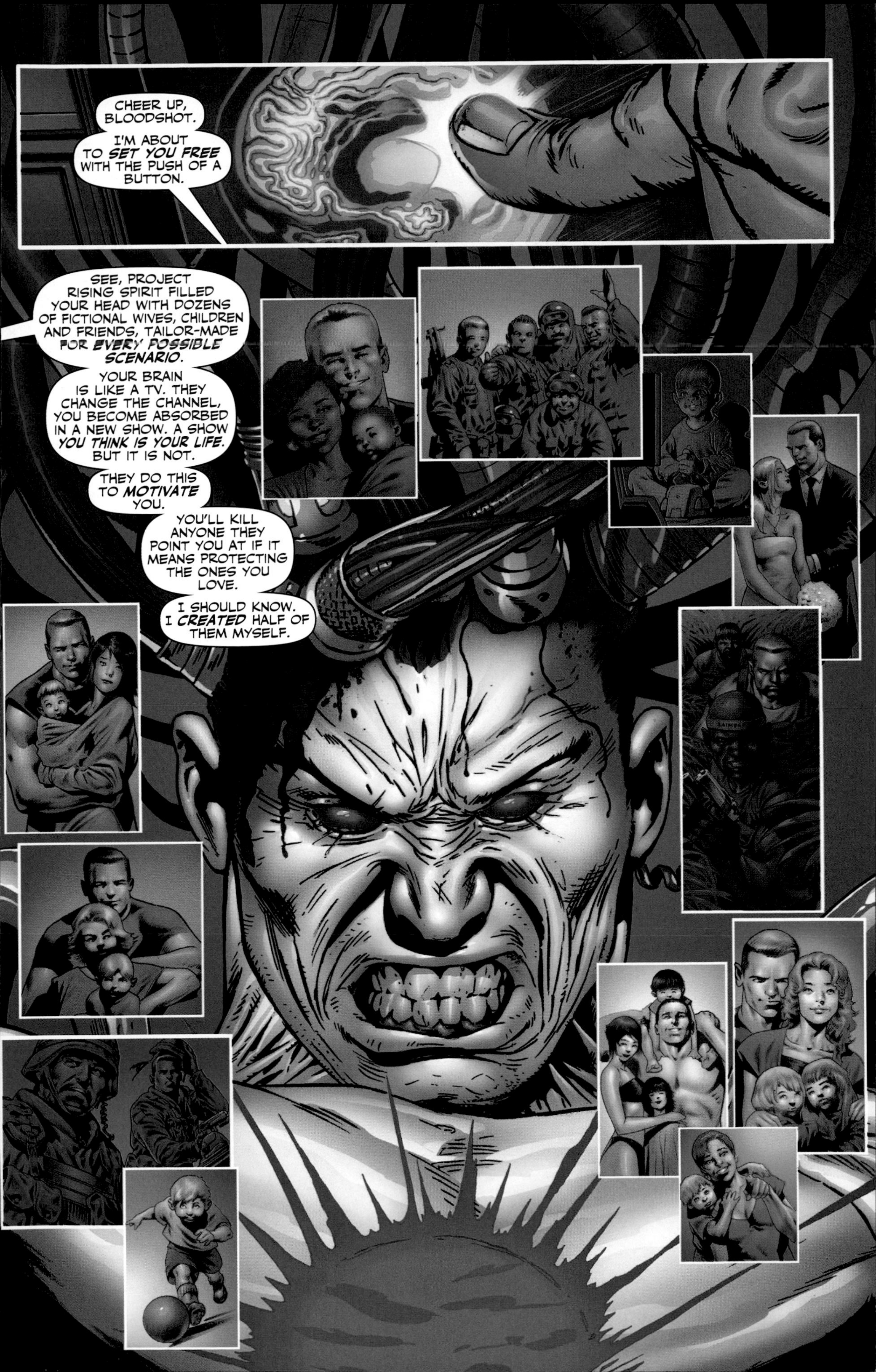
CHEER UP, BLOODSHOT.
I'M ABOUT TO SET YOU FREE WITH THE PUSH OF A BUTTON.
SEE, PROJECT RISING SPIRIT FILLED YOUR HEAD WITH DOZENS OF FICTIONAL WIVES, CHILDREN AND FRIENDS, TAILOR-MADE FOR EVERY POSSIBLE SCENARIO.
YOUR BRAIN IS LIKE A TV. THEY CHANGE THE CHANNEL, YOU BECOME ABSORBED IN A NEW SHOW. A SHOW YOU THINK IS YOUR LIFE. BUT IT IS NOT.
THEY DO THIS TO MOTIVATE YOU.
YOU'LL KILL ANYONE THEY POINT YOU AT IF IT MEANS PROTECTING THE ONES YOU LOVE.
I SHOULD KNOW. I CREATED HALF OF THEM MYSELF.

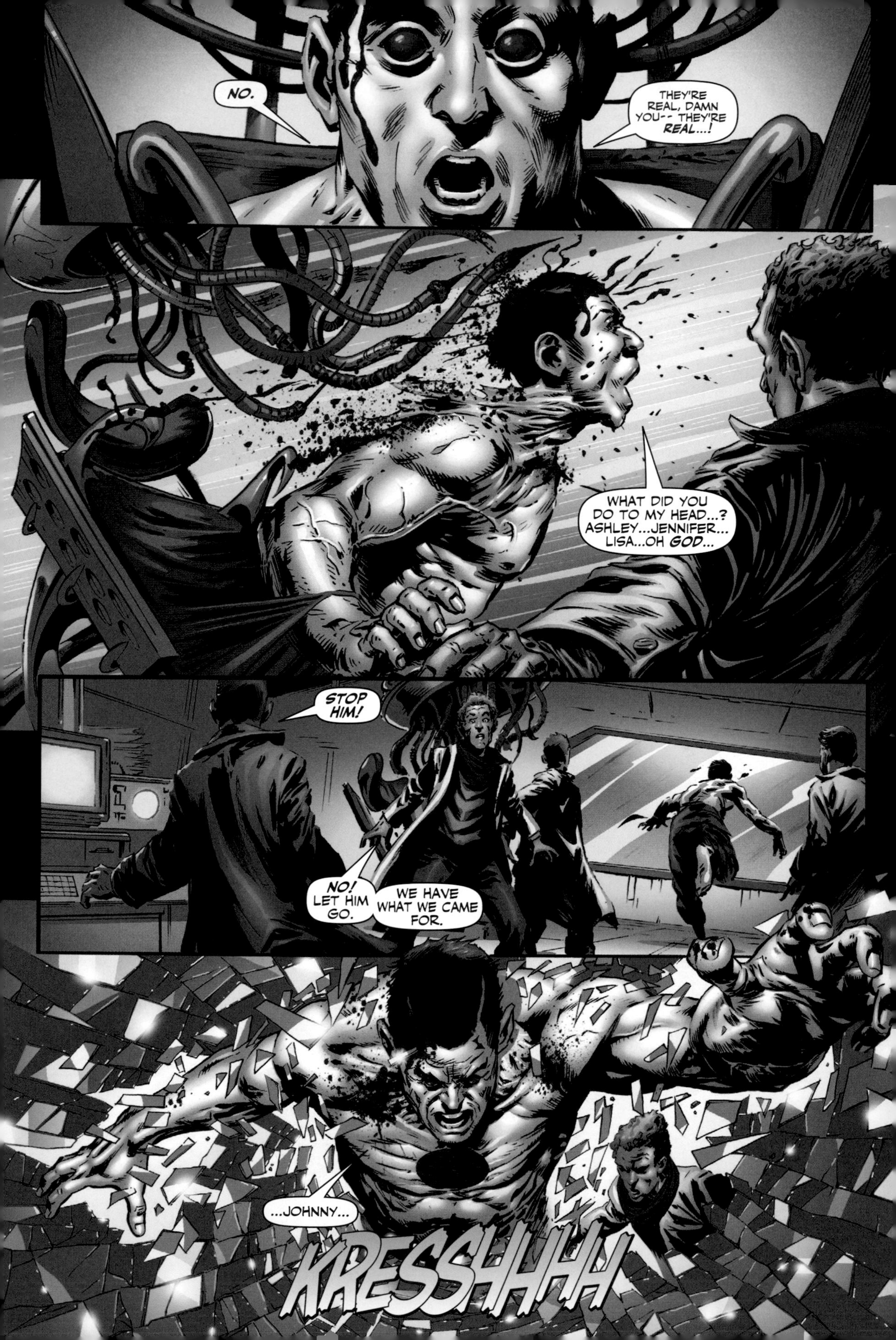

NO.
THEY'RE REAL, DAMN YOU-- THEY'RE REAL...!
WHAT DID YOU DO TO MY HEAD...? ASHLEY...JENNIFER... LISA...OH GOD...
STOP HIM!
NO! LET HIM GO.
WE HAVE WHAT WE CAME FOR.
...JOHNNY...
KRESSHHH

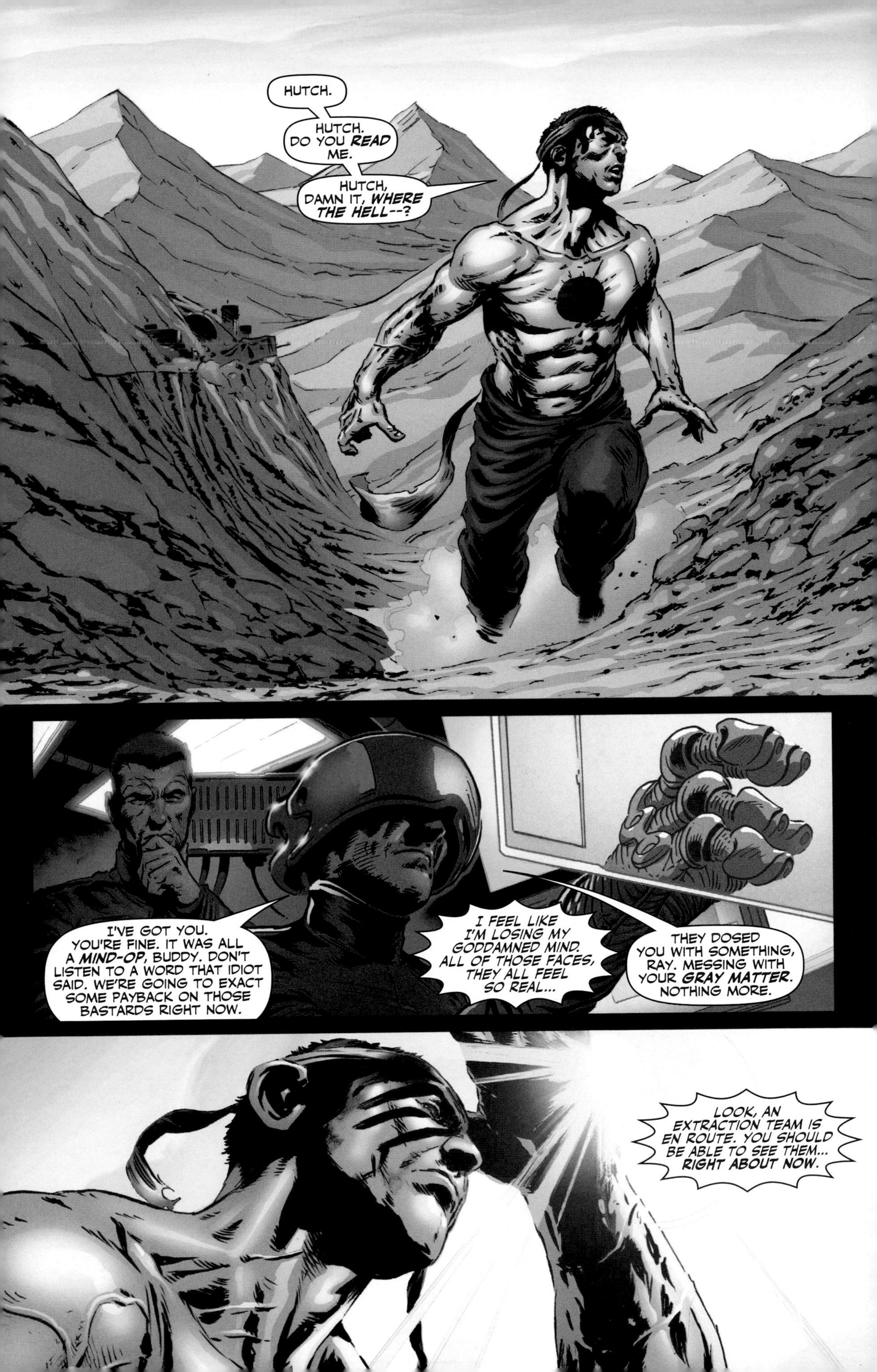
HUTCH.
HUTCH. DO YOU READ ME.
HUTCH, DAMN IT, WHERE THE HELL--?
I'VE GOT YOU. YOU'RE FINE. IT WAS ALL A MIND-OP, BUDDY. DON'T LISTEN TO A WORD THAT IDIOT SAID. WE'RE GOING TO EXACT SOME PAYBACK ON THOSE BASTARDS RIGHT NOW.
I FEEL LIKE I'M LOSING MY GODDAMNED MIND. ALL OF THOSE FACES, THEY ALL FEEL SO REAL...
THEY DOSED YOU WITH SOMETHING, RAY. MESSING WITH YOUR GRAY MATTER. NOTHING MORE.
LOOK, AN EXTRACTION TEAM IS EN ROUTE. YOU SHOULD BE ABLE TO SEE THEM... RIGHT ABOUT NOW.

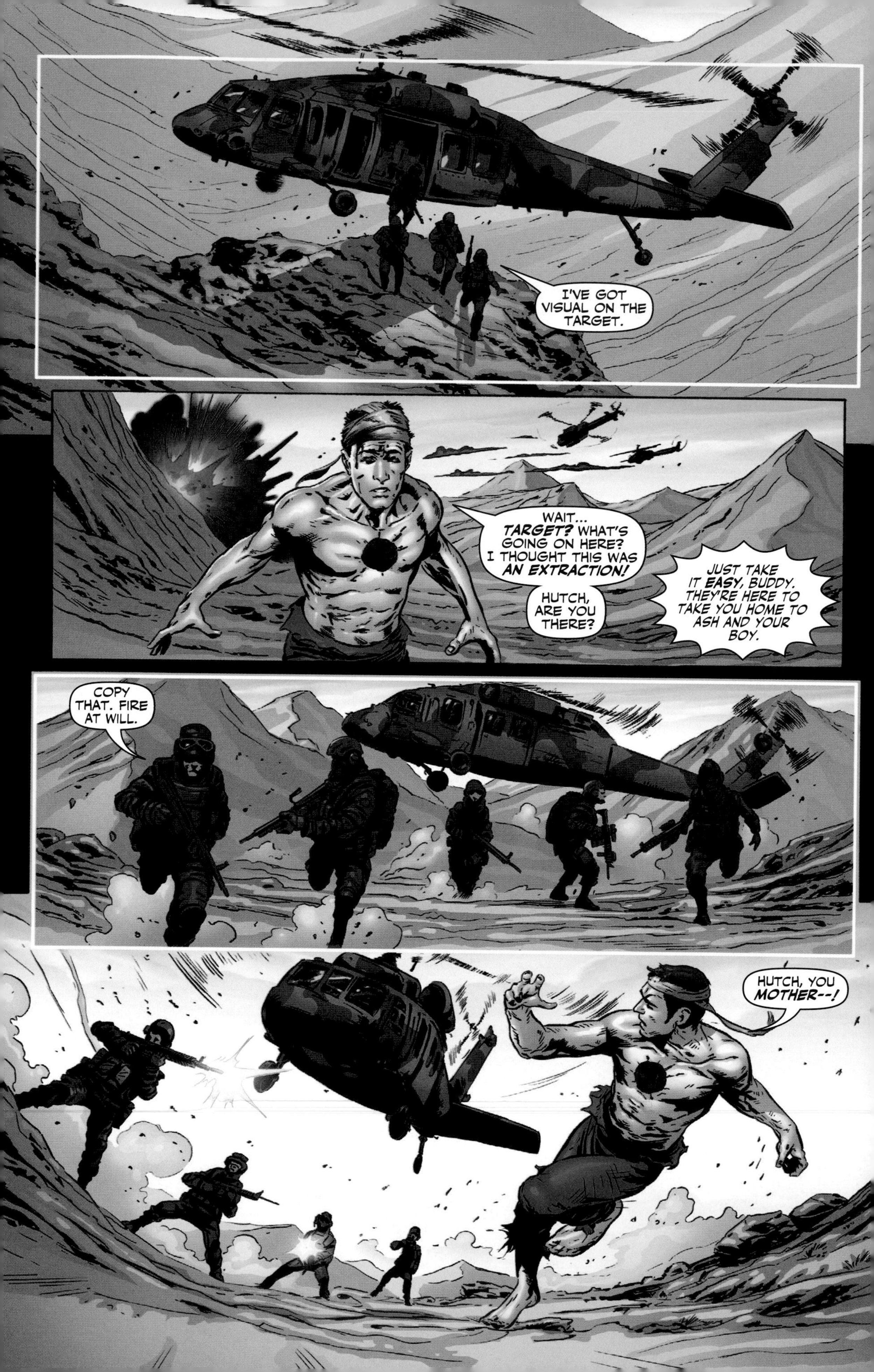
I'VE GOT VISUAL ON THE TARGET.
WAIT... TARGET? WHAT'S GOING ON HERE? I THOUGHT THIS WAS AN EXTRACTION!
HUTCH, ARE YOU THERE?
JUST TAKE IT EASY, BUDDY. THEY'RE HERE TO TAKE YOU HOME TO ASH AND YOUR BOY.
COPY THAT. FIRE AT WILL.
HUTCH, YOU MOTHER--!

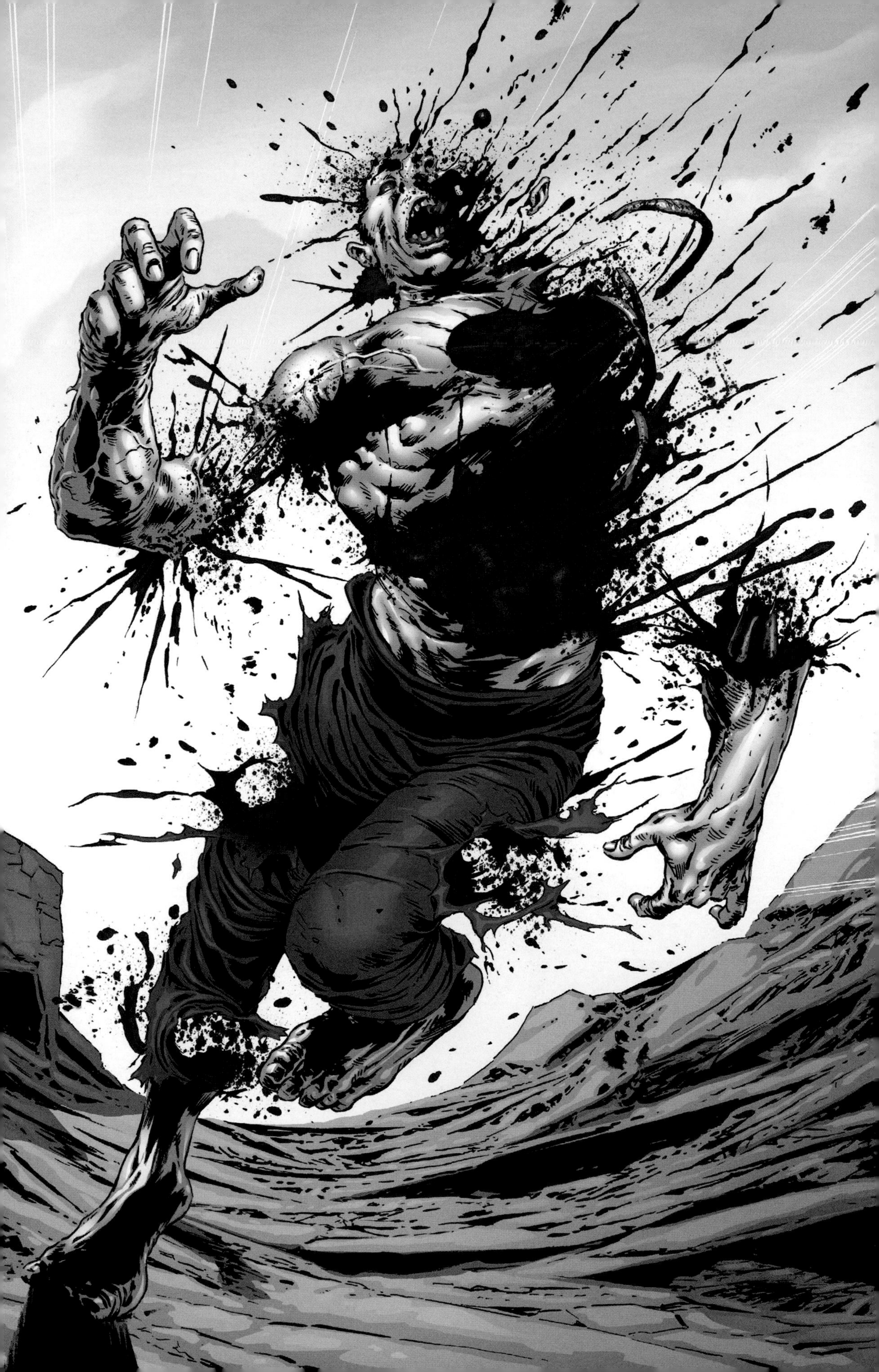

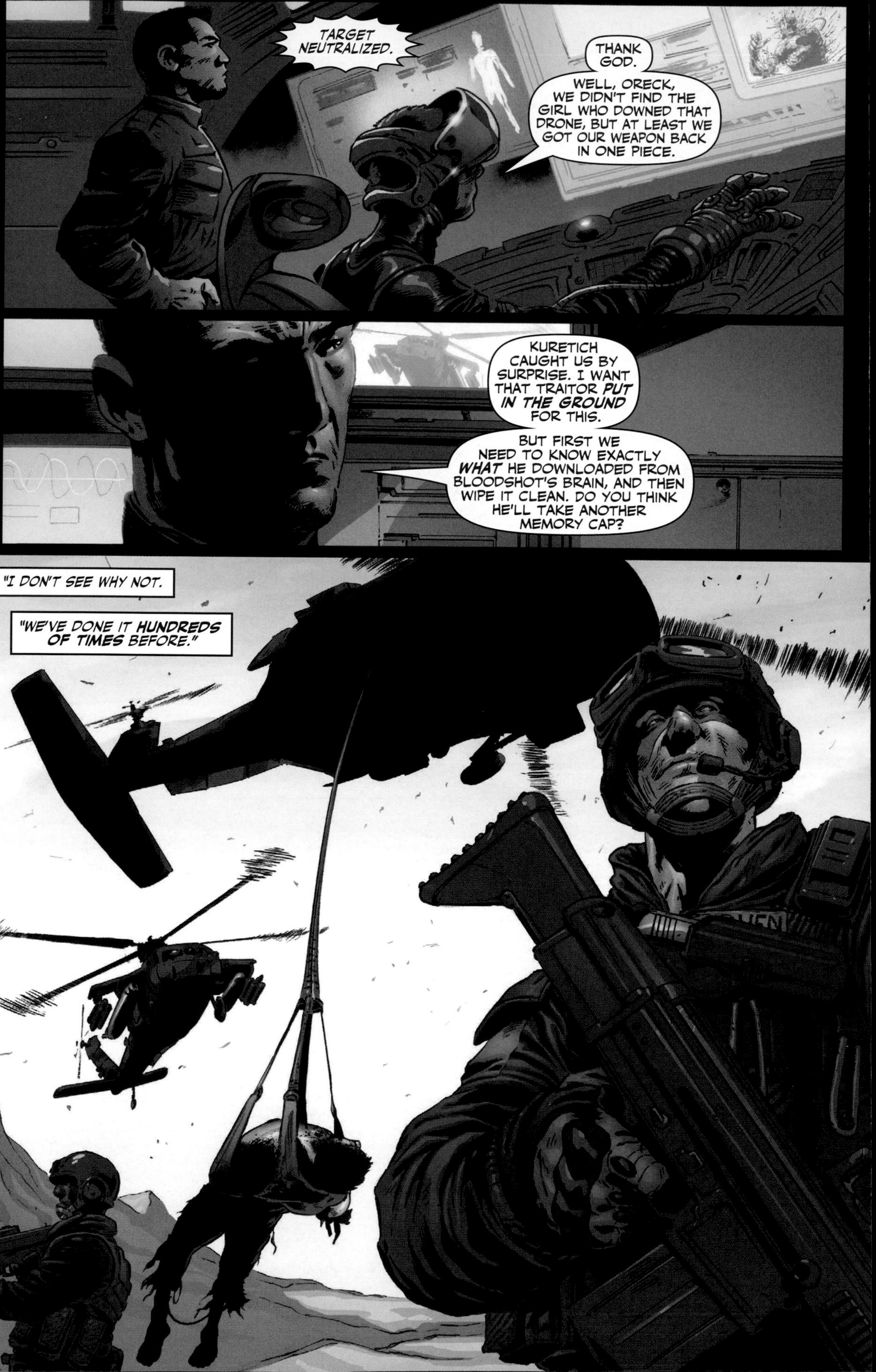
TARGET NEUTRALIZED.
THANK GOD.
WELL, ORECK, WE DIDN'T FIND THE GIRL WHO DOWNED THAT DRONE, BUT AT LEAST WE GOT OUR WEAPON BACK IN ONE PIECE.
KURETICH CAUGHT US BY SURPRISE. I WANT THAT TRAITOR PUT IN THE GROUND FOR THIS.
BUT FIRST WE NEED TO KNOW EXACTLY WHAT HE DOWNLOADED FROM BLOODSHOT'S BRAIN, AND THEN WIPE IT CLEAN. DO YOU THINK HE'LL TAKE ANOTHER MEMORY CAP?
"I DON'T SEE WHY NOT.
"WE'VE DONE IT HUNDREDS OF TIMES BEFORE."

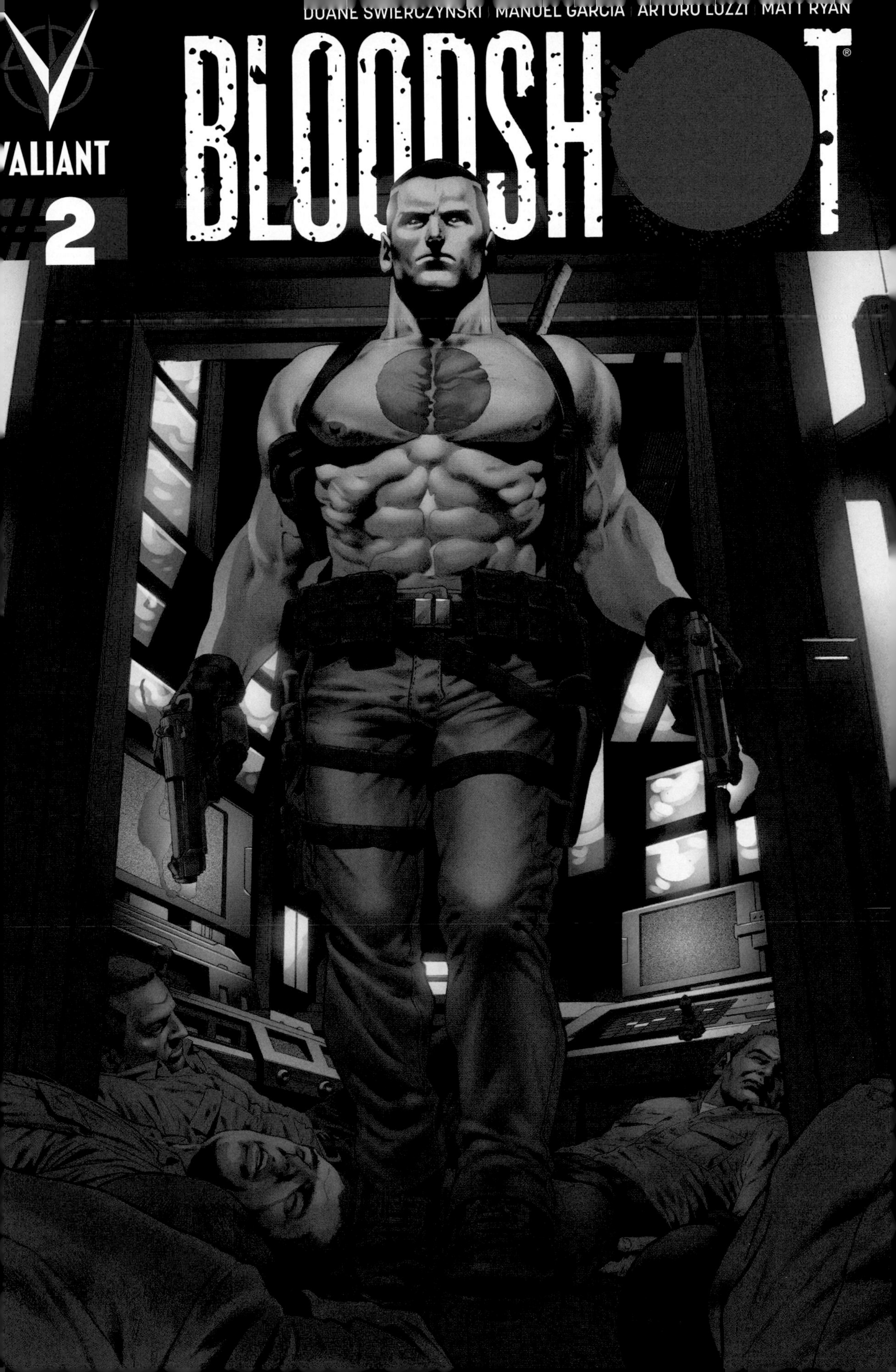
DUANE SWIERCZYNSKI | MANUEL GARCIA | ARTURO LOZZI | MATT RYAN
BLOODSHOT®
VALIANT
#2

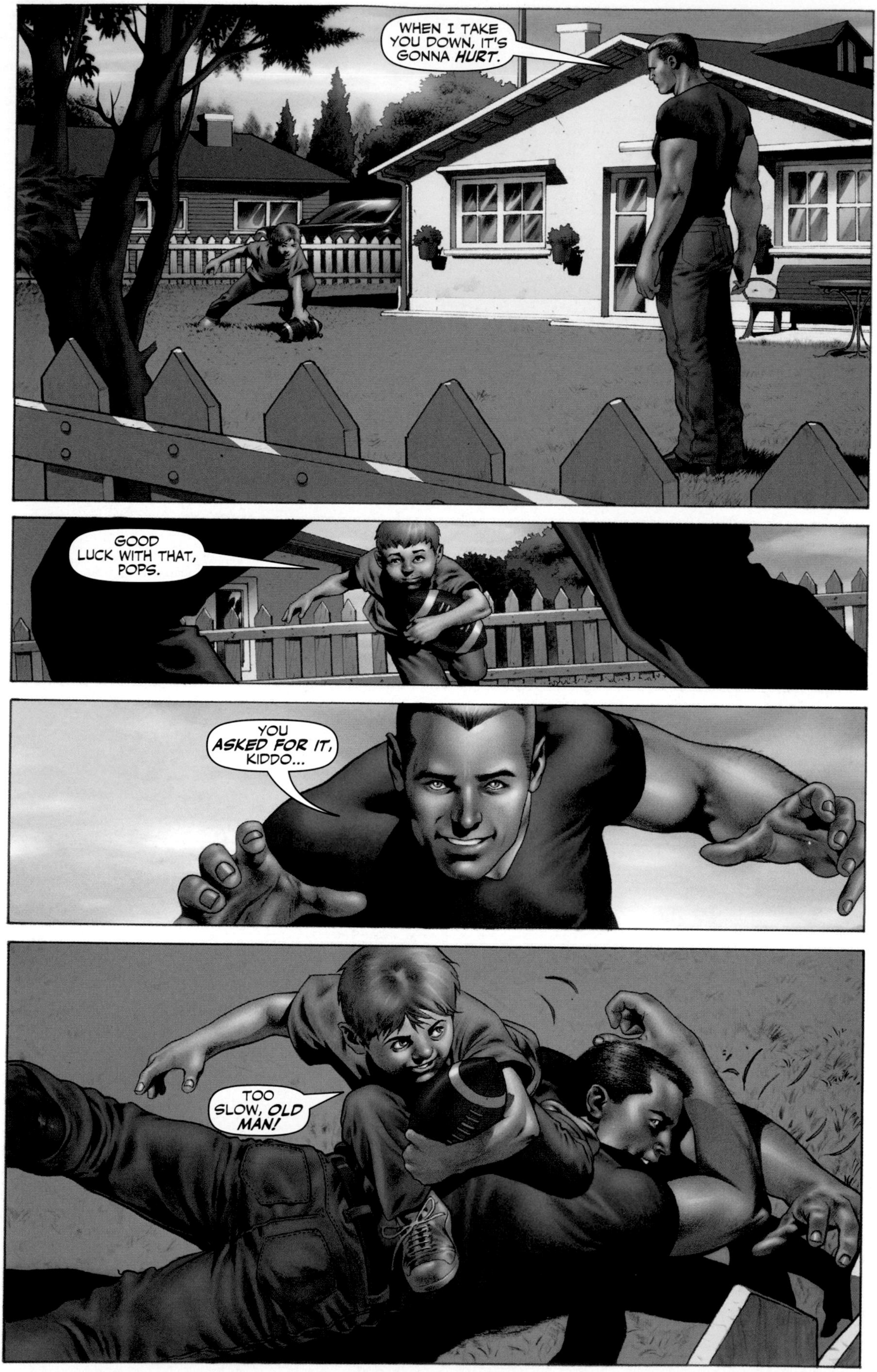
WHEN I TAKE YOU DOWN, IT'S GONNA *HURT*.
GOOD LUCK WITH THAT, POPS.
YOU *ASKED FOR IT*, KIDDO...
TOO SLOW, *OLD MAN!*

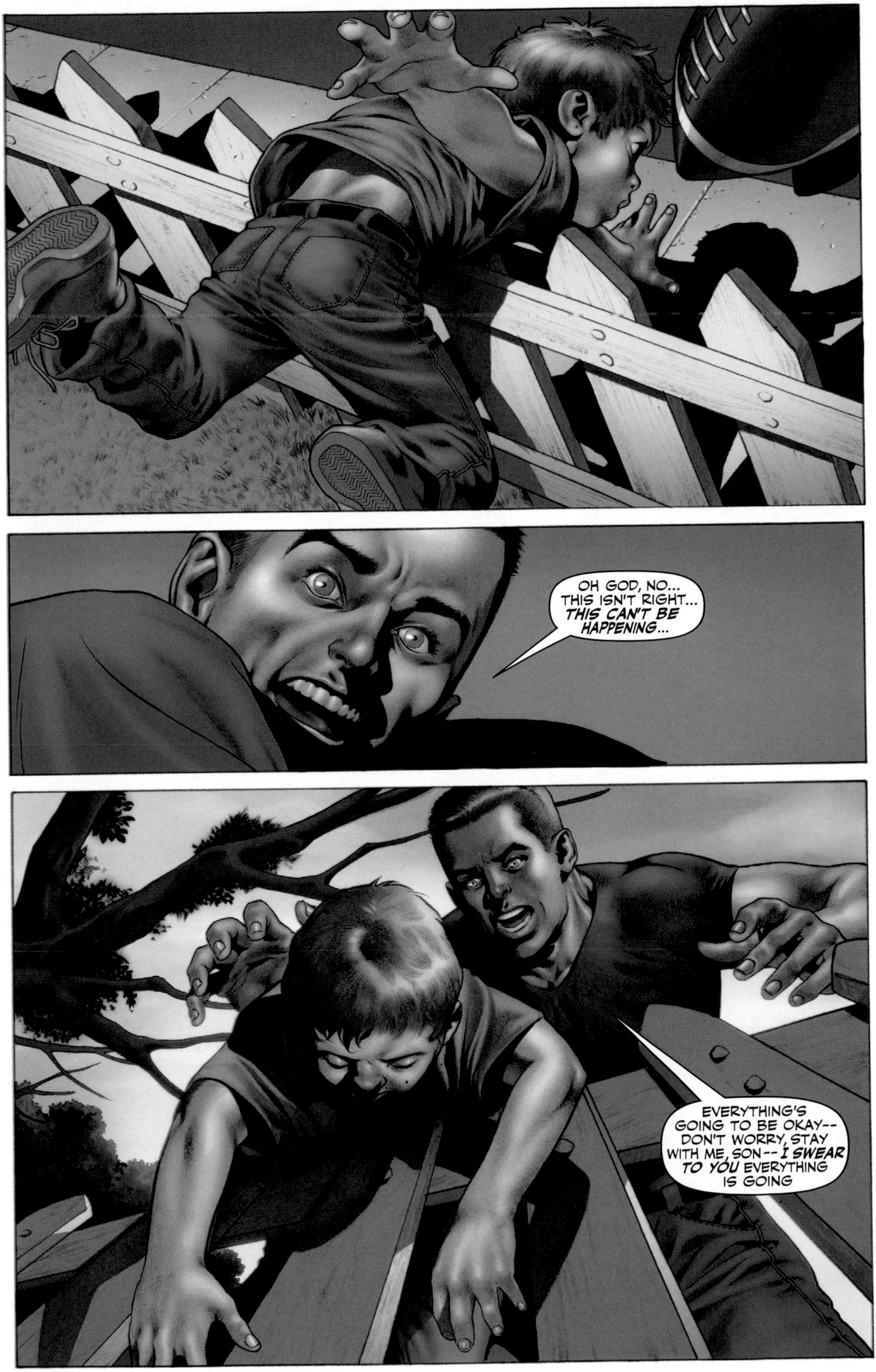
OH GOD, NO... THIS ISN'T RIGHT... THIS CAN'T BE HAPPENING...
EVERYTHING'S GOING TO BE OKAY-- DON'T WORRY, STAY WITH ME, SON-- I SWEAR TO YOU EVERYTHING IS GOING

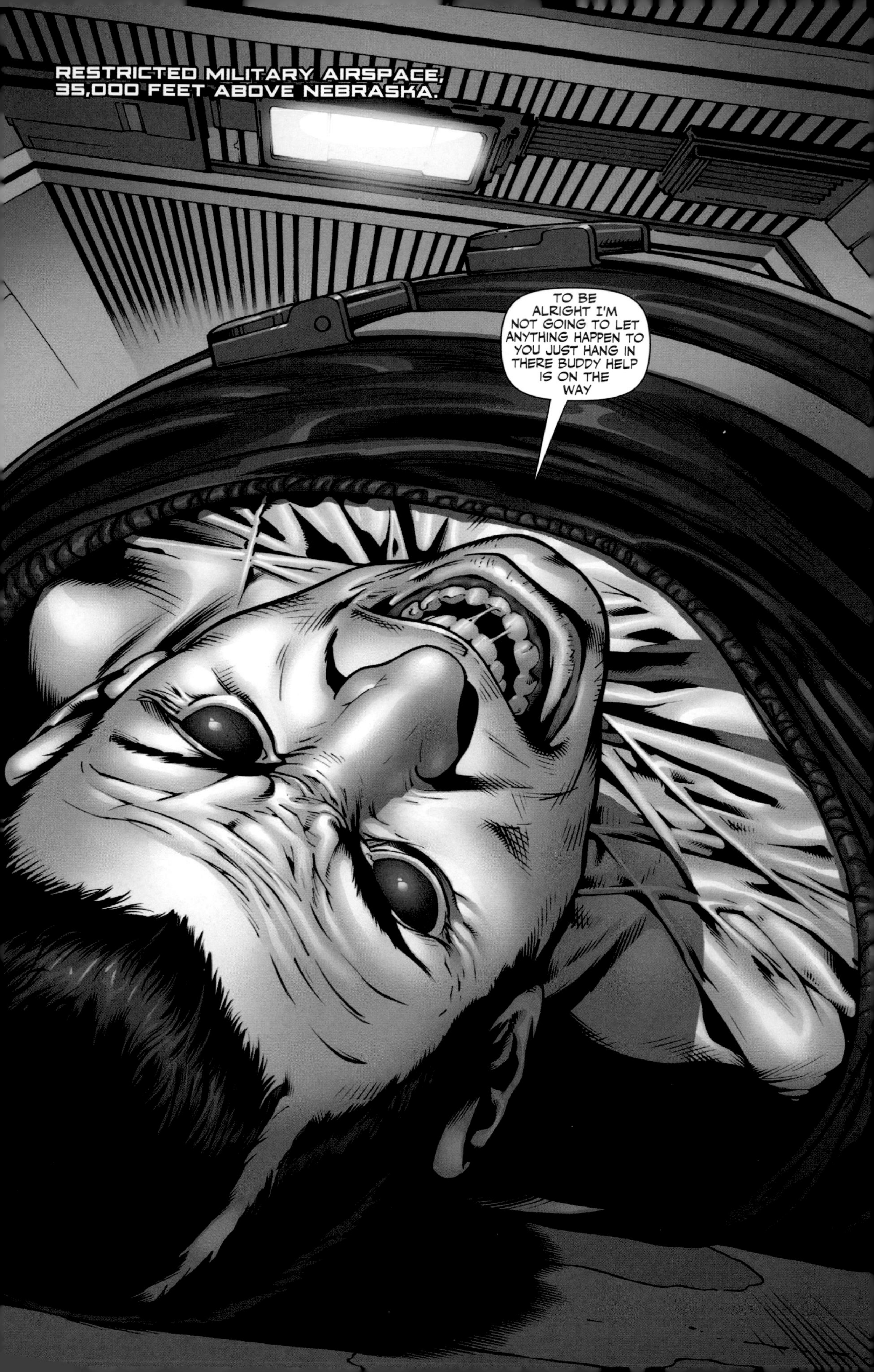
RESTRICTED MILITARY AIRSPACE,
35,000 FEET ABOVE NEBRASKA.
TO BE ALRIGHT I'M NOT GOING TO LET ANYTHING HAPPEN TO YOU JUST HANG IN THERE BUDDY HELP IS ON THE WAY

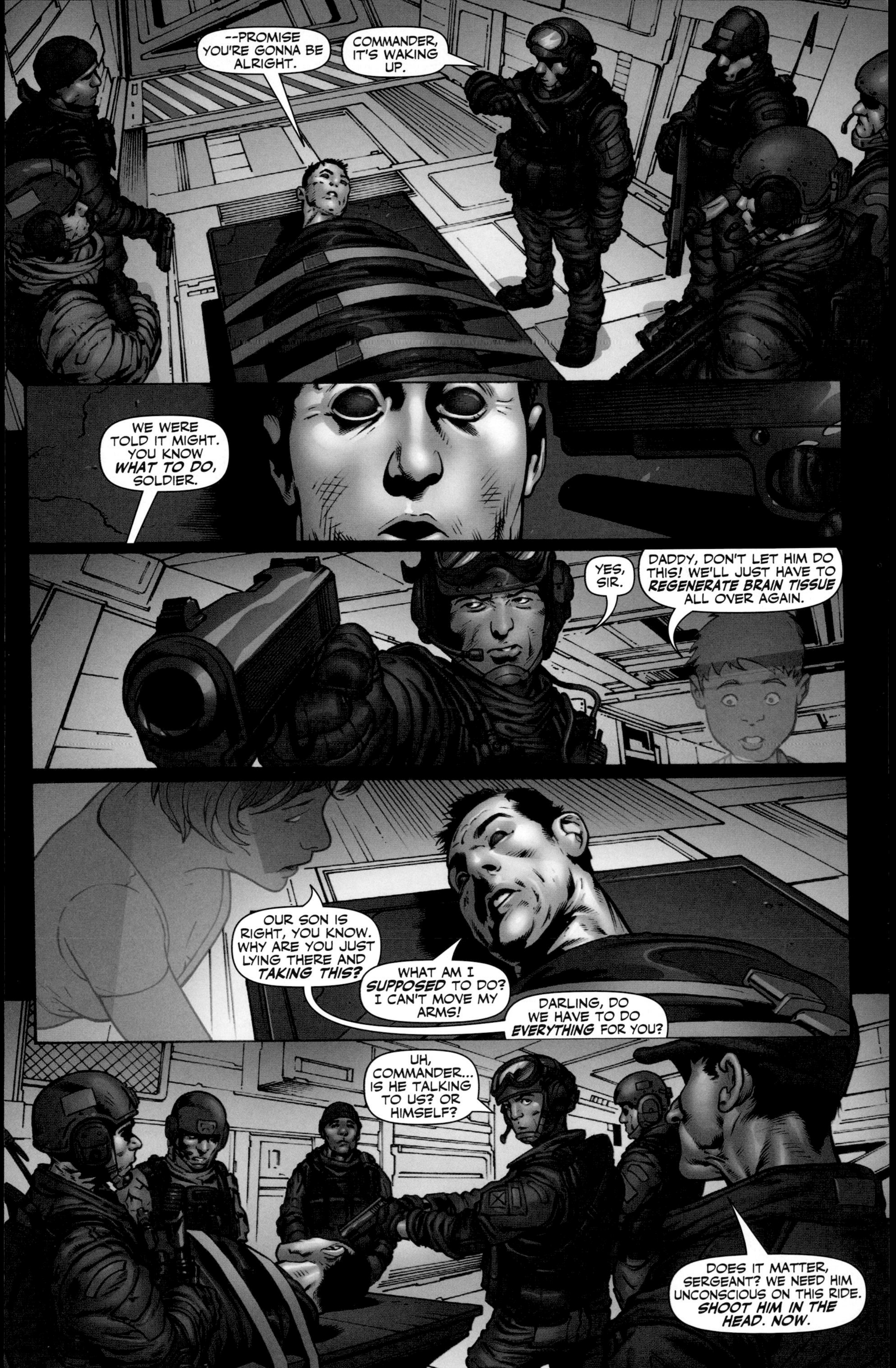
--PROMISE YOU'RE GONNA BE ALRIGHT.
COMMANDER, IT'S WAKING UP.
WE WERE TOLD IT MIGHT. YOU KNOW *WHAT TO DO,* SOLDIER.
YES, SIR.
DADDY, DON'T LET HIM DO THIS! WE'LL JUST HAVE TO *REGENERATE BRAIN TISSUE* ALL OVER AGAIN.
OUR SON IS RIGHT, YOU KNOW. WHY ARE YOU JUST LYING THERE AND *TAKING THIS?*
WHAT AM I *SUPPOSED* TO DO? I CAN'T MOVE MY ARMS!
DARLING, DO WE HAVE TO DO *EVERYTHING* FOR YOU?
UH, COMMANDER... IS HE TALKING TO US? OR HIMSELF?
DOES IT MATTER, SERGEANT? WE NEED HIM UNCONSCIOUS ON THIS RIDE. *SHOOT HIM IN THE HEAD. NOW.*

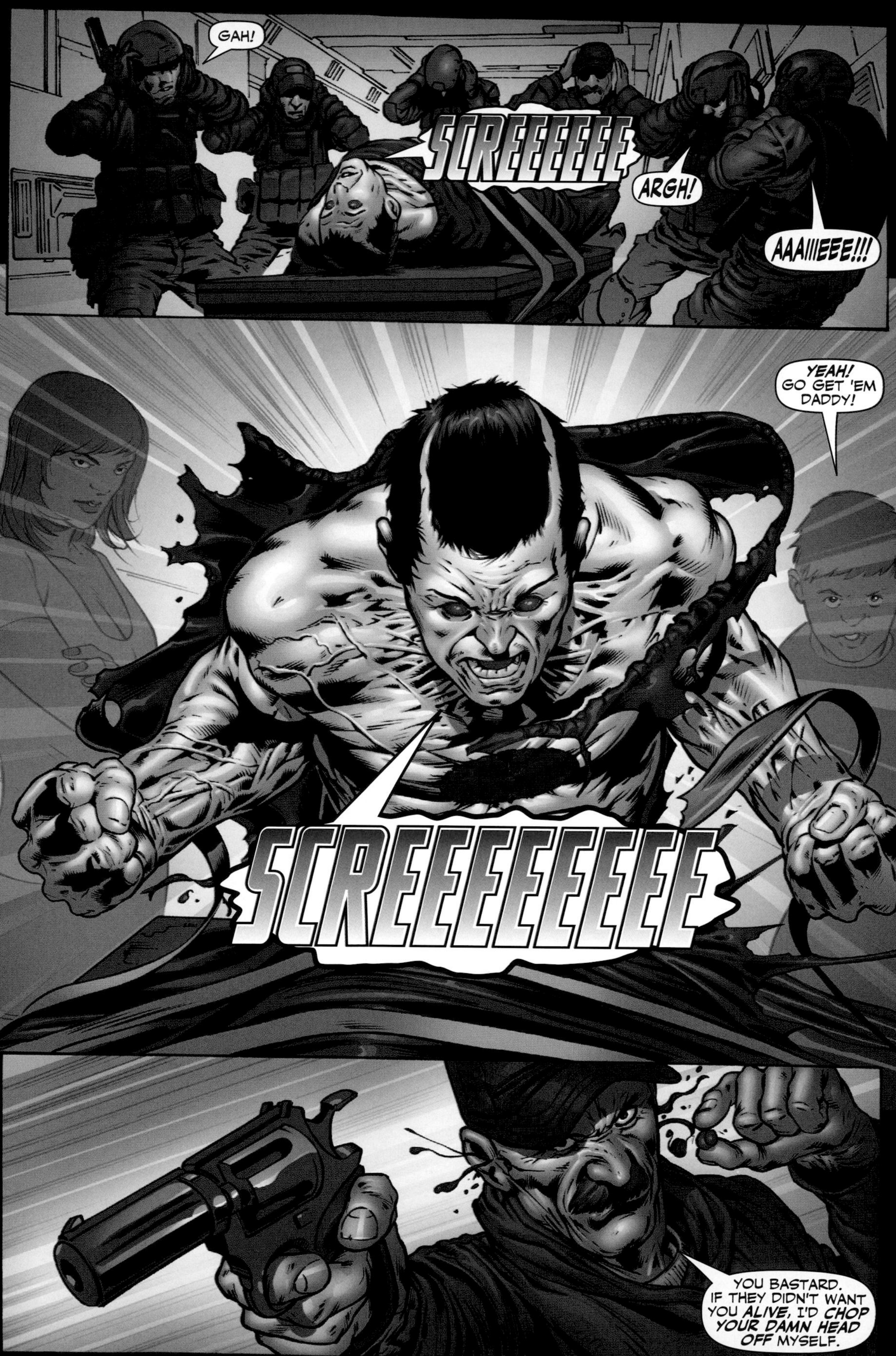
GAH!
SCREEEEEEE
ARGH!
AAAIIIEEE!!!
YEAH! GO GET 'EM DADDY!
SCREEEEEEEEE
YOU BASTARD. IF THEY DIDN'T WANT YOU *ALIVE*, I'D *CHOP YOUR DAMN HEAD OFF* MYSELF.

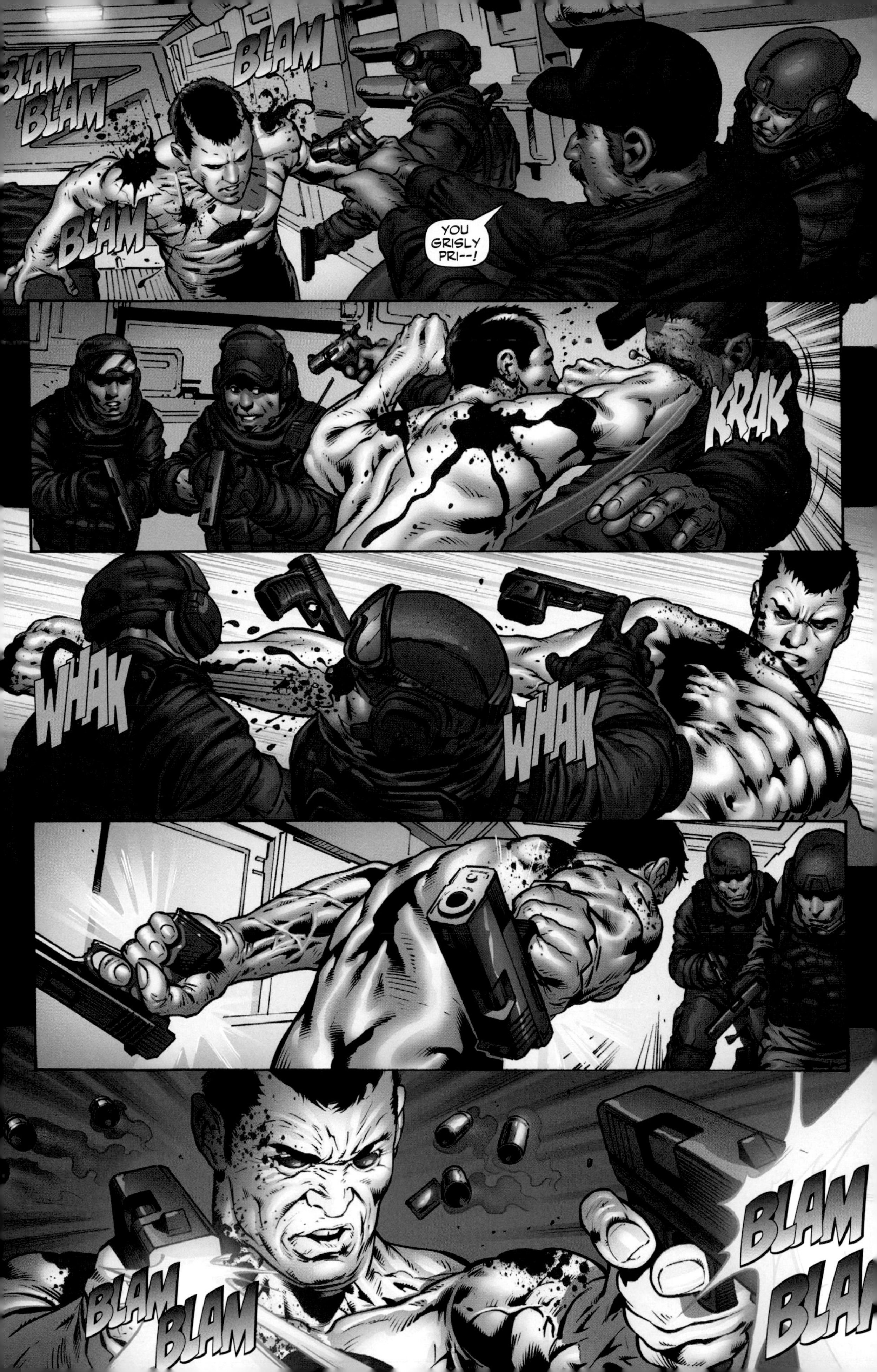
BLAM
BLAM
BLAM
BLAM
YOU GRISLY PRI--!
KRAK
WHAK
WHAK
BLAM
BLAM
BLAM

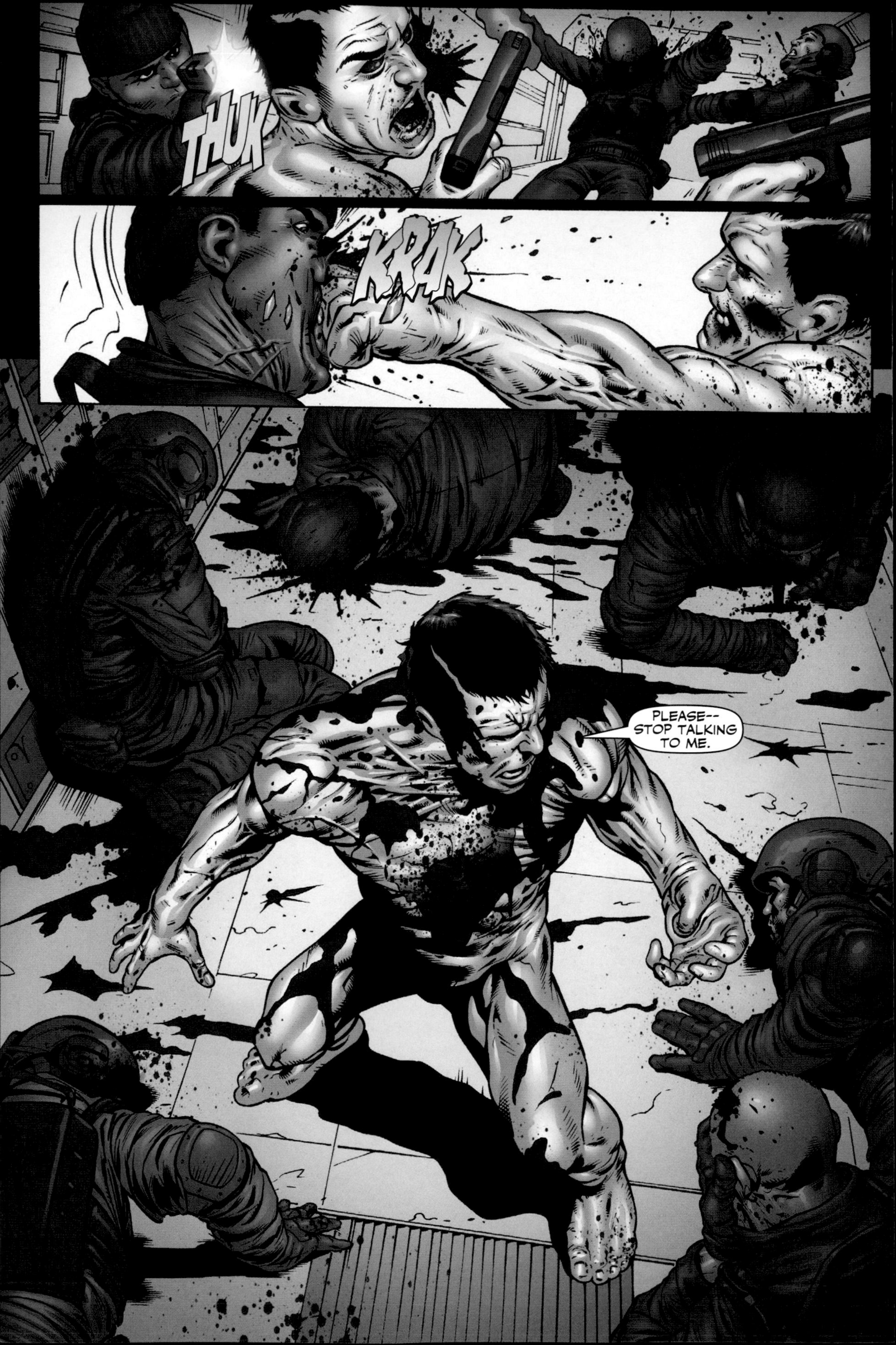
THUK
KRAK
PLEASE--
STOP TALKING
TO ME.

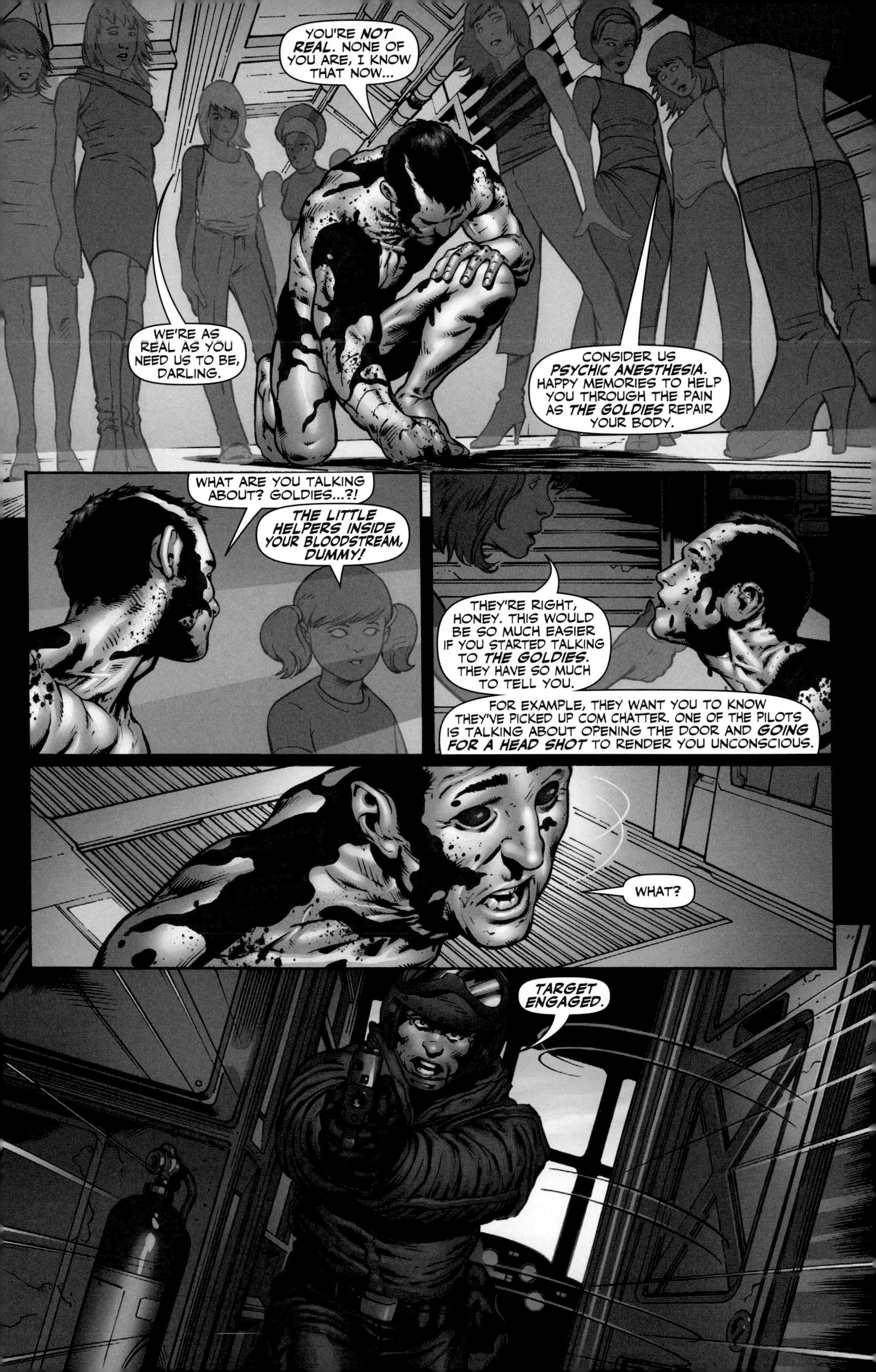
YOU'RE NOT REAL. NONE OF YOU ARE, I KNOW THAT NOW...
WE'RE AS REAL AS YOU NEED US TO BE, DARLING.
CONSIDER US PSYCHIC ANESTHESIA. HAPPY MEMORIES TO HELP YOU THROUGH THE PAIN AS THE GOLDIES REPAIR YOUR BODY.
WHAT ARE YOU TALKING ABOUT? GOLDIES...?!
THE LITTLE HELPERS INSIDE YOUR BLOODSTREAM, DUMMY!
THEY'RE RIGHT, HONEY. THIS WOULD BE SO MUCH EASIER IF YOU STARTED TALKING TO THE GOLDIES. THEY HAVE SO MUCH TO TELL YOU.
FOR EXAMPLE, THEY WANT YOU TO KNOW THEY'VE PICKED UP COM CHATTER. ONE OF THE PILOTS IS TALKING ABOUT OPENING THE DOOR AND GOING FOR A HEAD SHOT TO RENDER YOU UNCONSCIOUS.
WHAT?
TARGET ENGAGED.

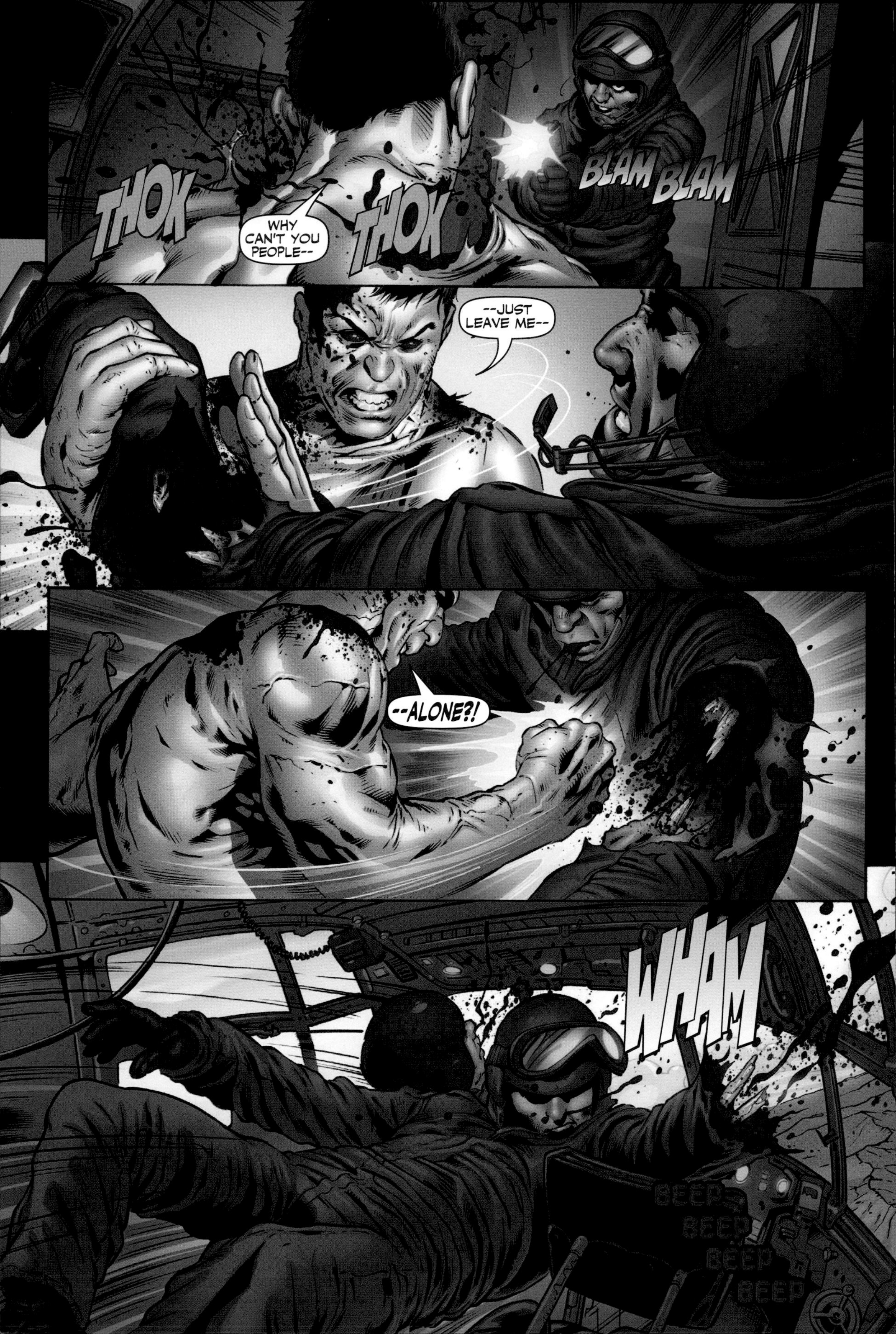
THOK
WHY CAN'T YOU PEOPLE--
THOK
BLAM BLAM
--JUST LEAVE ME--
--ALONE?!
WHAM
BEEP
BEEP
BEEP
BEEP

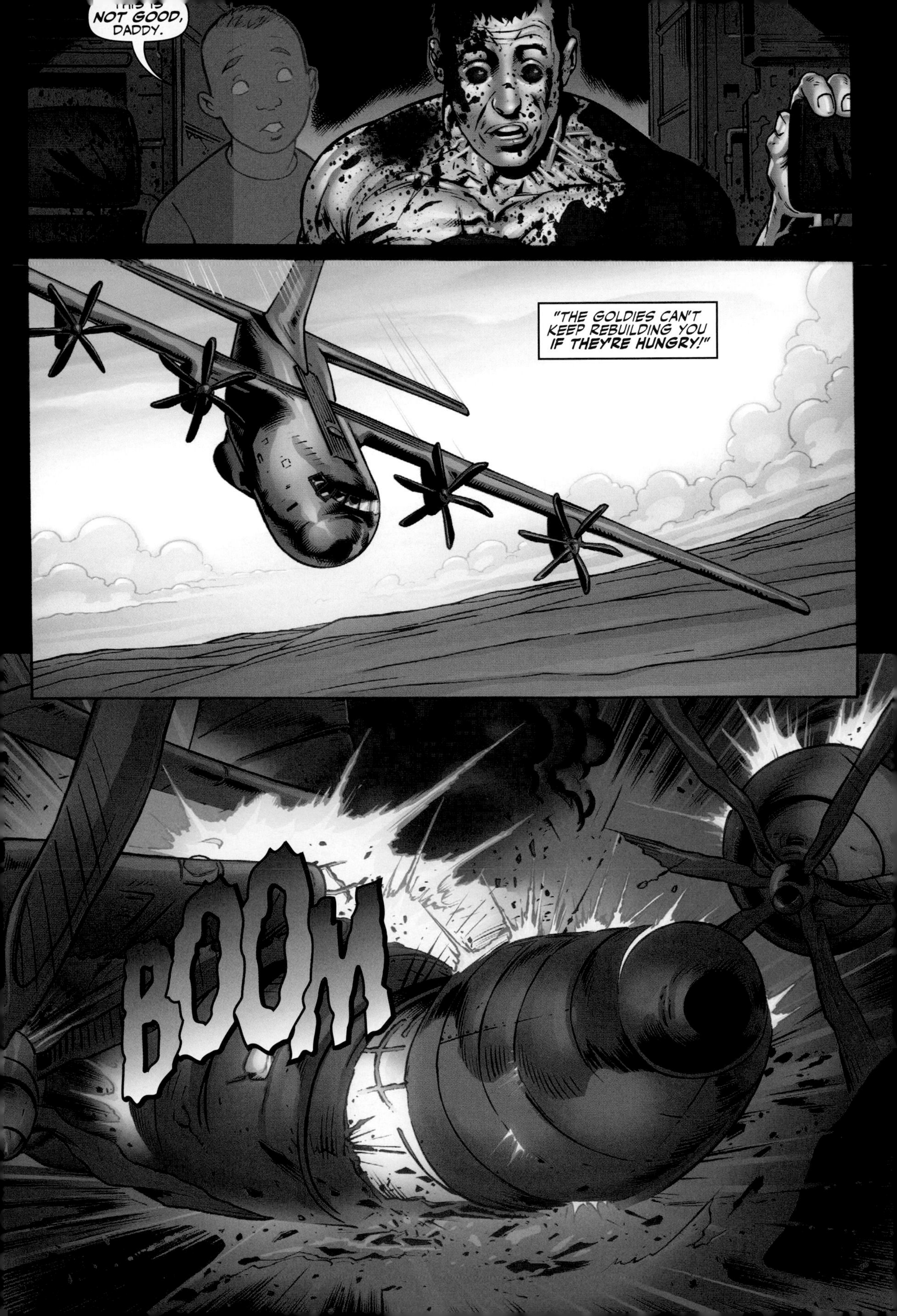
THIS IS NOT GOOD, DADDY.
"THE GOLDIES CAN'T KEEP REBUILDING YOU IF THEY'RE HUNGRY!"
BOOM

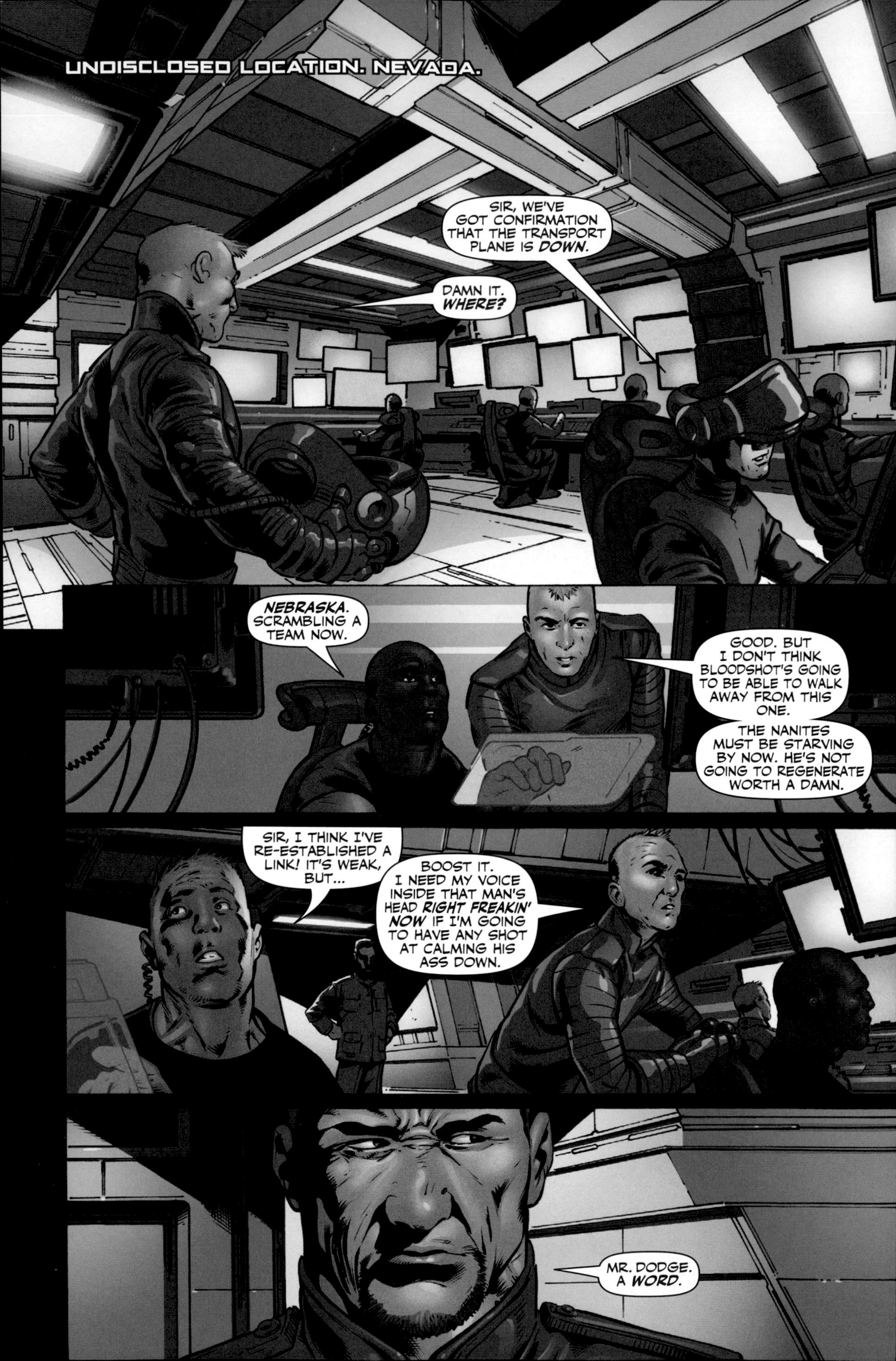
UNDISCLOSED LOCATION. NEVADA.
SIR, WE'VE GOT CONFIRMATION THAT THE TRANSPORT PLANE IS *DOWN*.
DAMN IT. *WHERE?*
NEBRASKA. SCRAMBLING A TEAM NOW.
GOOD. BUT I DON'T THINK BLOODSHOT'S GOING TO BE ABLE TO WALK AWAY FROM THIS ONE.
THE NANITES MUST BE STARVING BY NOW. HE'S NOT GOING TO REGENERATE WORTH A DAMN.
SIR, I THINK I'VE RE-ESTABLISHED A LINK! IT'S WEAK, BUT...
BOOST IT. I NEED MY VOICE INSIDE THAT MAN'S HEAD *RIGHT FREAKIN' NOW* IF I'M GOING TO HAVE ANY SHOT AT CALMING HIS ASS DOWN.
MR. DODGE. A *WORD*.

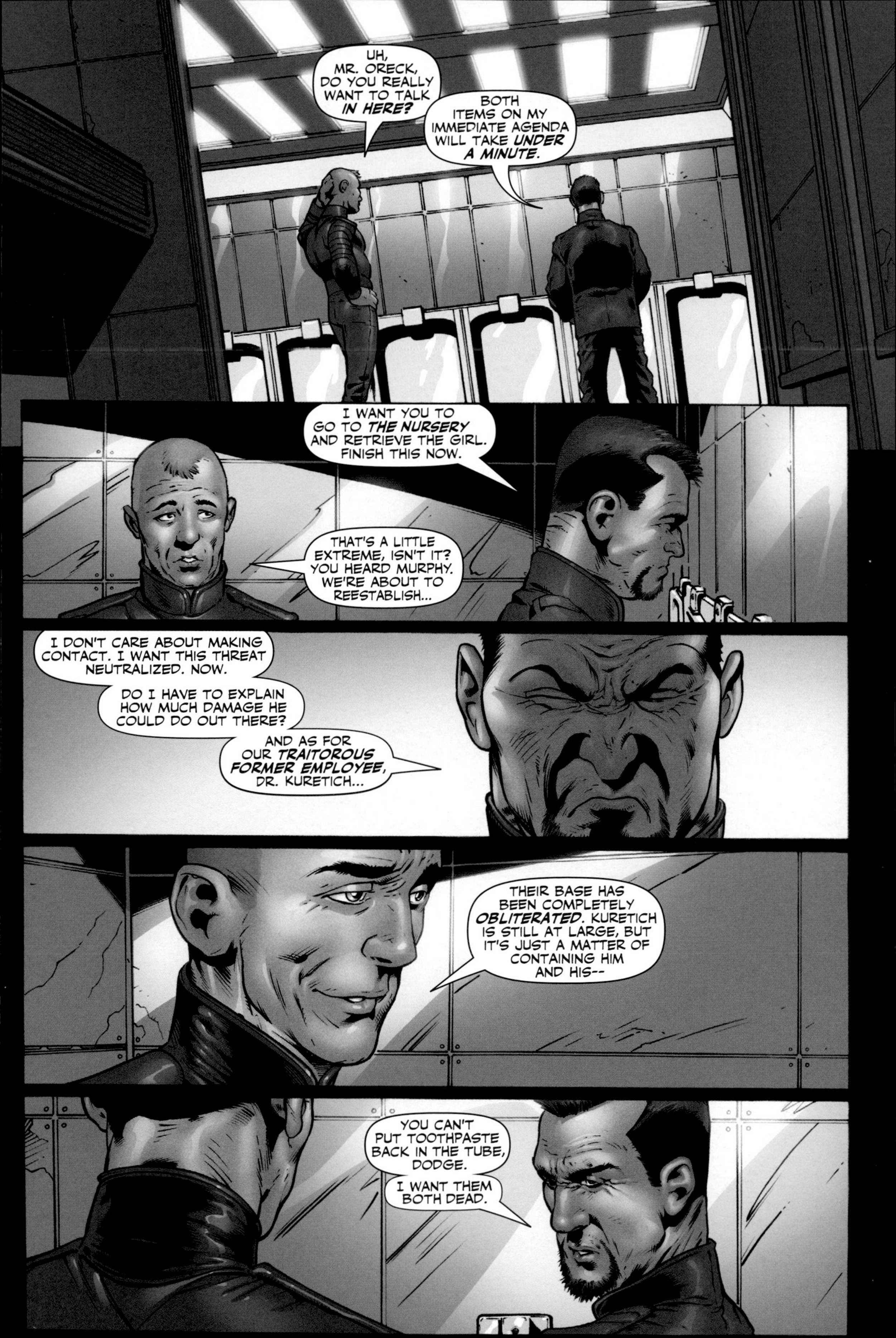
UH, MR. ORECK, DO YOU REALLY WANT TO TALK *IN HERE?*
BOTH ITEMS ON MY IMMEDIATE AGENDA WILL TAKE *UNDER A MINUTE*.
I WANT YOU TO GO TO *THE NURSERY* AND RETRIEVE THE GIRL. FINISH THIS NOW.
THAT'S A LITTLE EXTREME, ISN'T IT? YOU HEARD MURPHY. WE'RE ABOUT TO REESTABLISH...
I DON'T CARE ABOUT MAKING CONTACT. I WANT THIS THREAT NEUTRALIZED. NOW.
DO I HAVE TO EXPLAIN HOW MUCH DAMAGE HE COULD DO OUT THERE?
AND AS FOR OUR *TRAITOROUS FORMER EMPLOYEE*, DR. KURETICH...
THEIR BASE HAS BEEN COMPLETELY *OBLITERATED*. KURETICH IS STILL AT LARGE, BUT IT'S JUST A MATTER OF CONTAINING HIM AND HIS--
YOU CAN'T PUT TOOTHPASTE BACK IN THE TUBE, DODGE.
I WANT THEM BOTH DEAD.

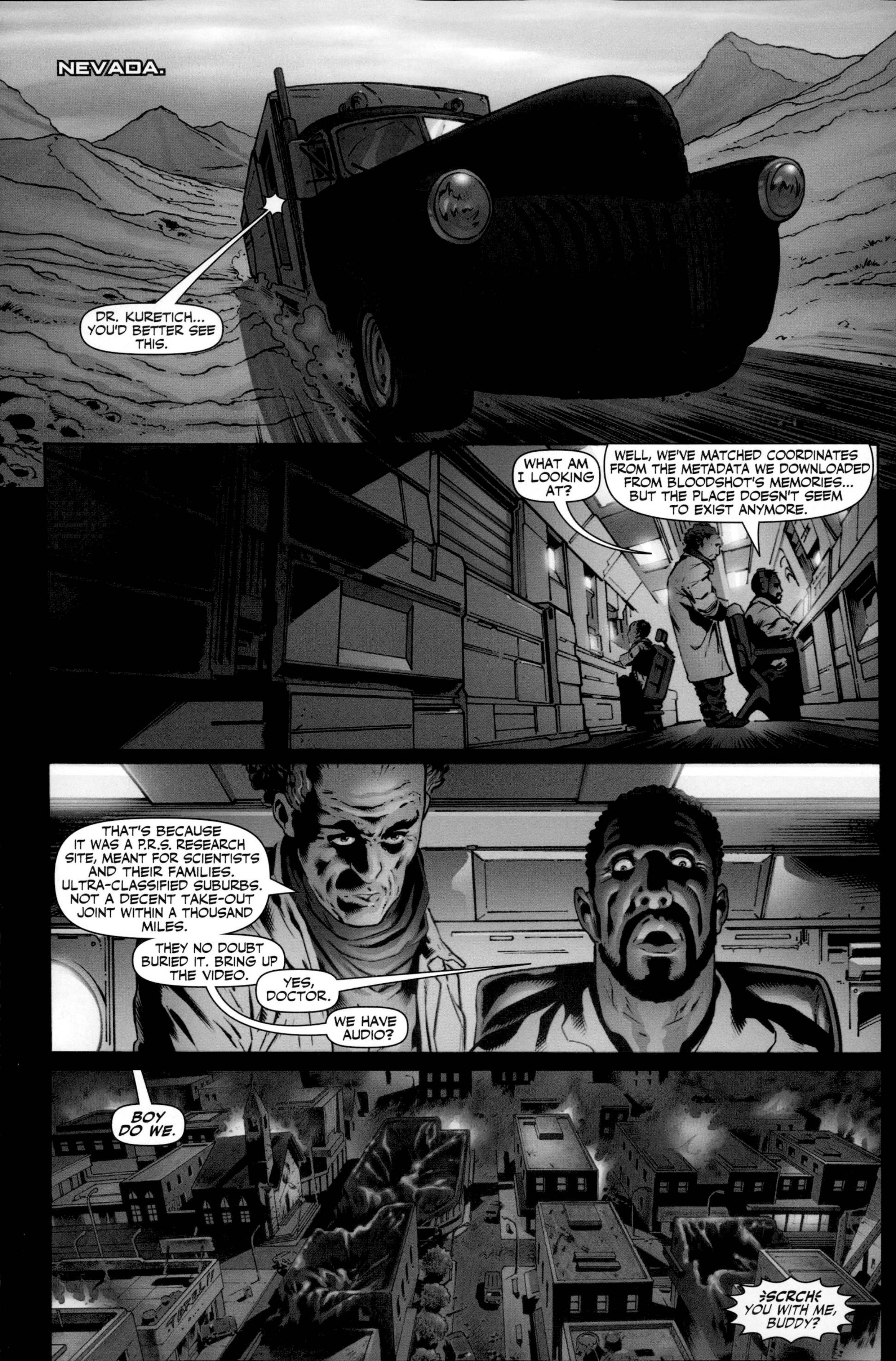
NEVADA.
DR. KURETICH... YOU'D BETTER SEE THIS.
WHAT AM I LOOKING AT?
WELL, WE'VE MATCHED COORDINATES FROM THE METADATA WE DOWNLOADED FROM BLOODSHOT'S MEMORIES... BUT THE PLACE DOESN'T SEEM TO EXIST ANYMORE.
THAT'S BECAUSE IT WAS A P.R.S. RESEARCH SITE, MEANT FOR SCIENTISTS AND THEIR FAMILIES. ULTRA-CLASSIFIED SUBURBS. NOT A DECENT TAKE-OUT JOINT WITHIN A THOUSAND MILES.
THEY NO DOUBT BURIED IT. BRING UP THE VIDEO.
YES, DOCTOR.
WE HAVE AUDIO?
BOY DO WE.
SCRCH YOU WITH ME, BUDDY?

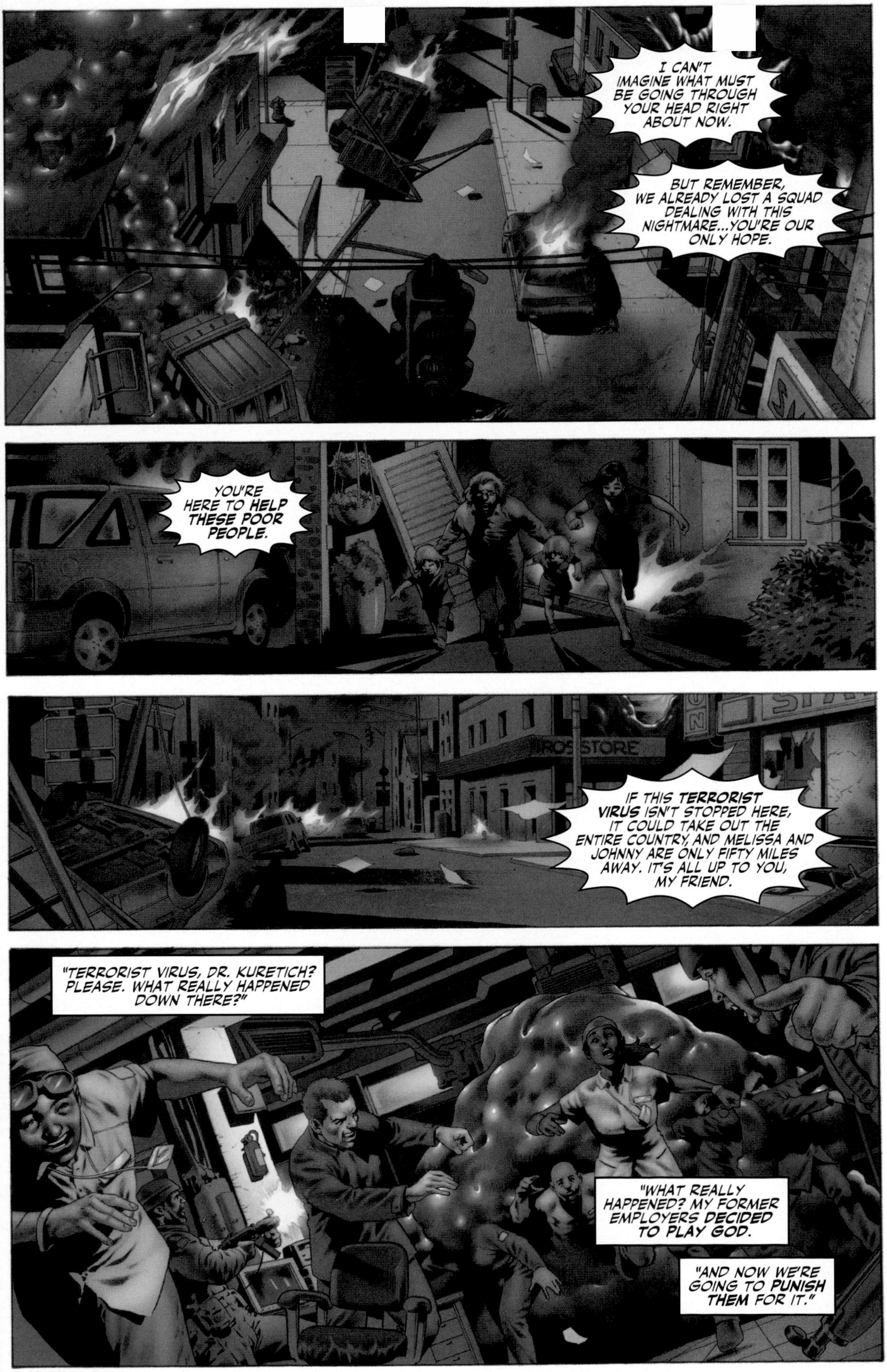
I CAN'T IMAGINE WHAT MUST BE GOING THROUGH YOUR HEAD RIGHT ABOUT NOW.
BUT REMEMBER, WE ALREADY LOST A SQUAD DEALING WITH THIS NIGHTMARE...YOU'RE OUR ONLY HOPE.
YOU'RE HERE TO **HELP THESE POOR PEOPLE**.
ROS STORE
IF THIS **TERRORIST VIRUS** ISN'T STOPPED HERE, IT COULD TAKE OUT THE ENTIRE COUNTRY, AND MELISSA AND JOHNNY ARE ONLY FIFTY MILES AWAY. IT'S ALL UP TO YOU, MY FRIEND.
"TERRORIST VIRUS, DR. KURETICH? PLEASE. WHAT REALLY HAPPENED DOWN THERE?"
"WHAT REALLY HAPPENED? MY FORMER EMPLOYERS **DECIDED TO PLAY GOD**.
"AND NOW WE'RE GOING TO **PUNISH THEM** FOR IT."

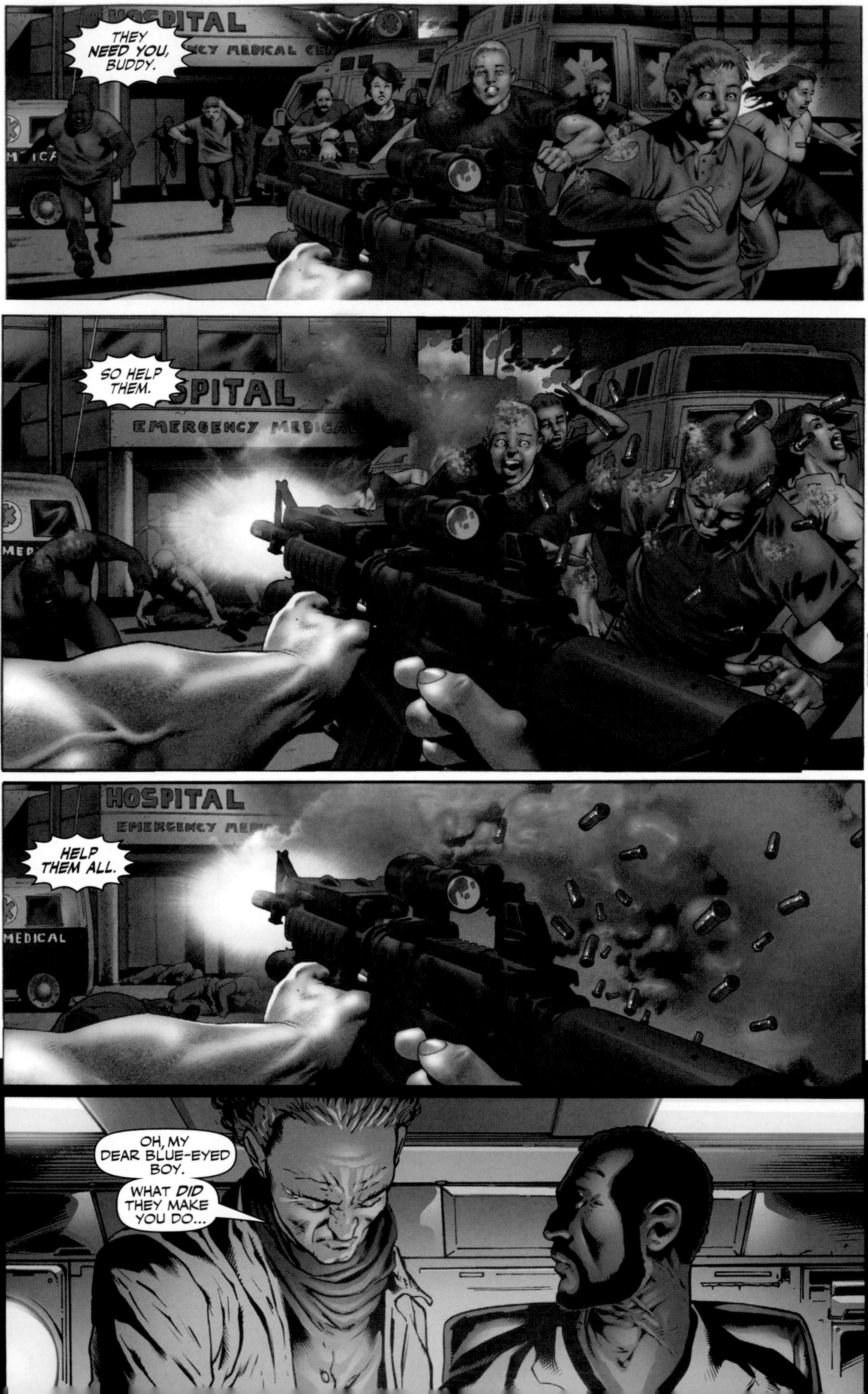
THEY NEED YOU, BUDDY.
SO HELP THEM.
EMERGENCY MEDICAL
HOSPITAL
HELP THEM ALL.
MEDICAL
OH, MY DEAR BLUE-EYED BOY.
WHAT DID THEY MAKE YOU DO...

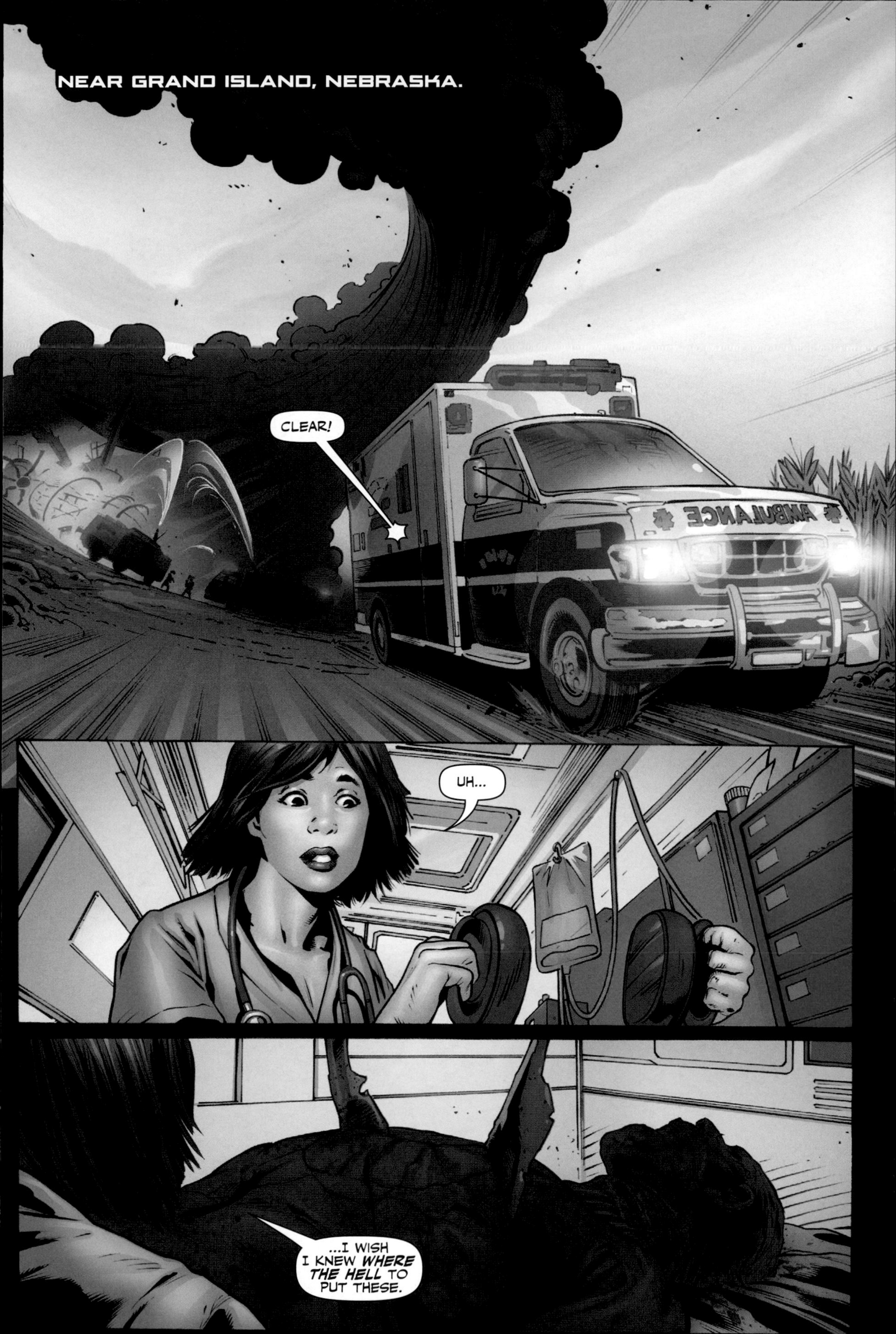
NEAR GRAND ISLAND, NEBRASKA.
CLEAR!
AMBULANCE
UH...
...I WISH I KNEW *WHERE THE HELL* TO PUT THESE.

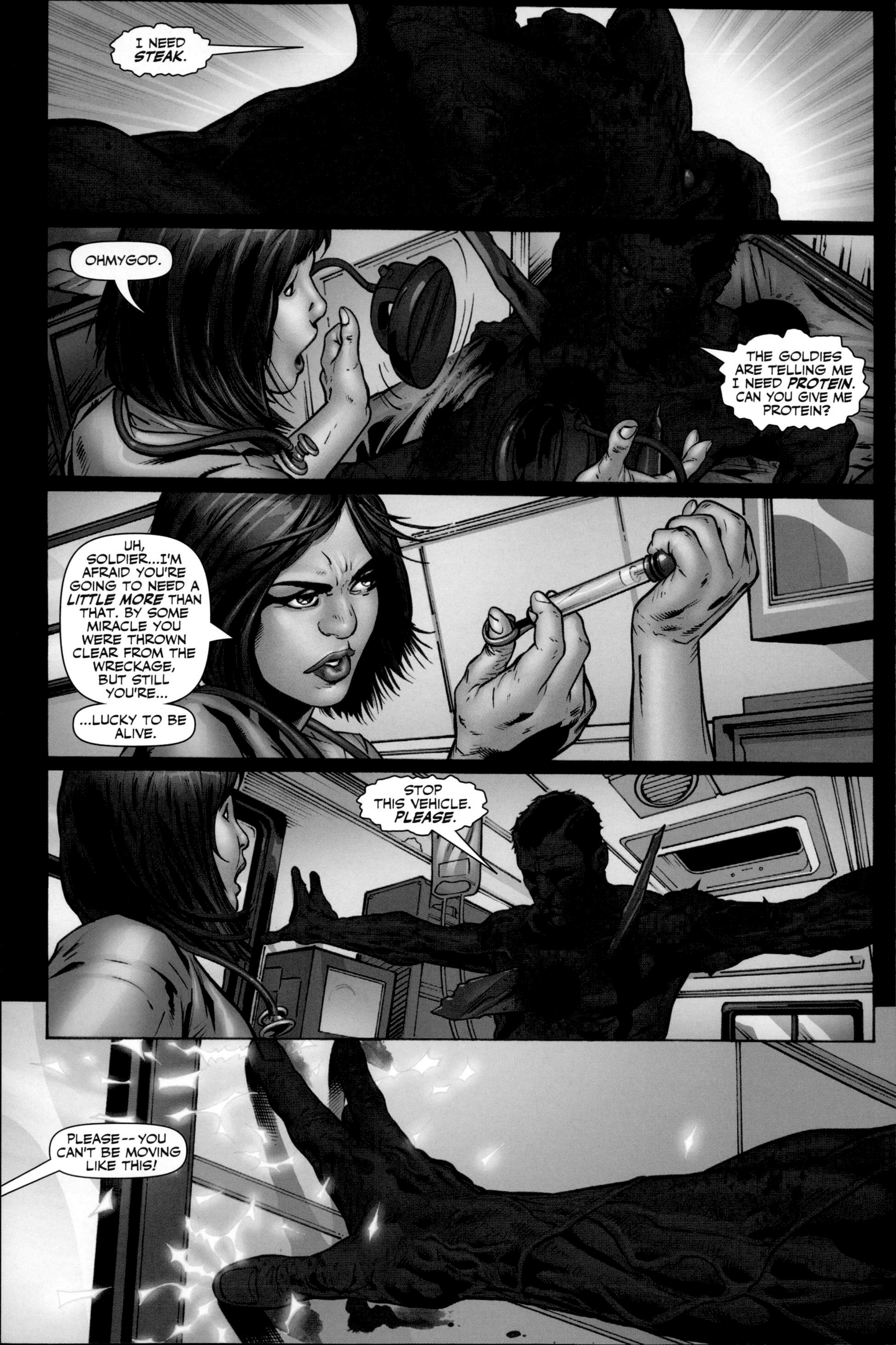
I NEED *STEAK.*
OHMYGOD.
THE GOLDIES ARE TELLING ME I NEED *PROTEIN.* CAN YOU GIVE ME PROTEIN?
UH, SOLDIER...I'M AFRAID YOU'RE GOING TO NEED A *LITTLE MORE* THAN THAT. BY SOME MIRACLE YOU WERE THROWN CLEAR FROM THE WRECKAGE, BUT STILL YOU'RE...
...LUCKY TO BE ALIVE.
STOP THIS VEHICLE. *PLEASE.*
PLEASE--YOU CAN'T BE MOVING LIKE THIS!

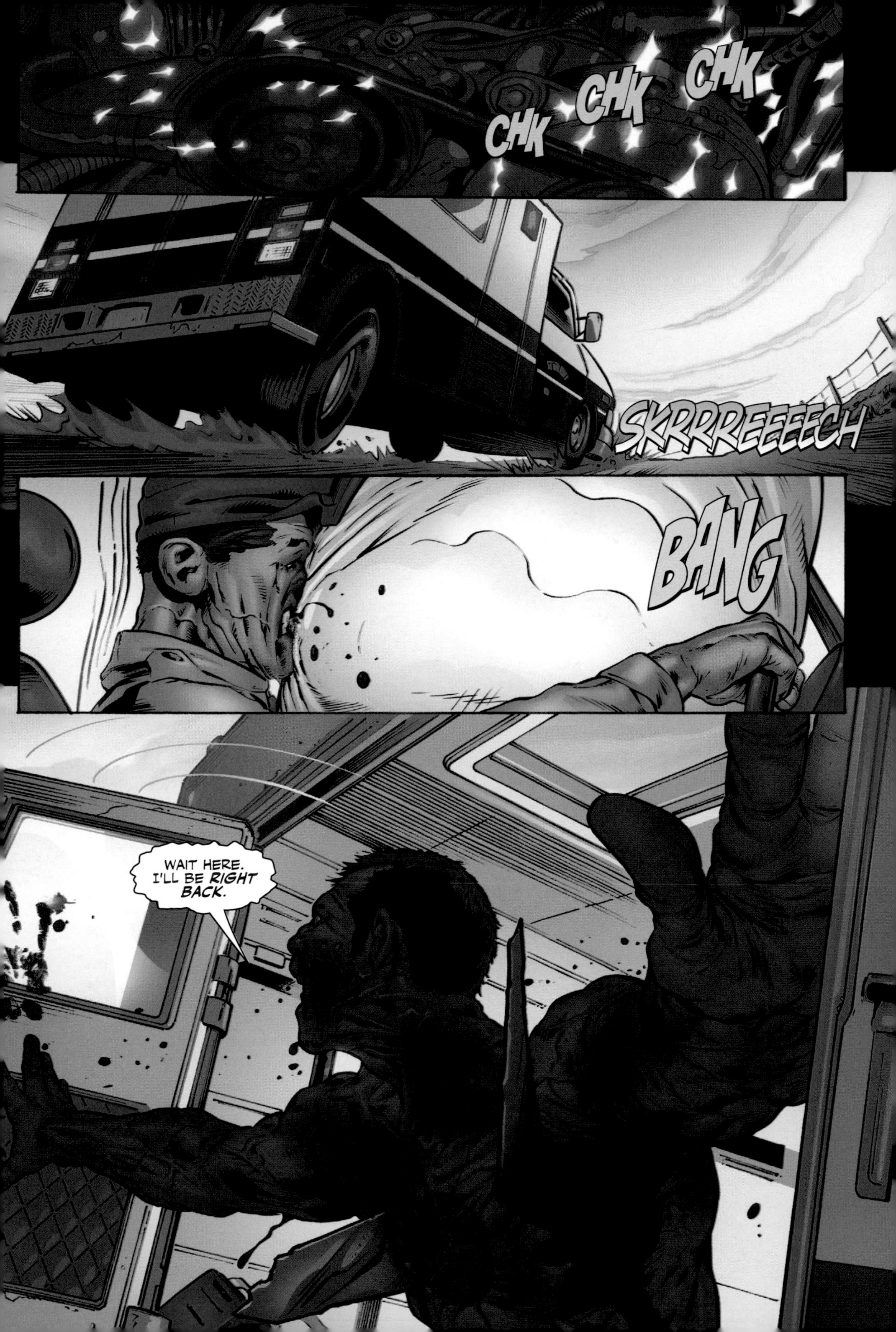
CHK
CHK
CHK
SKRRRREEEEECH
BANG
WAIT HERE. I'LL BE *RIGHT* BACK.

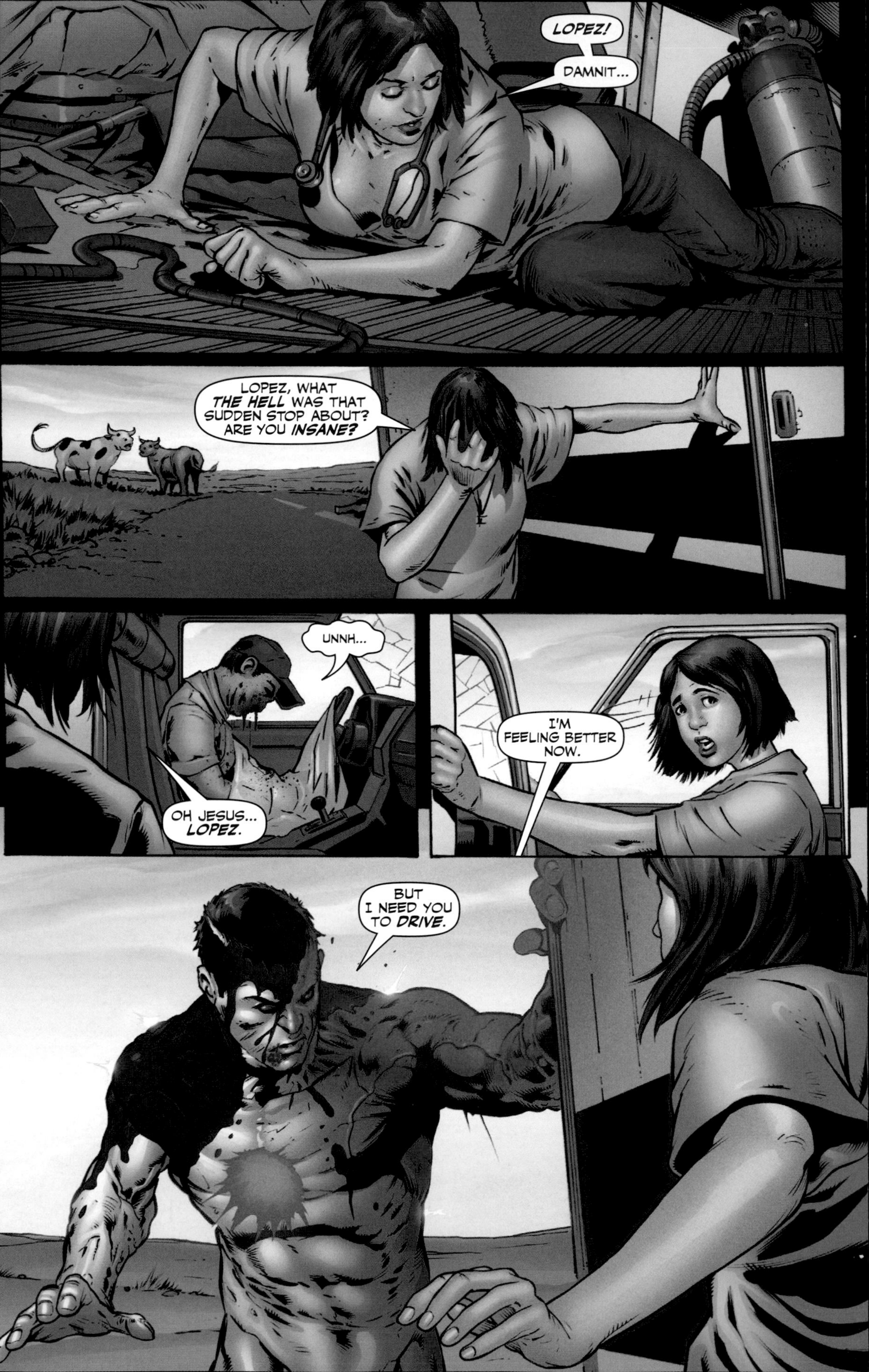
LOPEZ!
DAMNIT...
LOPEZ, WHAT THE HELL WAS THAT SUDDEN STOP ABOUT? ARE YOU INSANE?
UNNH...
OH JESUS... LOPEZ.
I'M FEELING BETTER NOW.
BUT I NEED YOU TO DRIVE.

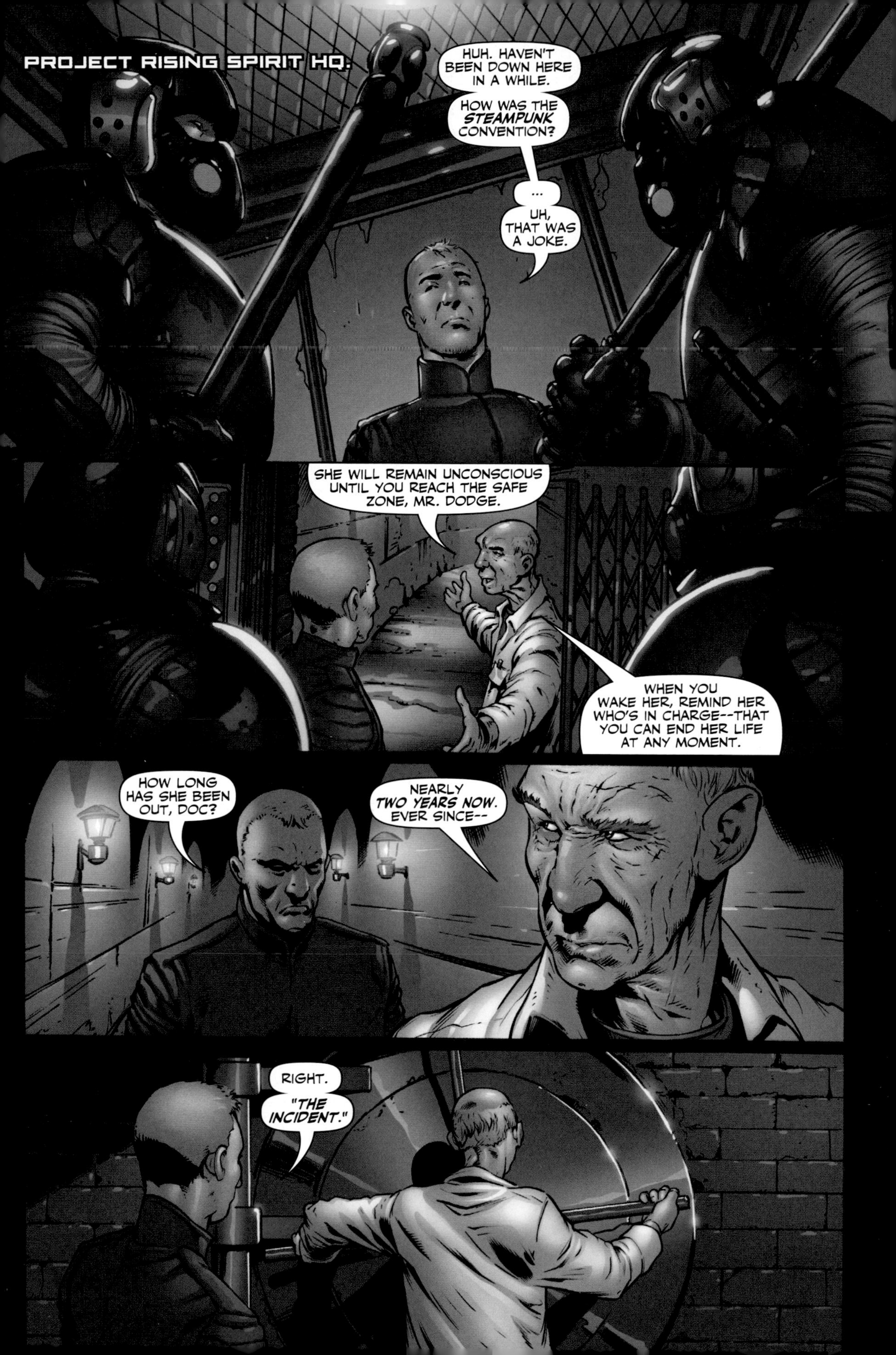
PROJECT RISING SPIRIT HQ.
HUH. HAVEN'T BEEN DOWN HERE IN A WHILE.
HOW WAS THE *STEAMPUNK* CONVENTION?
...
UH, THAT WAS A JOKE.
SHE WILL REMAIN UNCONSCIOUS UNTIL YOU REACH THE SAFE ZONE, MR. DODGE.
WHEN YOU WAKE HER, REMIND HER WHO'S IN CHARGE--THAT YOU CAN END HER LIFE AT ANY MOMENT.
HOW LONG HAS SHE BEEN OUT, DOC?
NEARLY *TWO YEARS NOW.* EVER SINCE--
RIGHT.
"THE INCIDENT."

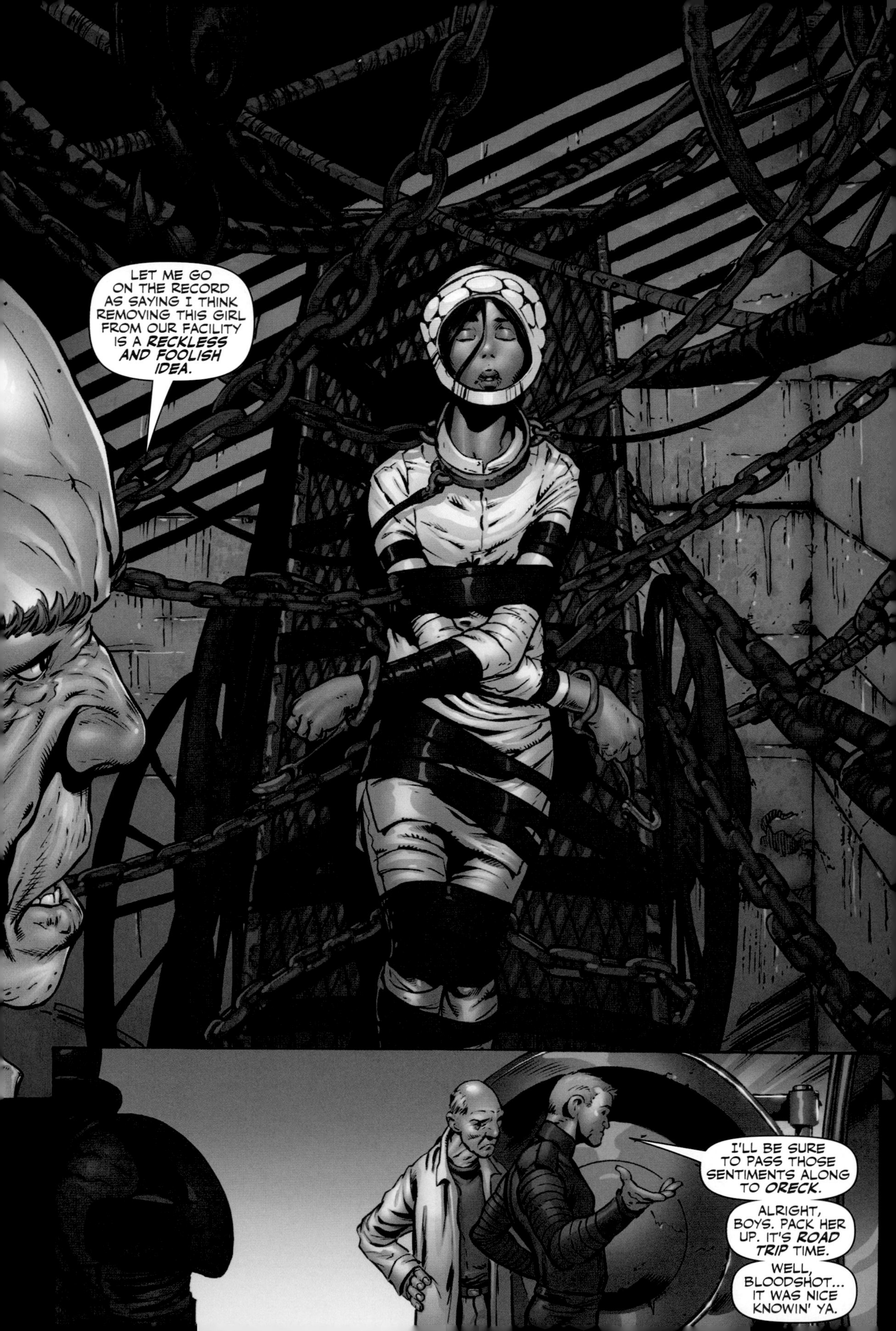
LET ME GO ON THE RECORD AS SAYING I THINK REMOVING THIS GIRL FROM OUR FACILITY IS A *RECKLESS AND FOOLISH IDEA*.
I'LL BE SURE TO PASS THOSE SENTIMENTS ALONG TO *ORECK*.
ALRIGHT, BOYS. PACK HER UP. IT'S *ROAD TRIP* TIME.
WELL, BLOODSHOT... IT WAS NICE KNOWIN' YA.

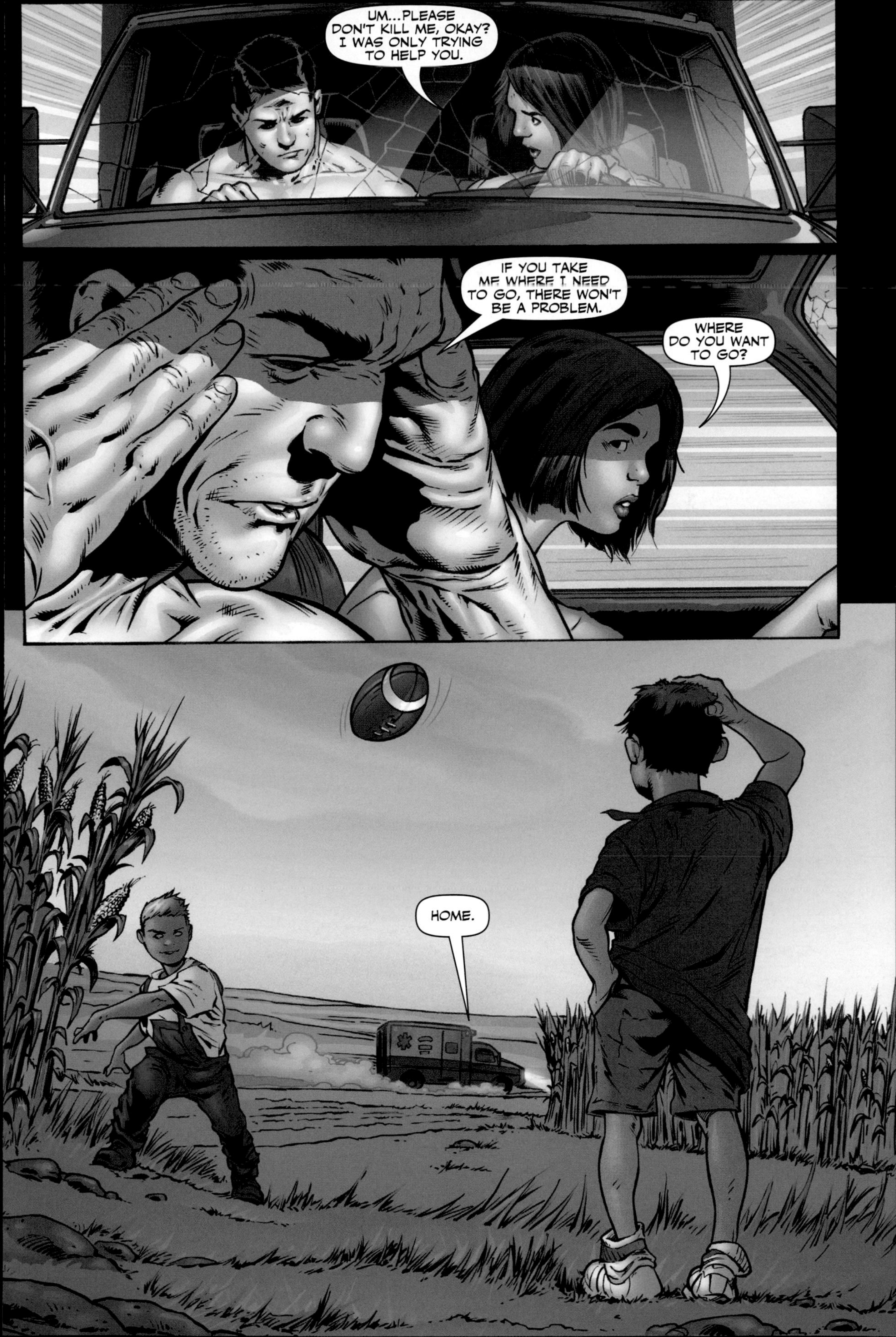
UM...PLEASE DON'T KILL ME, OKAY? I WAS ONLY TRYING TO HELP YOU.
IF YOU TAKE ME WHERE I NEED TO GO, THERE WON'T BE A PROBLEM.
WHERE DO YOU WANT TO GO?
HOME.

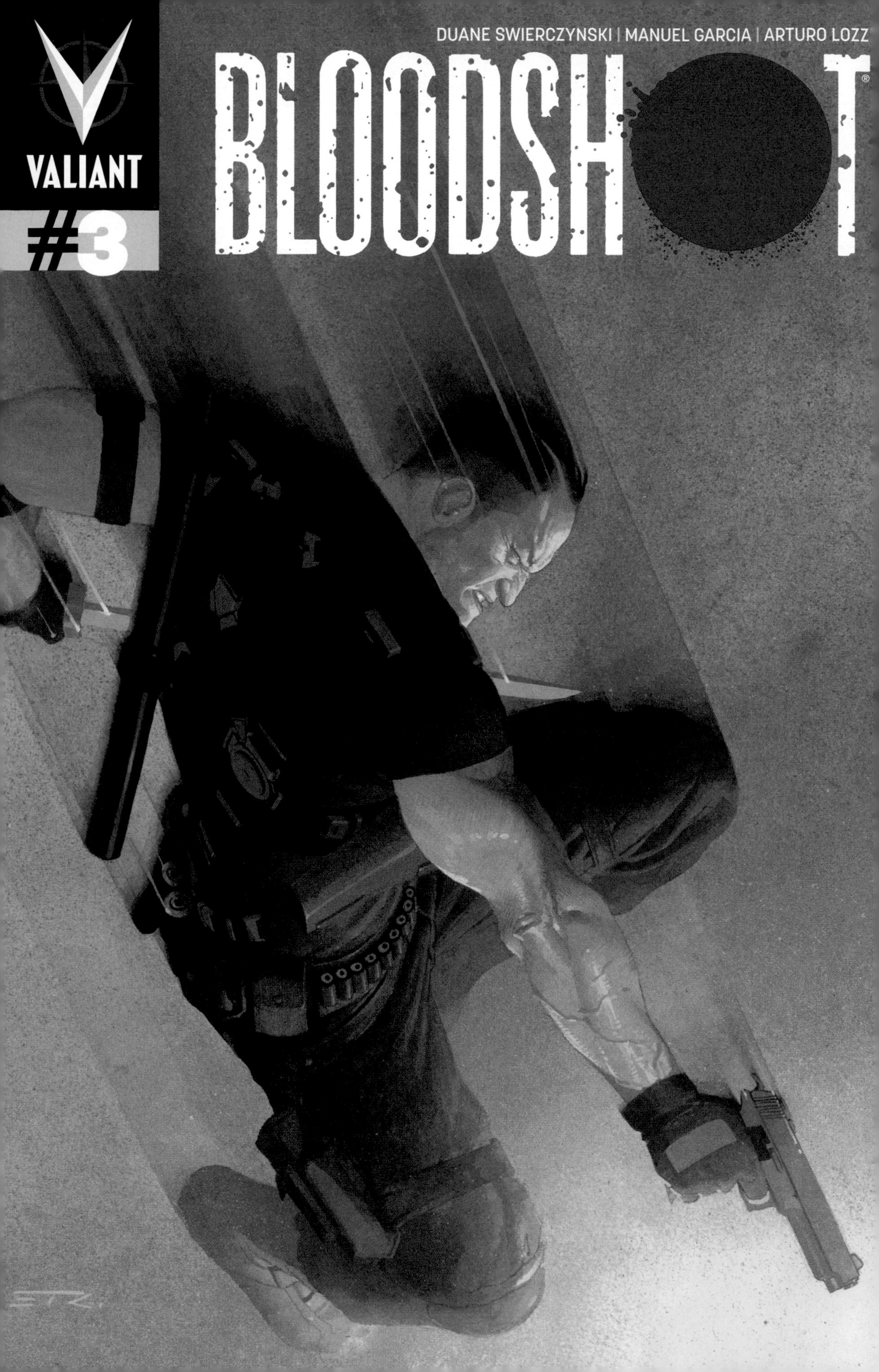
VALIANT
#3
DUANE SWIERCZYNSKI | MANUEL GARCIA | ARTURO LOZZ
BLOODSHOT

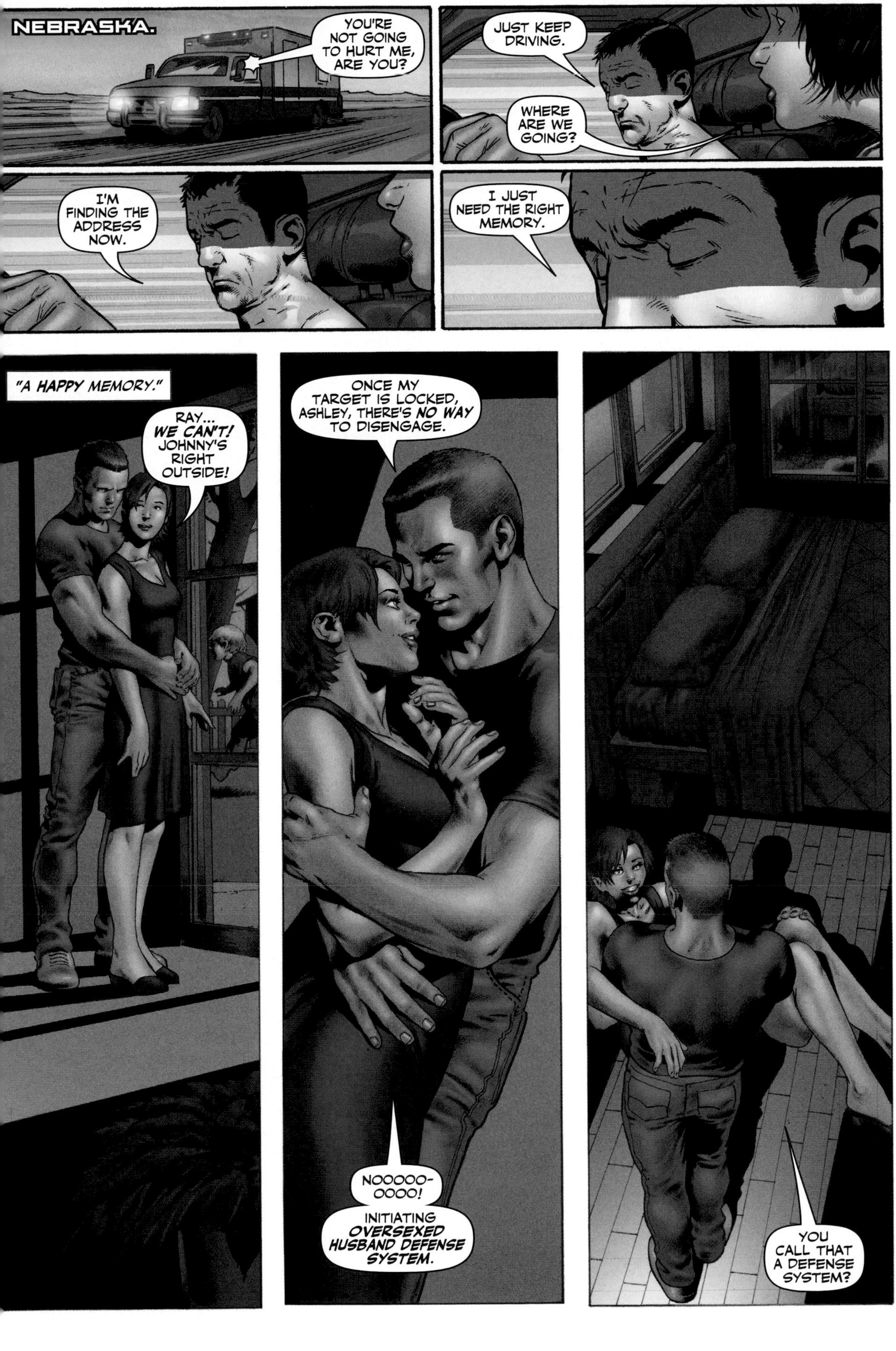
NEBRASKA.
YOU'RE NOT GOING TO HURT ME, ARE YOU?
JUST KEEP DRIVING.
WHERE ARE WE GOING?
I'M FINDING THE ADDRESS NOW.
I JUST NEED THE RIGHT MEMORY.
"A HAPPY MEMORY."
RAY... WE CAN'T! JOHNNY'S RIGHT OUTSIDE!
ONCE MY TARGET IS LOCKED, ASHLEY, THERE'S NO WAY TO DISENGAGE.
NOOOOO-OOOO!
INITIATING OVERSEXED HUSBAND DEFENSE SYSTEM.
YOU CALL THAT A DEFENSE SYSTEM?

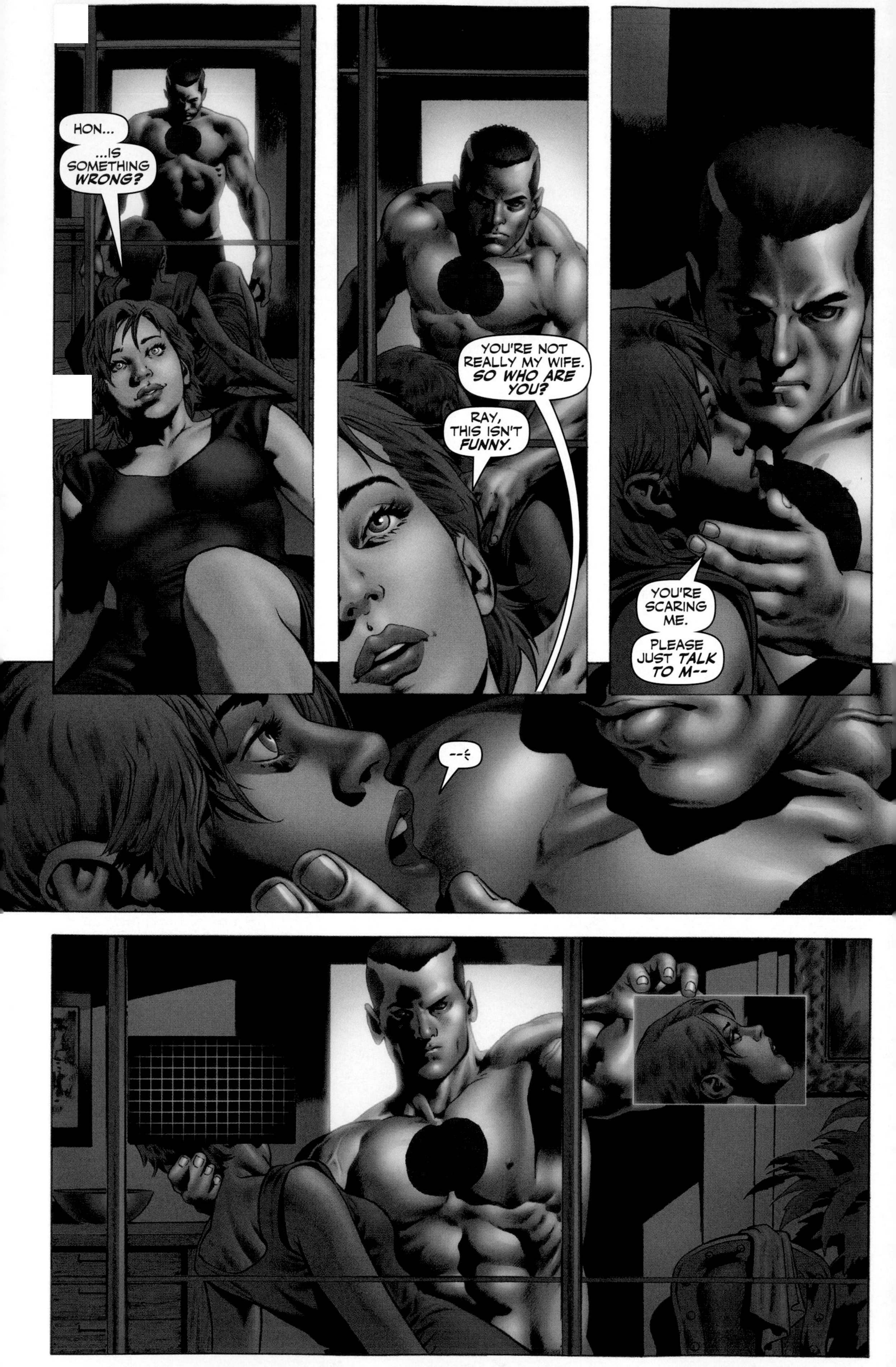
HON...
...IS SOMETHING WRONG?
YOU'RE NOT REALLY MY WIFE. SO WHO ARE YOU?
RAY, THIS ISN'T FUNNY.
YOU'RE SCARING ME.
PLEASE JUST TALK TO M--
--!

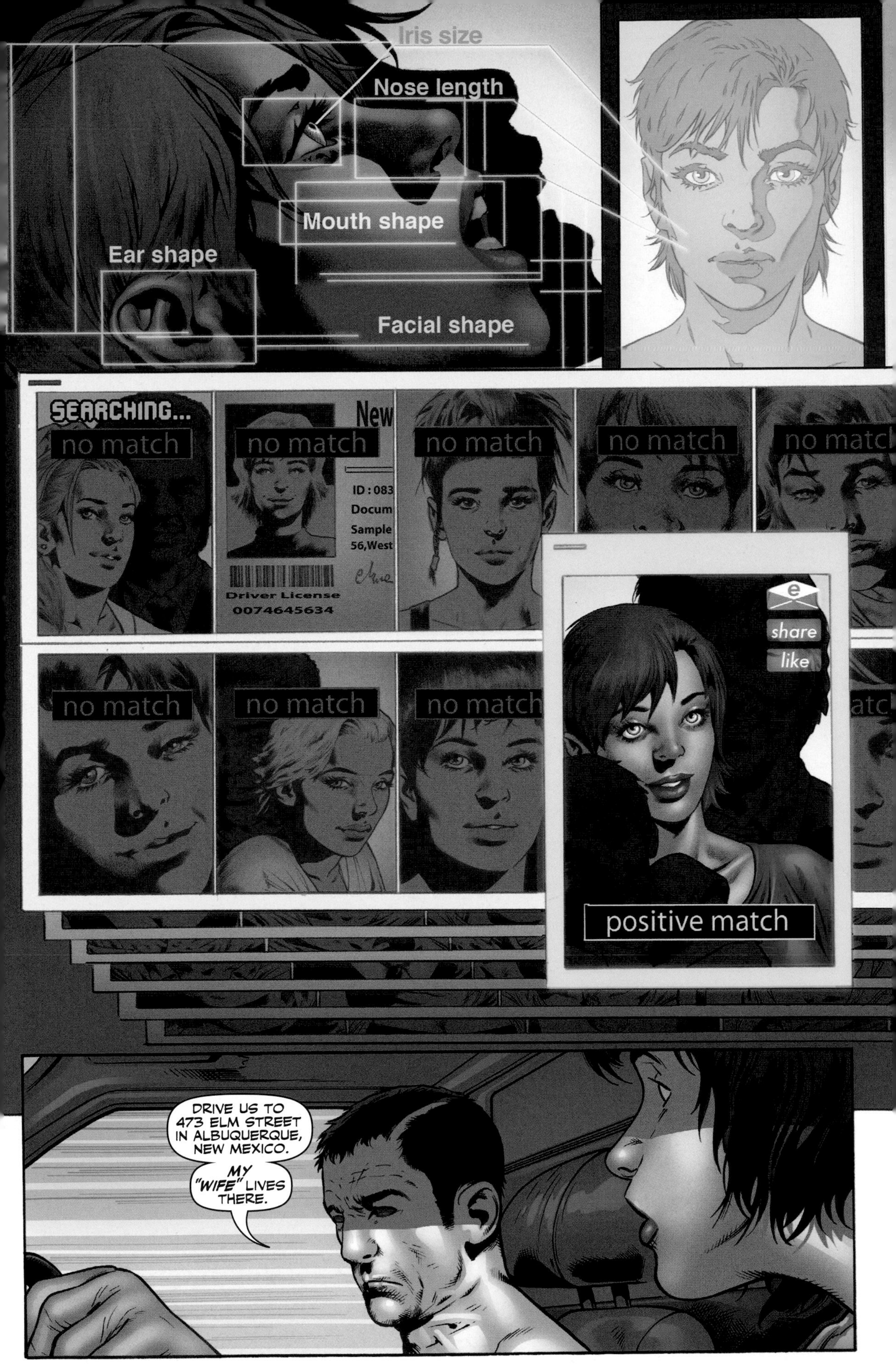

Iris size
Nose length
Mouth shape
Ear shape
Facial shape
SEARCHING...
no match
New
no match
ID : 083
Docum
Sample
56,West
Driver License
0074645634
no match
no match
no match
no match
no match
share
like
positive match
DRIVE US TO 473 ELM STREET IN ALBUQUERQUE, NEW MEXICO.
MY "WIFE" LIVES THERE.

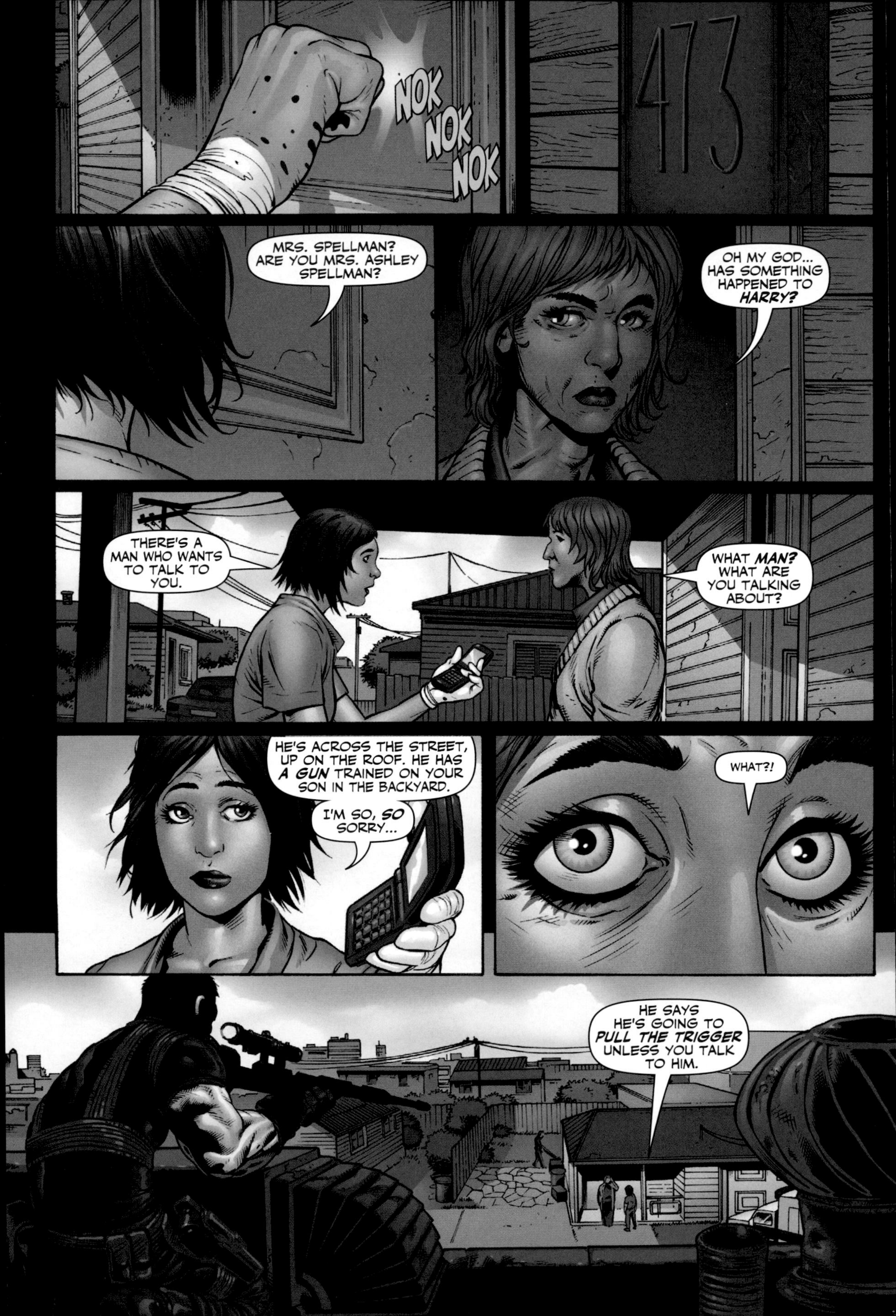
NOK
NOK
NOK
473
MRS. SPELLMAN? ARE YOU MRS. ASHLEY SPELLMAN?
OH MY GOD... HAS SOMETHING HAPPENED TO HARRY?
THERE'S A MAN WHO WANTS TO TALK TO YOU.
WHAT MAN? WHAT ARE YOU TALKING ABOUT?
HE'S ACROSS THE STREET, UP ON THE ROOF. HE HAS A GUN TRAINED ON YOUR SON IN THE BACKYARD.
I'M SO, SO SORRY...
WHAT?!
HE SAYS HE'S GOING TO PULL THE TRIGGER UNLESS YOU TALK TO HIM.

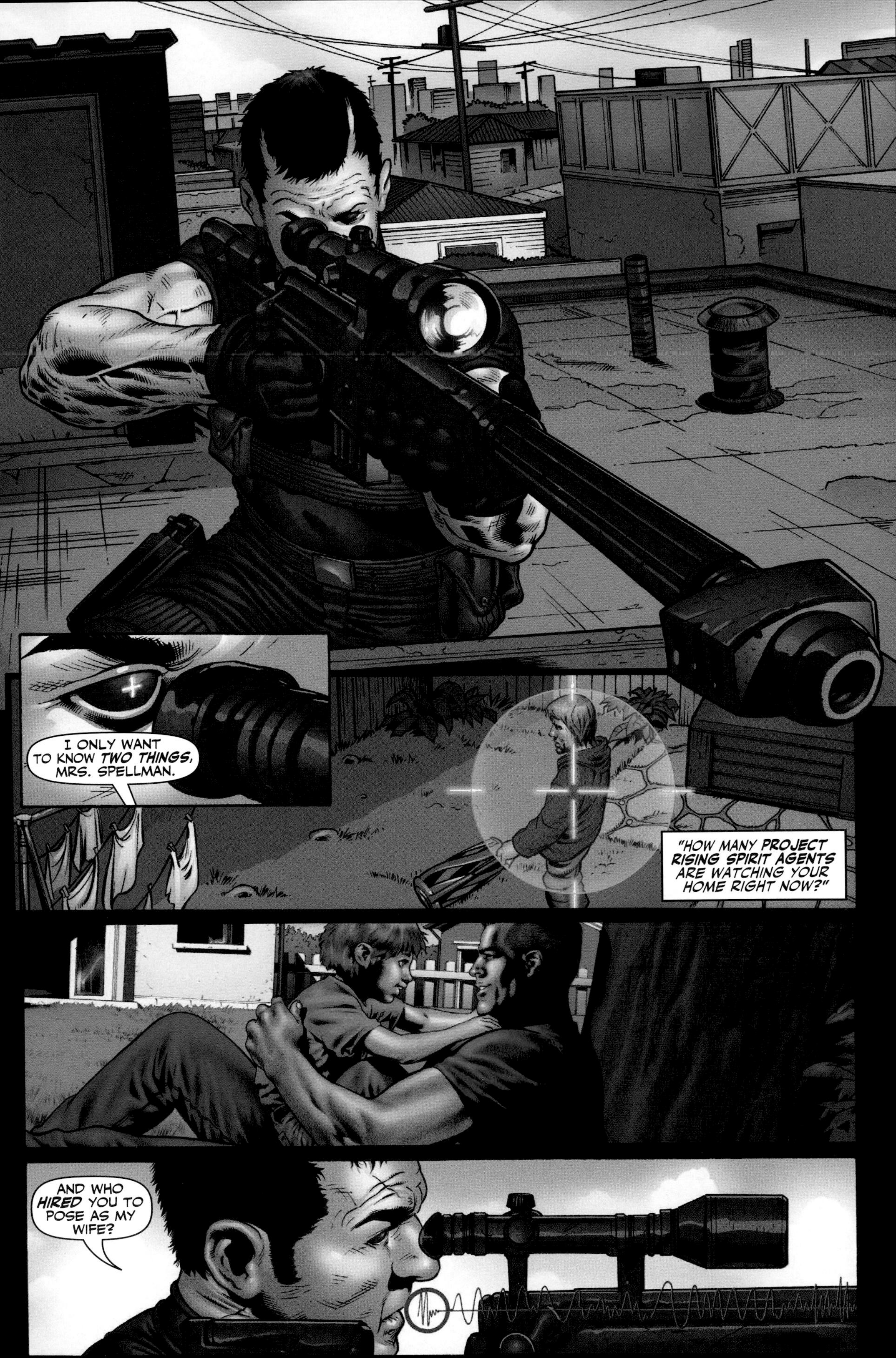
I ONLY WANT TO KNOW *TWO THINGS*, MRS. SPELLMAN.
"HOW MANY *PROJECT RISING SPIRIT AGENTS* ARE WATCHING YOUR HOME RIGHT NOW?"
AND WHO *HIRED* YOU TO POSE AS MY WIFE?

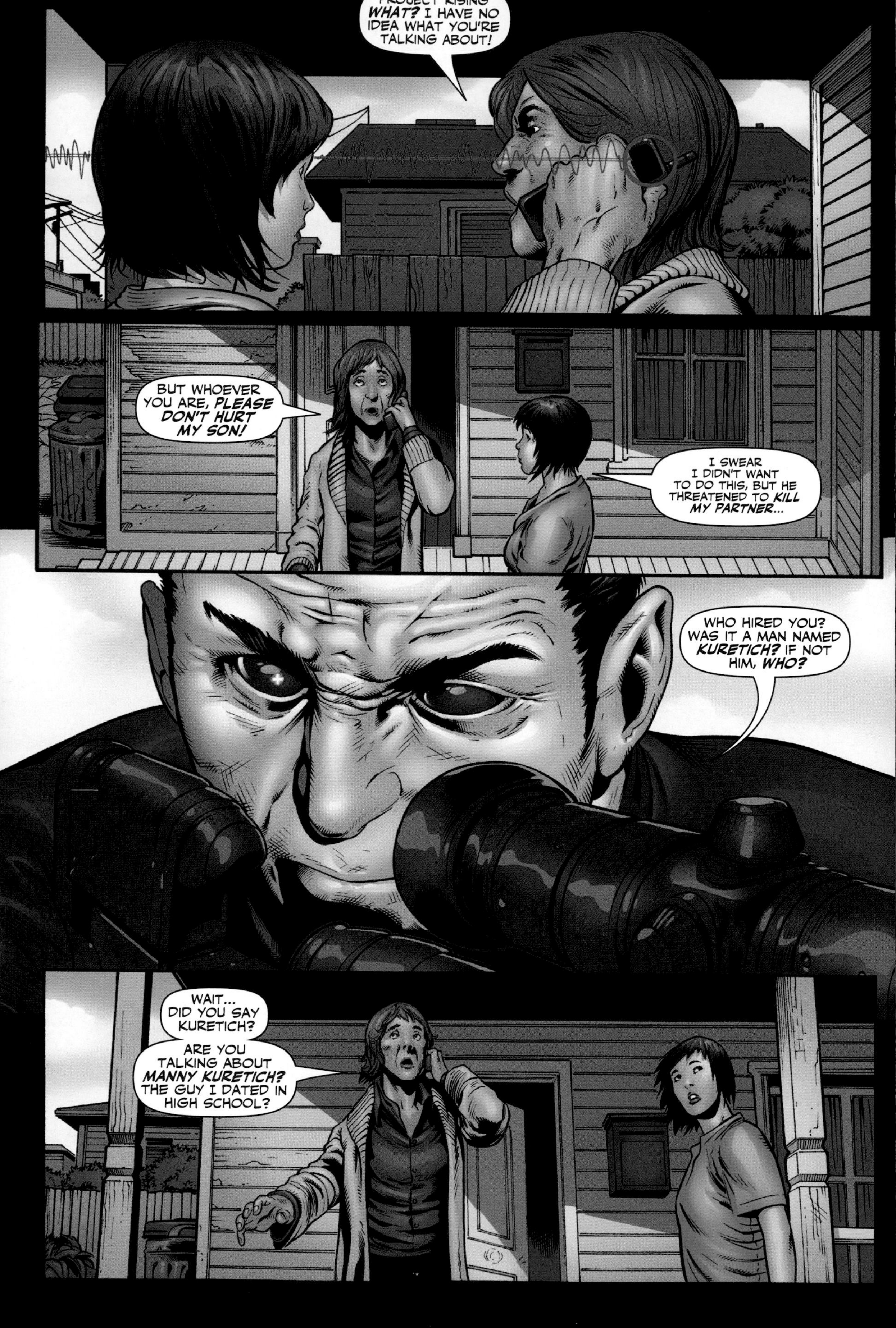
PROJECT RISING *WHAT?* I HAVE NO IDEA WHAT YOU'RE TALKING ABOUT!
BUT WHOEVER YOU ARE, *PLEASE DON'T HURT MY SON!*
I SWEAR I DIDN'T WANT TO DO THIS, BUT HE THREATENED TO *KILL MY PARTNER...*
WHO HIRED YOU? WAS IT A MAN NAMED *KURETICH?* IF NOT HIM, *WHO?*
WAIT... DID YOU SAY KURETICH?
ARE YOU TALKING ABOUT *MANNY KURETICH?* THE GUY I DATED IN HIGH SCHOOL?

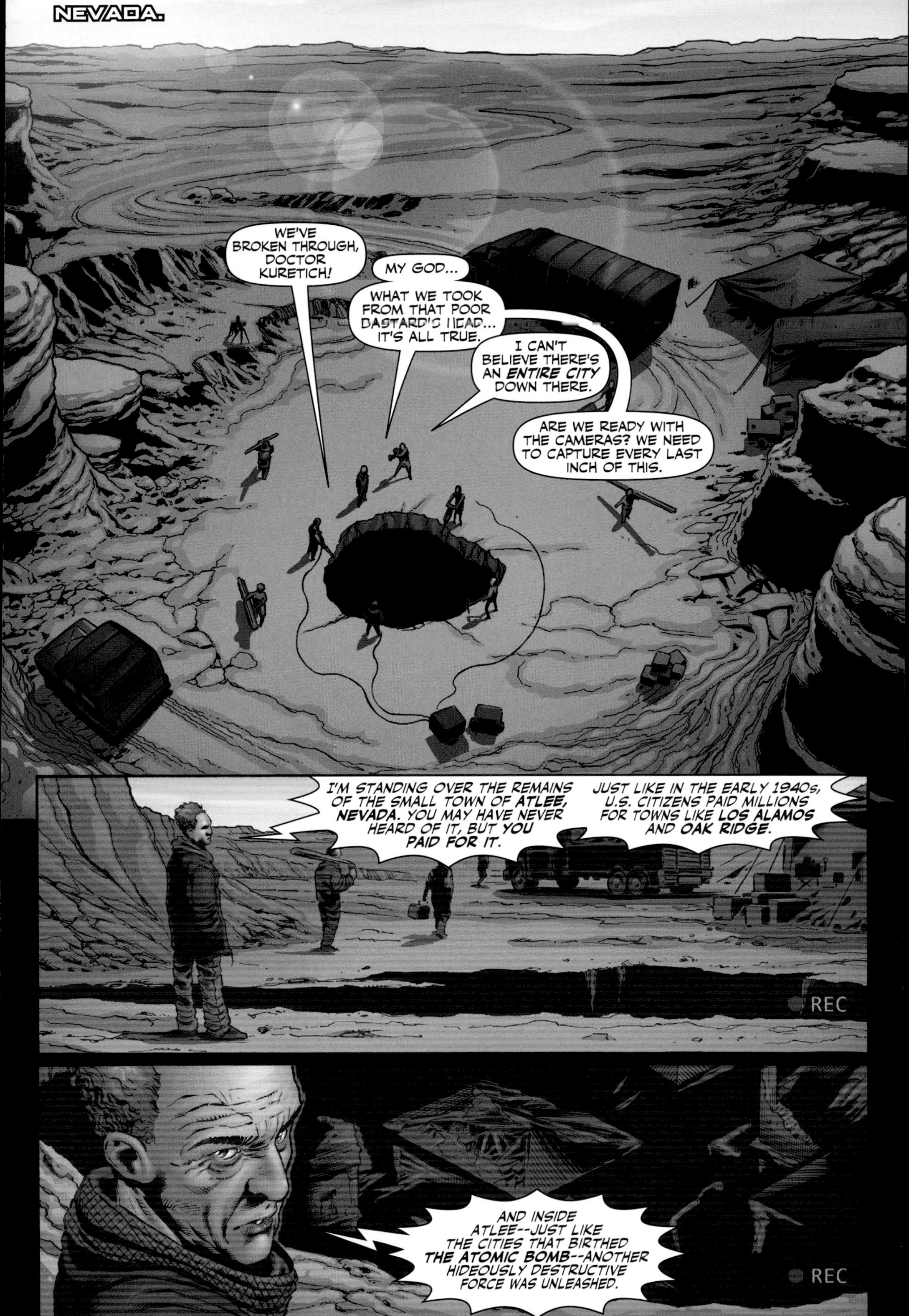

NEVADA.
WE'VE BROKEN THROUGH, DOCTOR KURETICH!
MY GOD...
WHAT WE TOOK FROM THAT POOR BASTARD'S HEAD... IT'S ALL TRUE.
I CAN'T BELIEVE THERE'S AN ENTIRE CITY DOWN THERE.
ARE WE READY WITH THE CAMERAS? WE NEED TO CAPTURE EVERY LAST INCH OF THIS.
I'M STANDING OVER THE REMAINS OF THE SMALL TOWN OF ATLEE, NEVADA. YOU MAY HAVE NEVER HEARD OF IT, BUT YOU PAID FOR IT.
JUST LIKE IN THE EARLY 1940s, U.S. CITIZENS PAID MILLIONS FOR TOWNS LIKE LOS ALAMOS AND OAK RIDGE.
REC
AND INSIDE ATLEE--JUST LIKE THE CITIES THAT BIRTHED THE ATOMIC BOMB--ANOTHER HIDEOUSLY DESTRUCTIVE FORCE WAS UNLEASHED.
REC

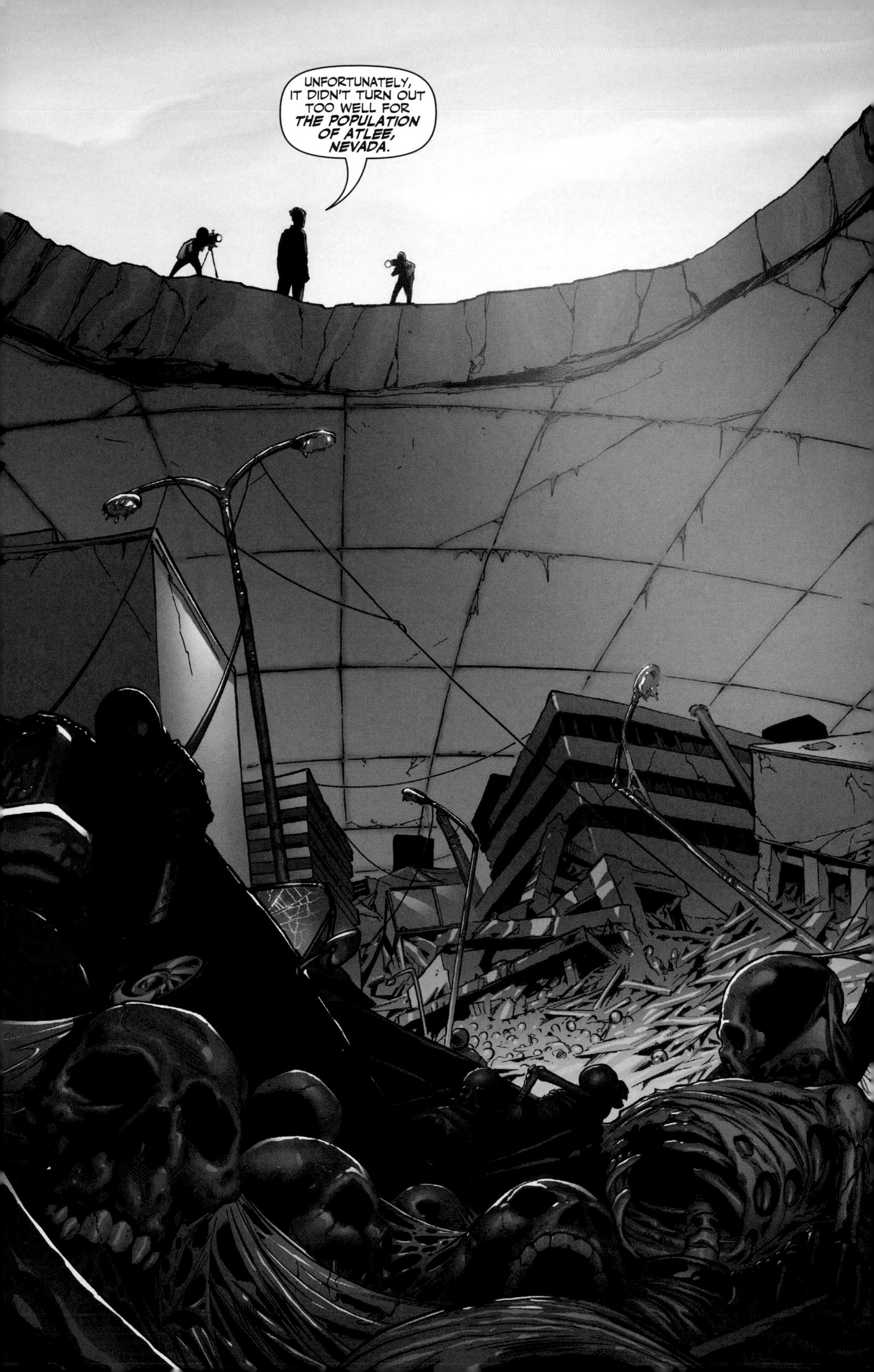
UNFORTUNATELY, IT DIDN'T TURN OUT TOO WELL FOR *THE POPULATION OF ATLEE, NEVADA.*

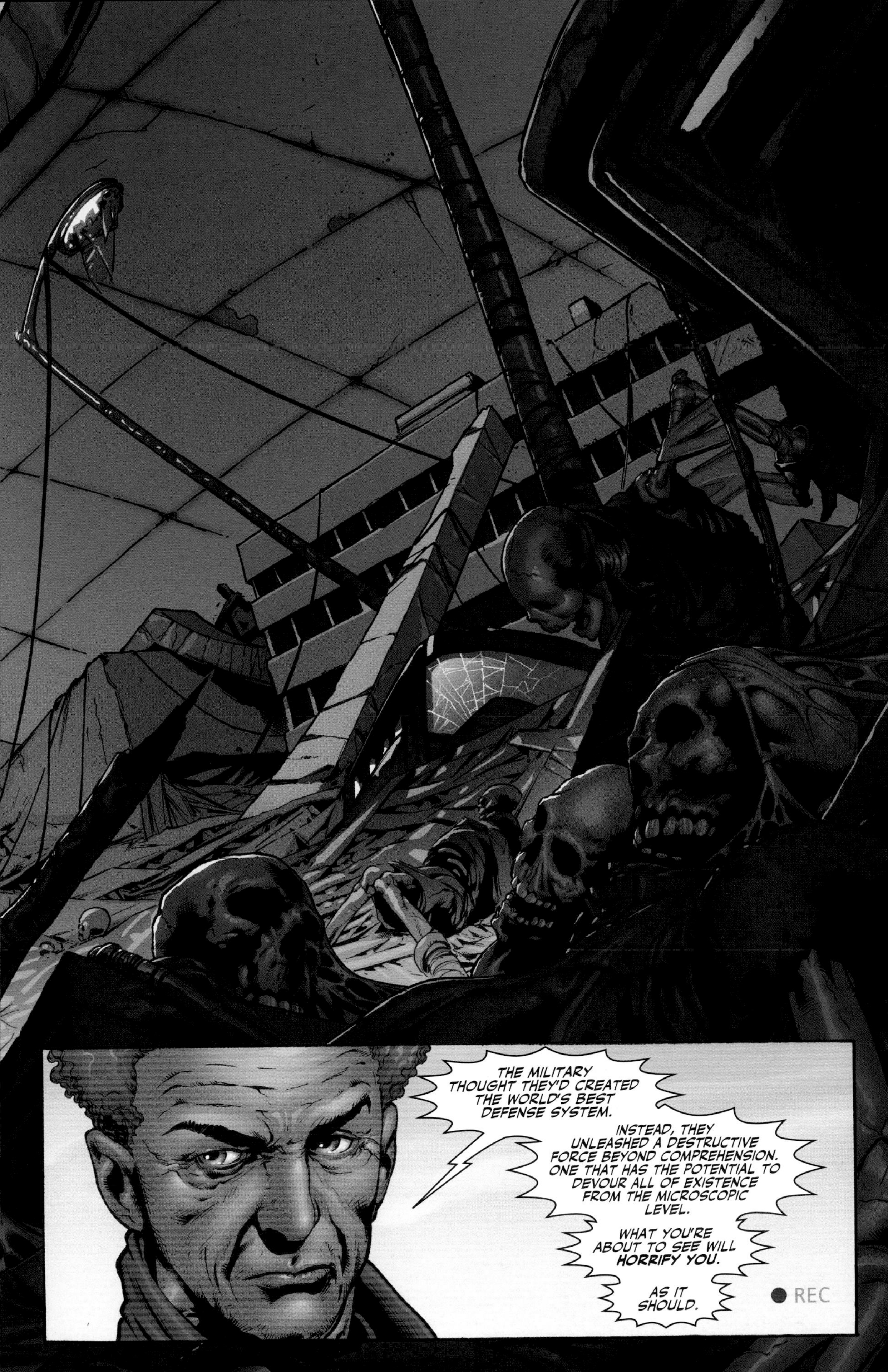
THE MILITARY THOUGHT THEY'D CREATED THE WORLD'S BEST DEFENSE SYSTEM.
INSTEAD, THEY UNLEASHED A DESTRUCTIVE FORCE BEYOND COMPREHENSION. ONE THAT HAS THE POTENTIAL TO DEVOUR ALL OF EXISTENCE FROM THE MICROSCOPIC LEVEL.
WHAT YOU'RE ABOUT TO SEE WILL **HORRIFY YOU**.
AS IT SHOULD.
REC

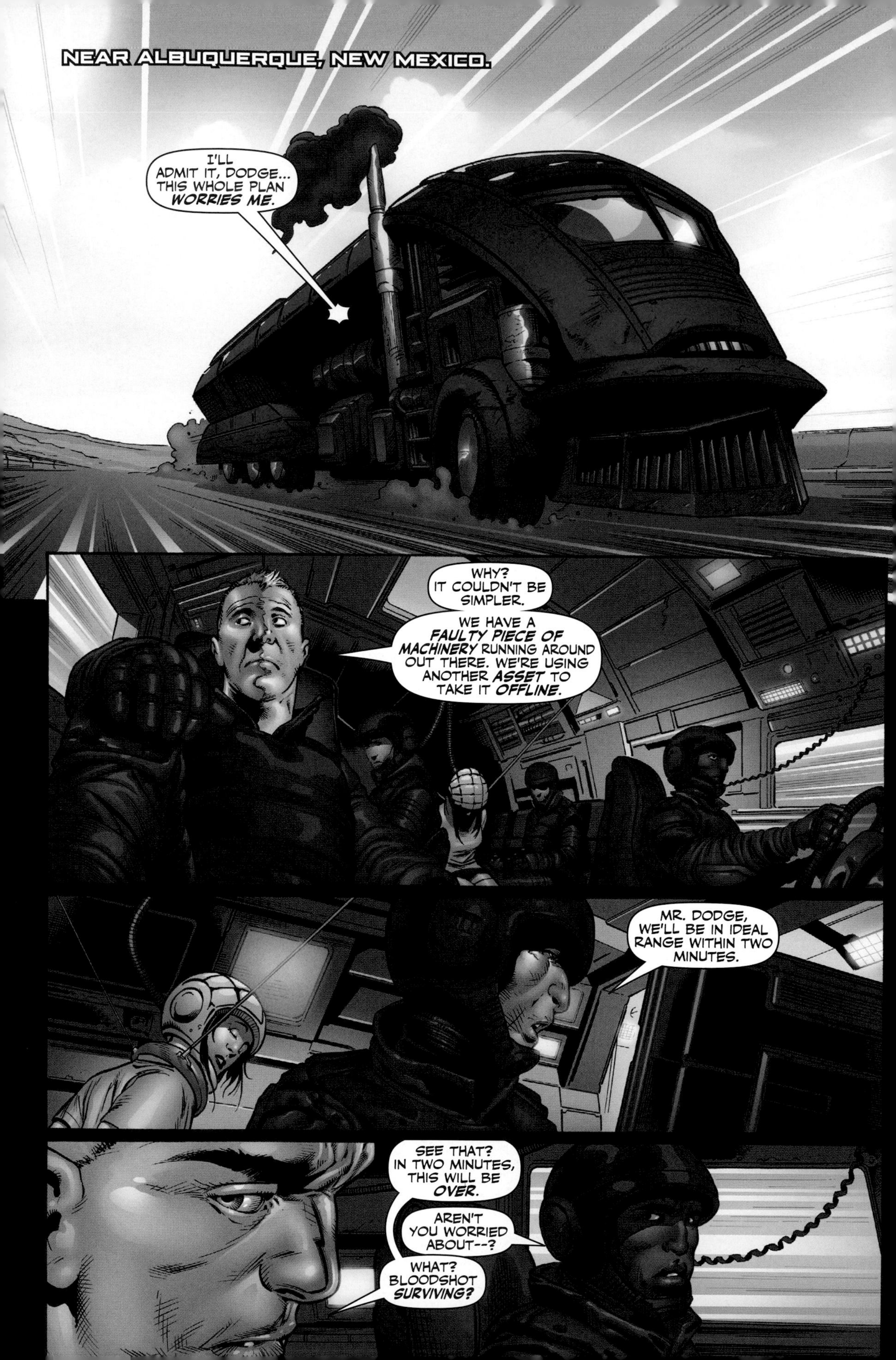
NEAR ALBUQUERQUE, NEW MEXICO.
I'LL ADMIT IT, DODGE... THIS WHOLE PLAN WORRIES ME.
WHY? IT COULDN'T BE SIMPLER.
WE HAVE A FAULTY PIECE OF MACHINERY RUNNING AROUND OUT THERE. WE'RE USING ANOTHER ASSET TO TAKE IT OFFLINE.
MR. DODGE, WE'LL BE IN IDEAL RANGE WITHIN TWO MINUTES.
SEE THAT? IN TWO MINUTES, THIS WILL BE OVER.
AREN'T YOU WORRIED ABOUT--?
WHAT? BLOODSHOT SURVIVING?

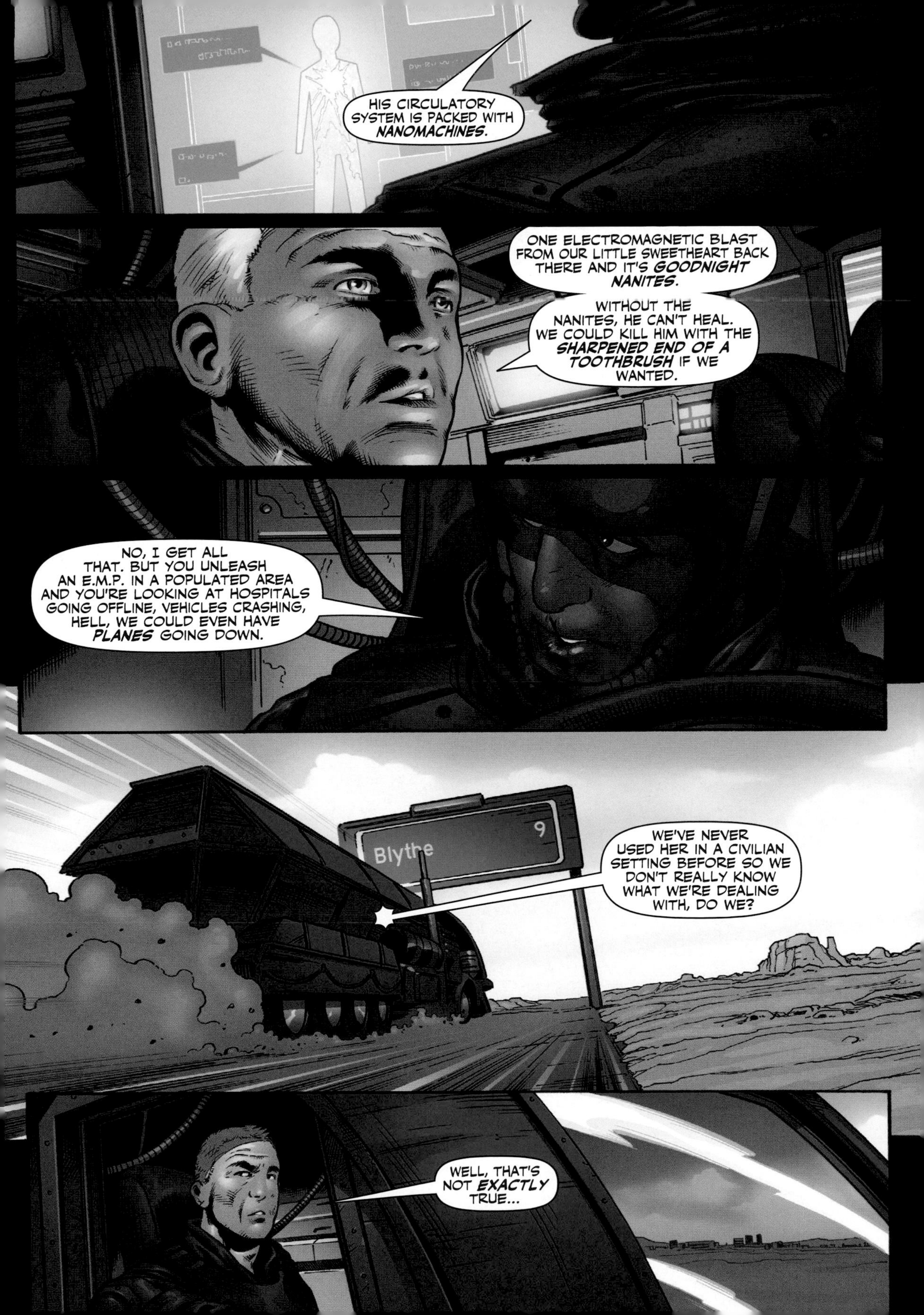
HIS CIRCULATORY SYSTEM IS PACKED WITH NANOMACHINES.
ONE ELECTROMAGNETIC BLAST FROM OUR LITTLE SWEETHEART BACK THERE AND IT'S GOODNIGHT NANITES.
WITHOUT THE NANITES, HE CAN'T HEAL. WE COULD KILL HIM WITH THE SHARPENED END OF A TOOTHBRUSH IF WE WANTED.
NO, I GET ALL THAT. BUT YOU UNLEASH AN E.M.P. IN A POPULATED AREA AND YOU'RE LOOKING AT HOSPITALS GOING OFFLINE, VEHICLES CRASHING, HELL, WE COULD EVEN HAVE PLANES GOING DOWN.
Blythe 9
WE'VE NEVER USED HER IN A CIVILIAN SETTING BEFORE SO WE DON'T REALLY KNOW WHAT WE'RE DEALING WITH, DO WE?
WELL, THAT'S NOT EXACTLY TRUE...

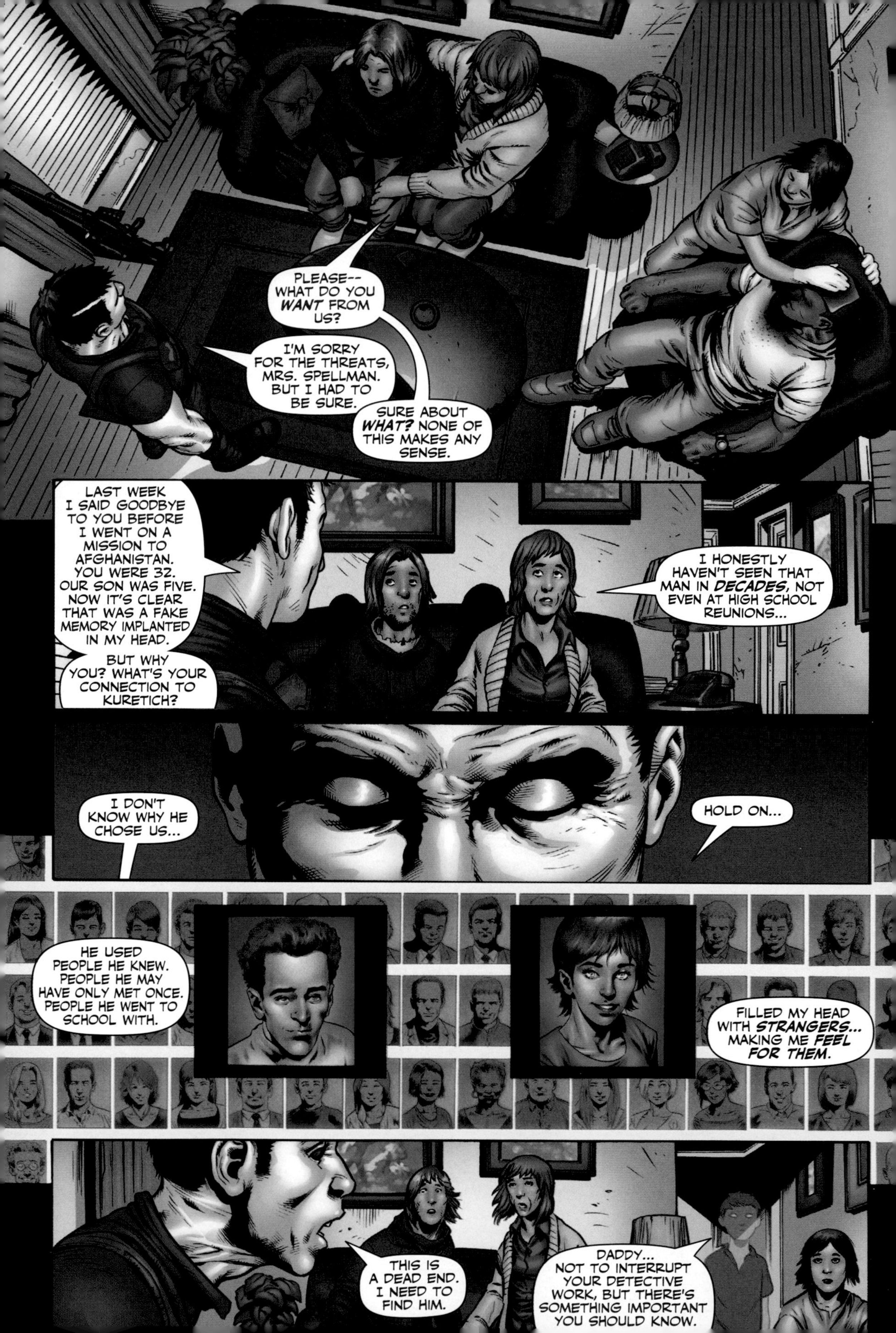
PLEASE-- WHAT DO YOU WANT FROM US?
I'M SORRY FOR THE THREATS, MRS. SPELLMAN. BUT I HAD TO BE SURE.
SURE ABOUT WHAT? NONE OF THIS MAKES ANY SENSE.
LAST WEEK I SAID GOODBYE TO YOU BEFORE I WENT ON A MISSION TO AFGHANISTAN. YOU WERE 32. OUR SON WAS FIVE. NOW IT'S CLEAR THAT WAS A FAKE MEMORY IMPLANTED IN MY HEAD.
BUT WHY YOU? WHAT'S YOUR CONNECTION TO KURETICH?
I HONESTLY HAVEN'T SEEN THAT MAN IN DECADES, NOT EVEN AT HIGH SCHOOL REUNIONS...
I DON'T KNOW WHY HE CHOSE US...
HOLD ON...
HE USED PEOPLE HE KNEW. PEOPLE HE MAY HAVE ONLY MET ONCE. PEOPLE HE WENT TO SCHOOL WITH.
FILLED MY HEAD WITH STRANGERS... MAKING ME FEEL FOR THEM.
THIS IS A DEAD END. I NEED TO FIND HIM.
DADDY... NOT TO INTERRUPT YOUR DETECTIVE WORK, BUT THERE'S SOMETHING IMPORTANT YOU SHOULD KNOW.

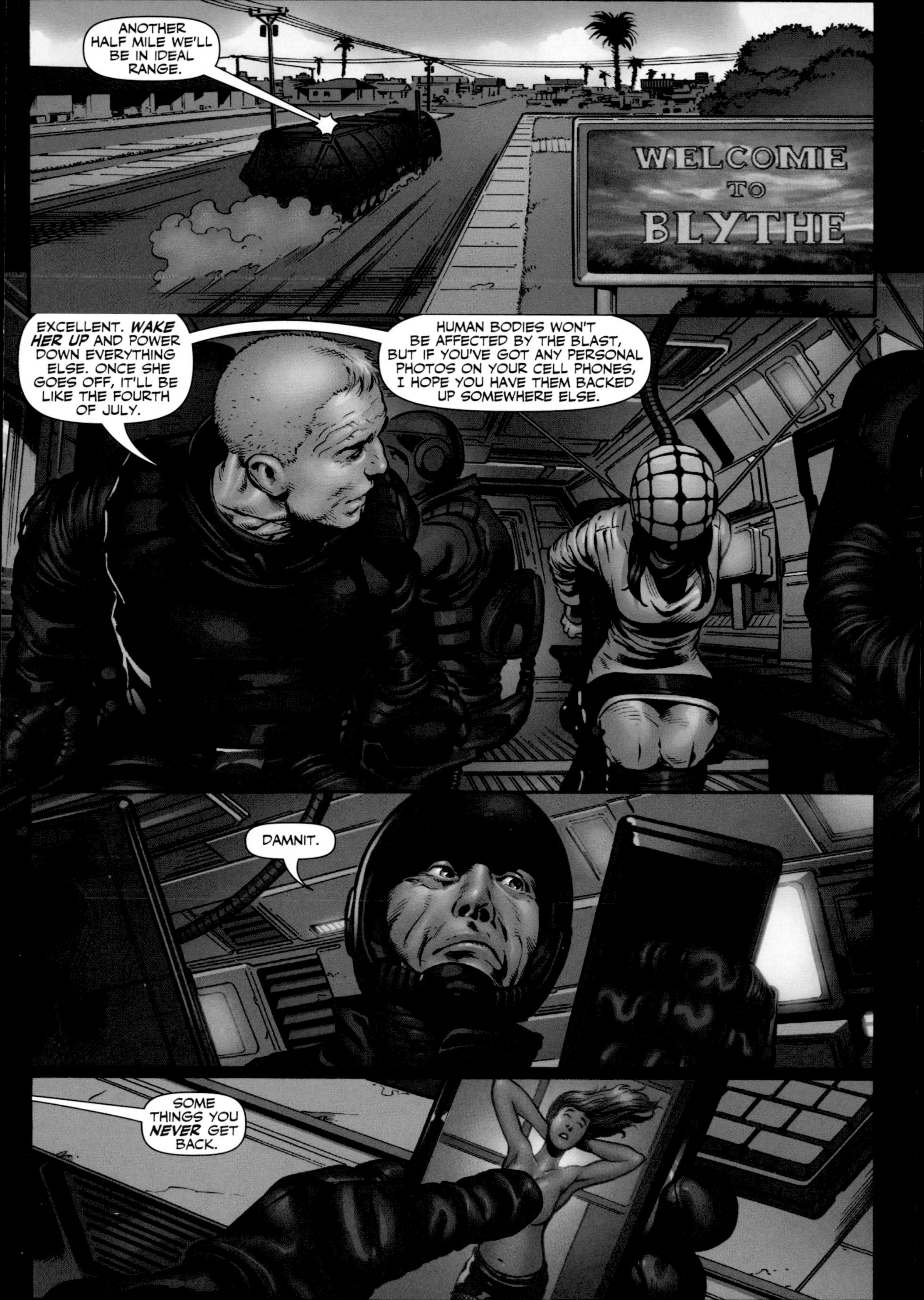
ANOTHER HALF MILE WE'LL BE IN IDEAL RANGE.
WELCOME TO BLYTHE
EXCELLENT. **WAKE HER UP** AND POWER DOWN EVERYTHING ELSE. ONCE SHE GOES OFF, IT'LL BE LIKE THE FOURTH OF JULY.
HUMAN BODIES WON'T BE AFFECTED BY THE BLAST, BUT IF YOU'VE GOT ANY PERSONAL PHOTOS ON YOUR CELL PHONES, I HOPE YOU HAVE THEM BACKED UP SOMEWHERE ELSE.
DAMNIT.
SOME THINGS YOU **NEVER** GET BACK.

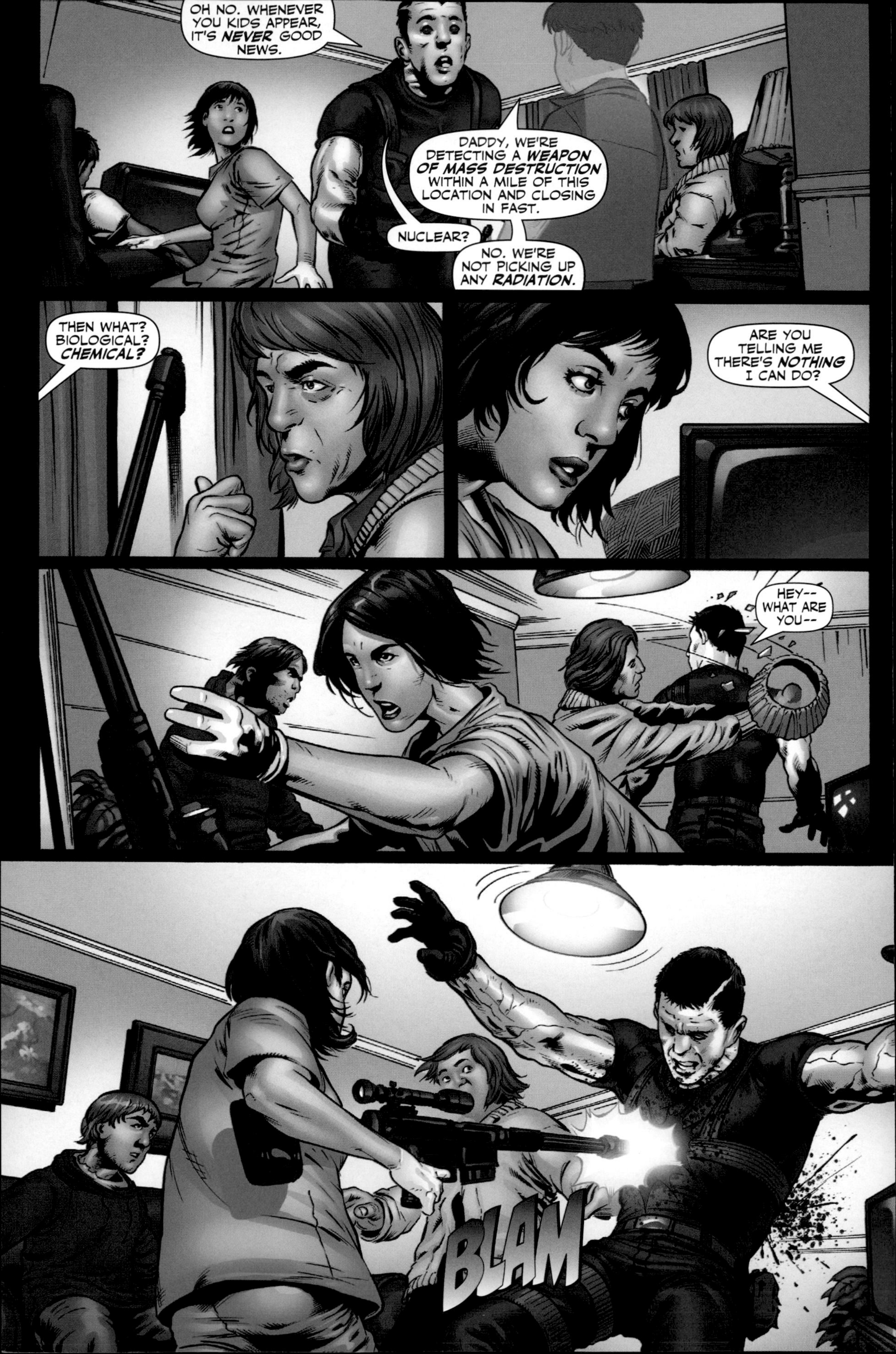
OH NO. WHENEVER YOU KIDS APPEAR, IT'S NEVER GOOD NEWS.
DADDY, WE'RE DETECTING A WEAPON OF MASS DESTRUCTION WITHIN A MILE OF THIS LOCATION AND CLOSING IN FAST.
NUCLEAR?
NO. WE'RE NOT PICKING UP ANY RADIATION.
THEN WHAT? BIOLOGICAL? CHEMICAL?
ARE YOU TELLING ME THERE'S NOTHING I CAN DO?
HEY-- WHAT ARE YOU--
BLAM

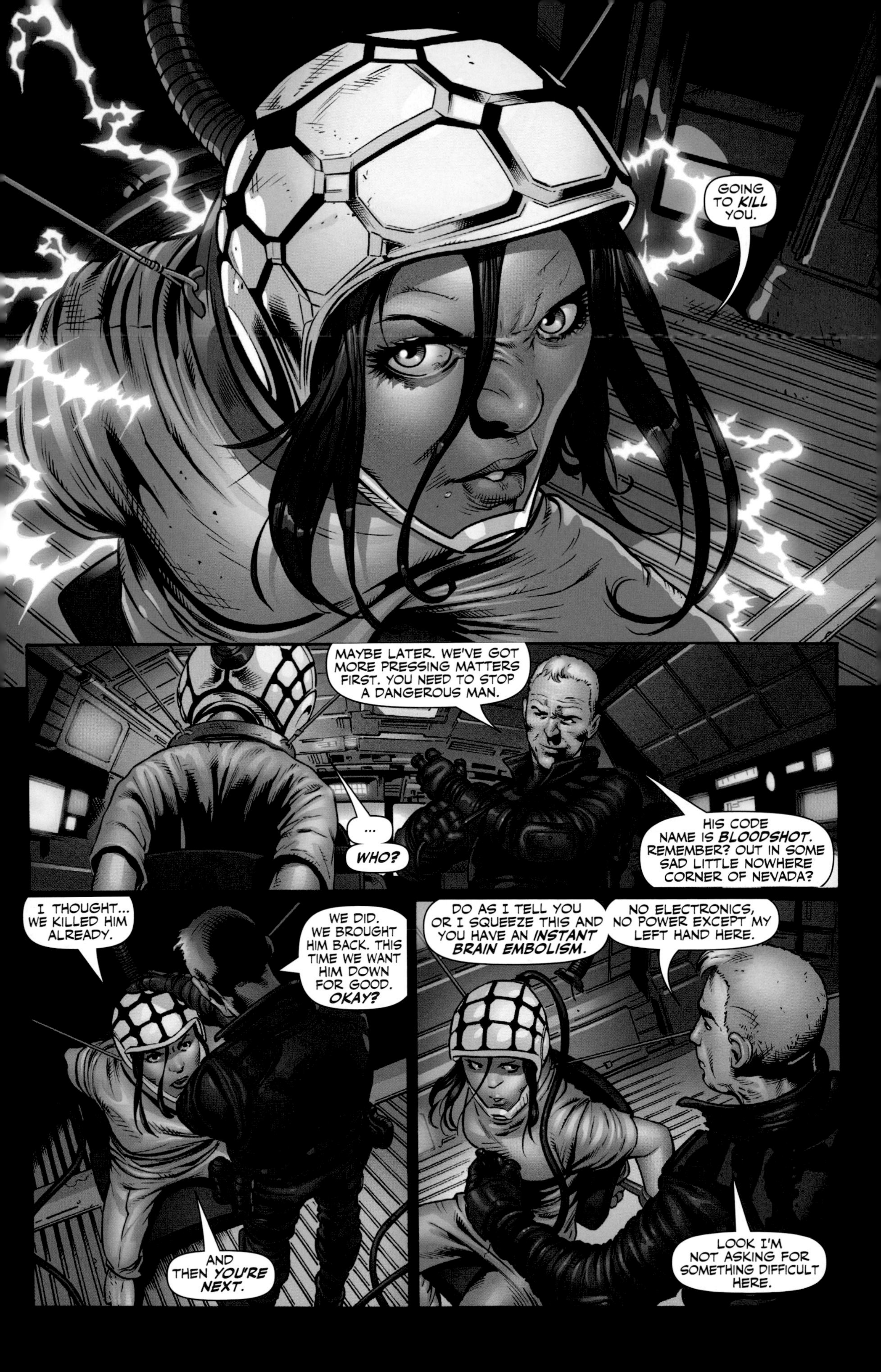
GOING TO *KILL* YOU.
MAYBE LATER. WE'VE GOT MORE PRESSING MATTERS FIRST. YOU NEED TO STOP A DANGEROUS MAN.
... *WHO?*
HIS CODE NAME IS *BLOODSHOT*. REMEMBER? OUT IN SOME SAD LITTLE NOWHERE CORNER OF NEVADA?
I THOUGHT... WE KILLED HIM ALREADY.
WE DID. WE BROUGHT HIM BACK. THIS TIME WE WANT HIM DOWN FOR GOOD. *OKAY?*
AND THEN *YOU'RE NEXT*.
DO AS I TELL YOU OR I SQUEEZE THIS AND YOU HAVE AN *INSTANT BRAIN EMBOLISM*.
NO ELECTRONICS, NO POWER EXCEPT MY LEFT HAND HERE.
LOOK I'M NOT ASKING FOR SOMETHING DIFFICULT HERE.

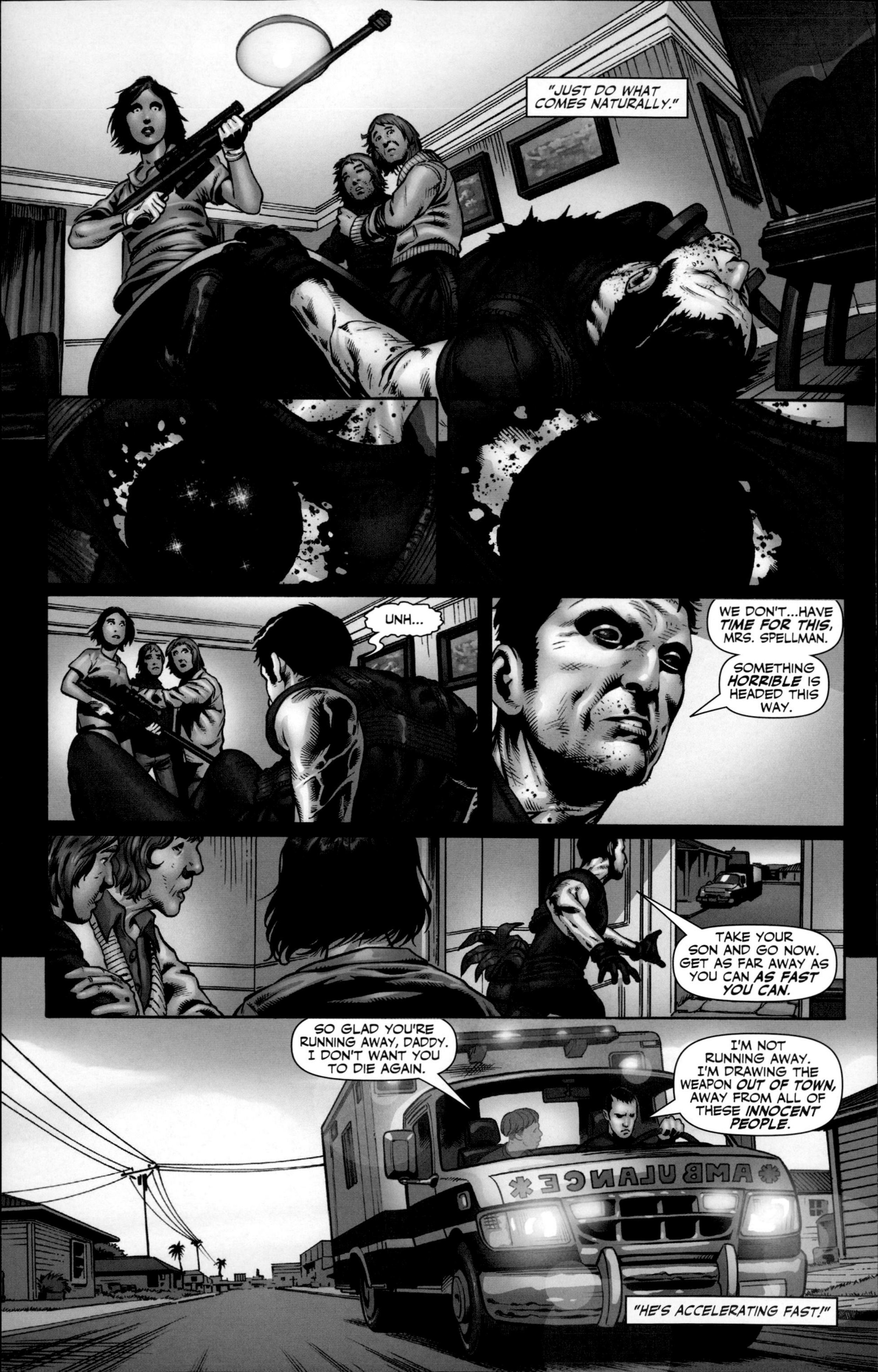
"JUST DO WHAT COMES NATURALLY."
UNH...
WE DON'T...HAVE TIME FOR THIS, MRS. SPELLMAN.
SOMETHING HORRIBLE IS HEADED THIS WAY.
TAKE YOUR SON AND GO NOW. GET AS FAR AWAY AS YOU CAN AS FAST YOU CAN.
SO GLAD YOU'RE RUNNING AWAY, DADDY. I DON'T WANT YOU TO DIE AGAIN.
I'M NOT RUNNING AWAY. I'M DRAWING THE WEAPON OUT OF TOWN, AWAY FROM ALL OF THESE INNOCENT PEOPLE.
AMBULANCE
"HE'S ACCELERATING FAST!"

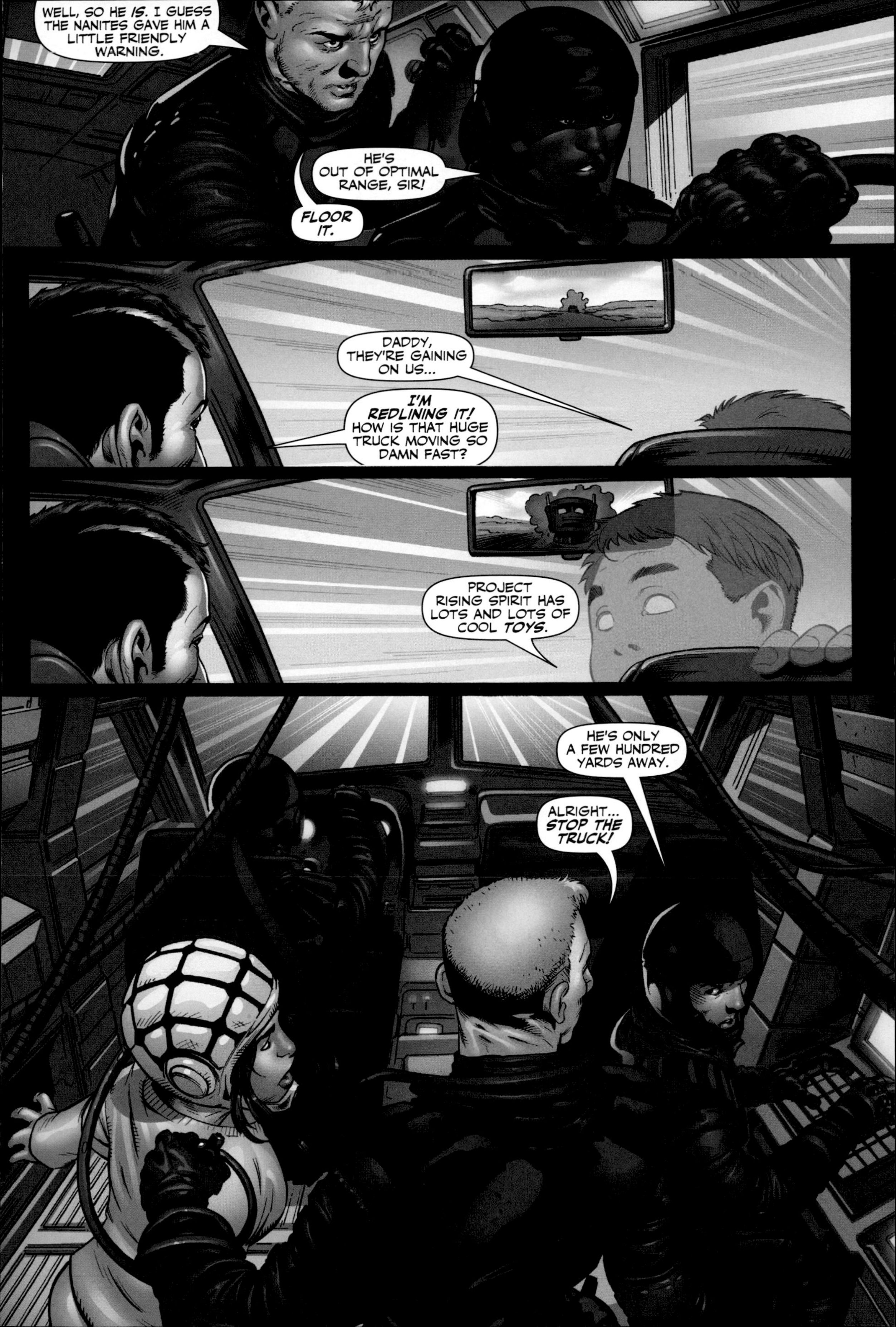
WELL, SO HE *IS*. I GUESS THE NANITES GAVE HIM A LITTLE FRIENDLY WARNING.
HE'S OUT OF OPTIMAL RANGE, SIR!
FLOOR IT.
DADDY, THEY'RE GAINING ON US...
I'M REDLINING IT! HOW IS THAT HUGE TRUCK MOVING SO DAMN FAST?
PROJECT RISING SPIRIT HAS LOTS AND LOTS OF COOL *TOYS*.
HE'S ONLY A FEW HUNDRED YARDS AWAY.
ALRIGHT... *STOP THE TRUCK!*

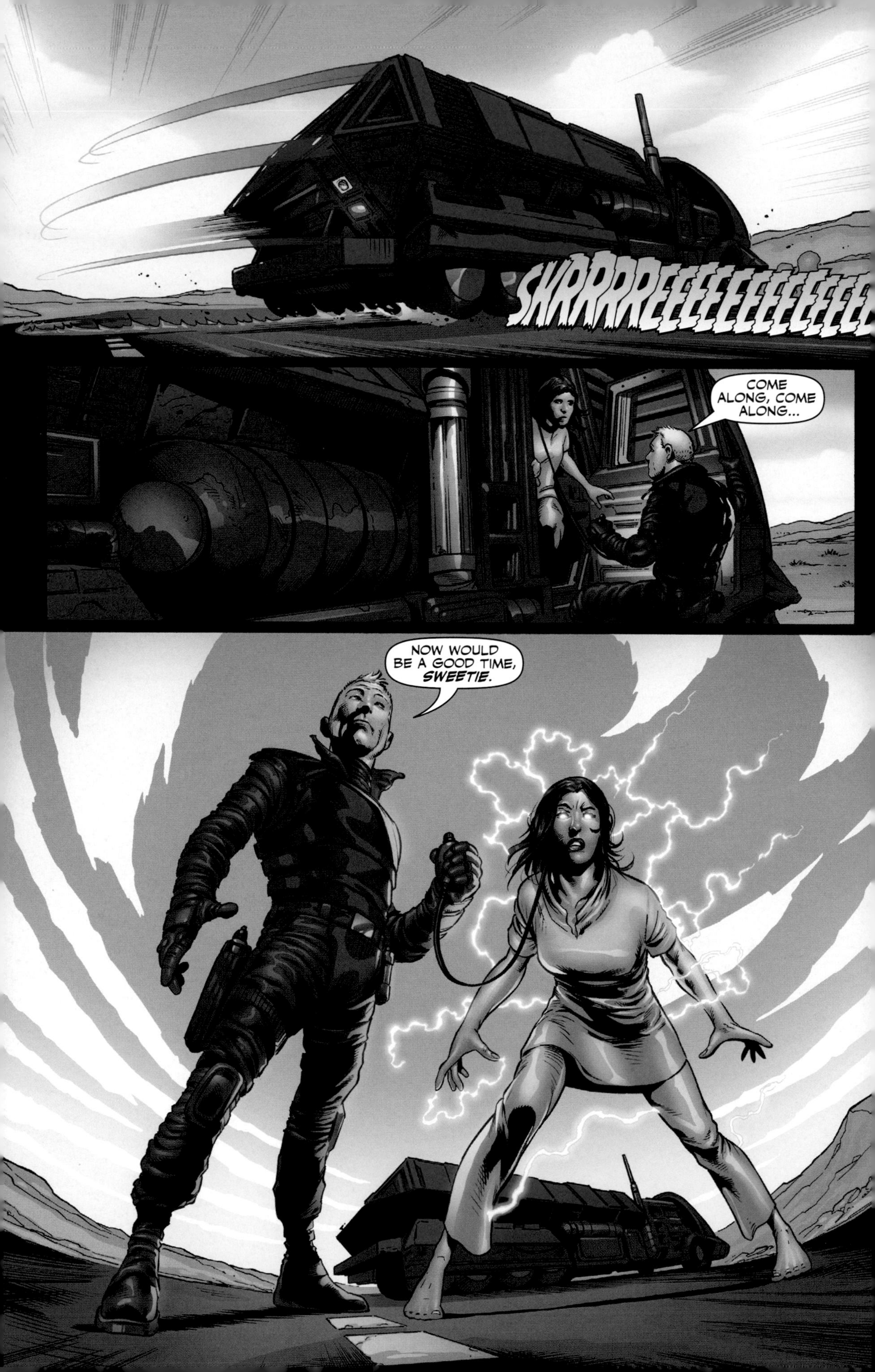
SKRRRRREEEEEEEEEEEEE
COME ALONG, COME ALONG...
NOW WOULD BE A GOOD TIME, SWEETIE.

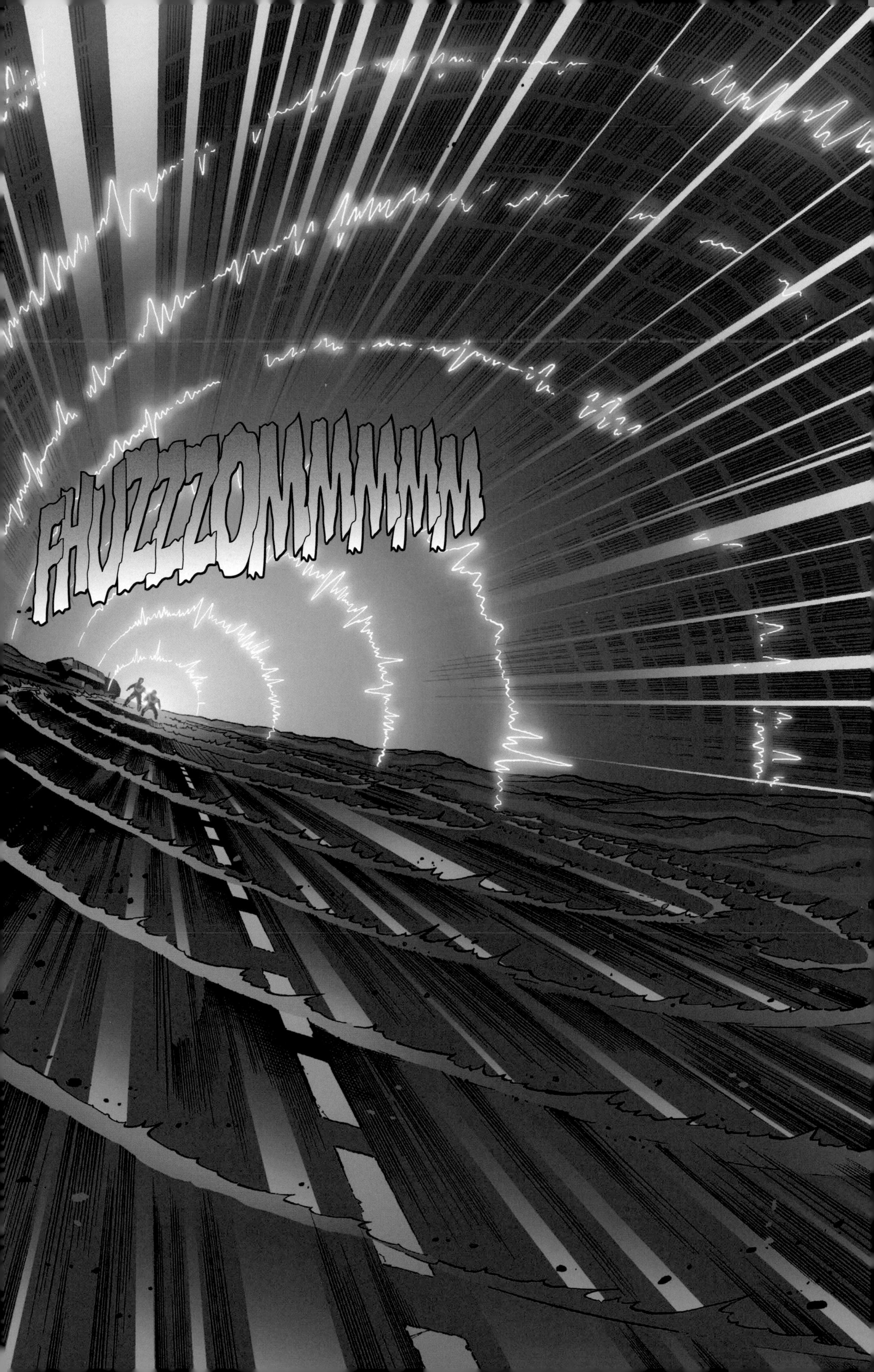
FHUZZZOMMMMM

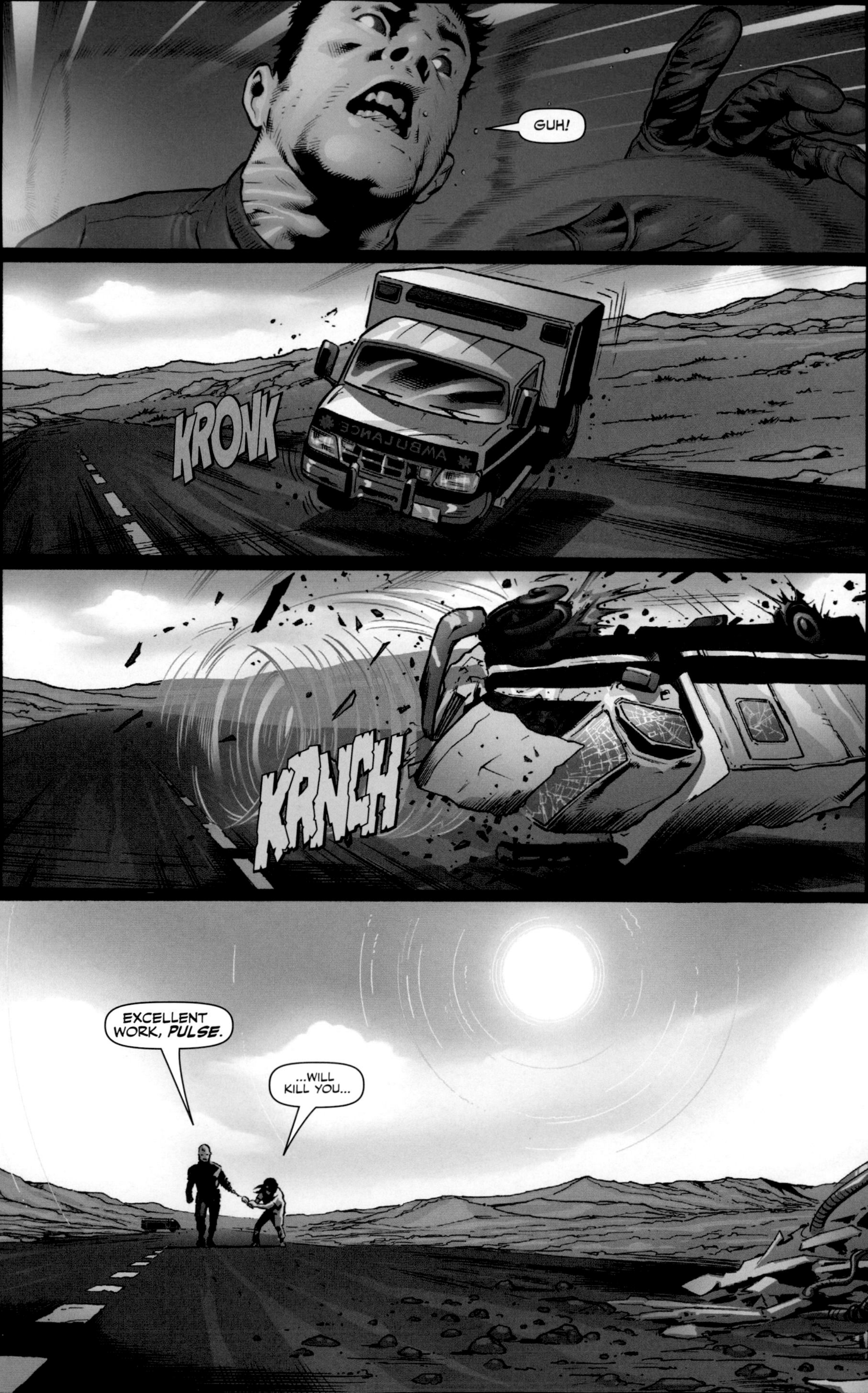
GUH!
KRONK
AMBULANCE
KRNCH
EXCELLENT WORK, *PULSE*.
...WILL KILL YOU...

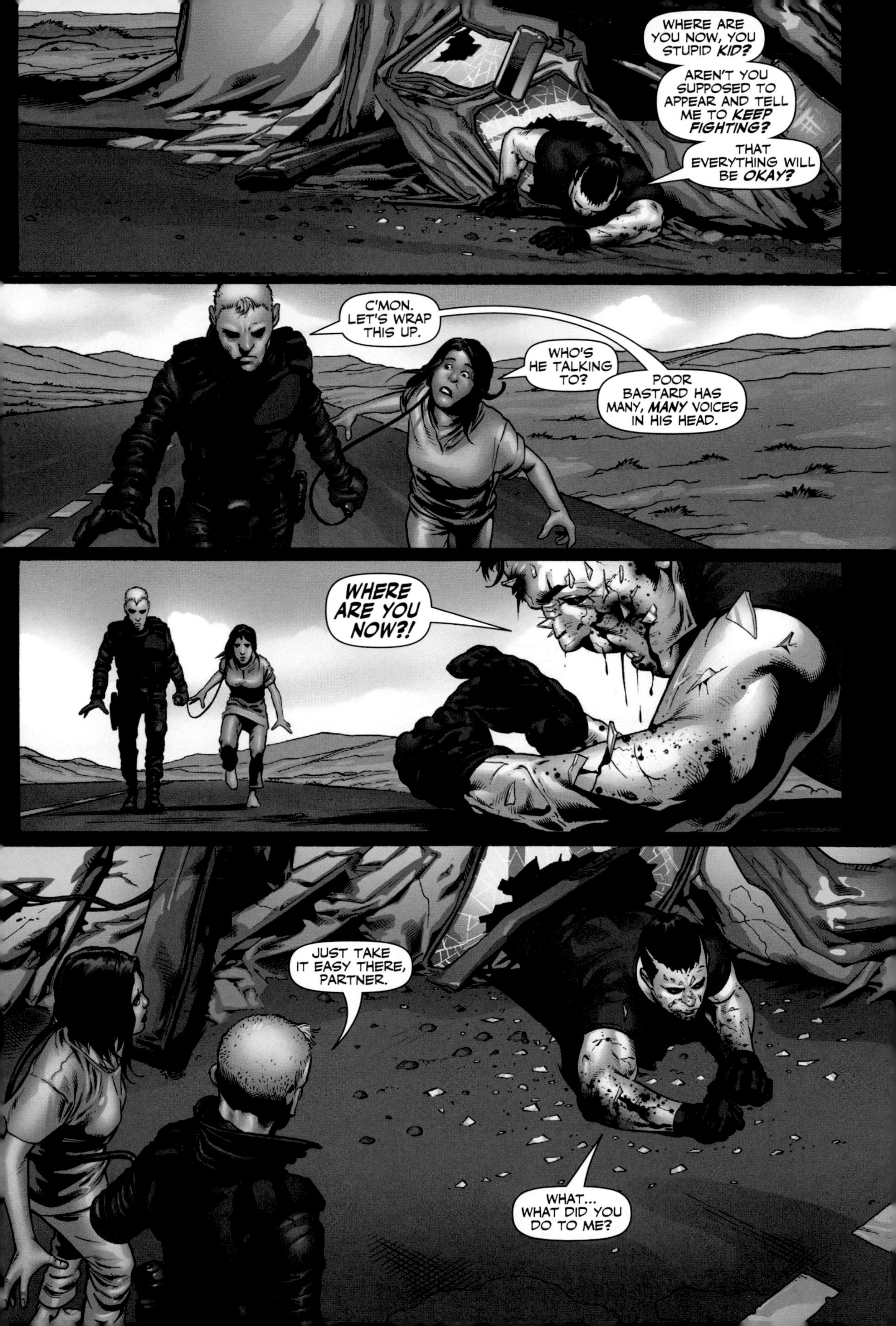
WHERE ARE YOU NOW, YOU STUPID KID?
AREN'T YOU SUPPOSED TO APPEAR AND TELL ME TO KEEP FIGHTING?
THAT EVERYTHING WILL BE OKAY?
C'MON. LET'S WRAP THIS UP.
WHO'S HE TALKING TO?
POOR BASTARD HAS MANY, MANY VOICES IN HIS HEAD.
WHERE ARE YOU NOW?!
JUST TAKE IT EASY THERE, PARTNER.
WHAT... WHAT DID YOU DO TO ME?

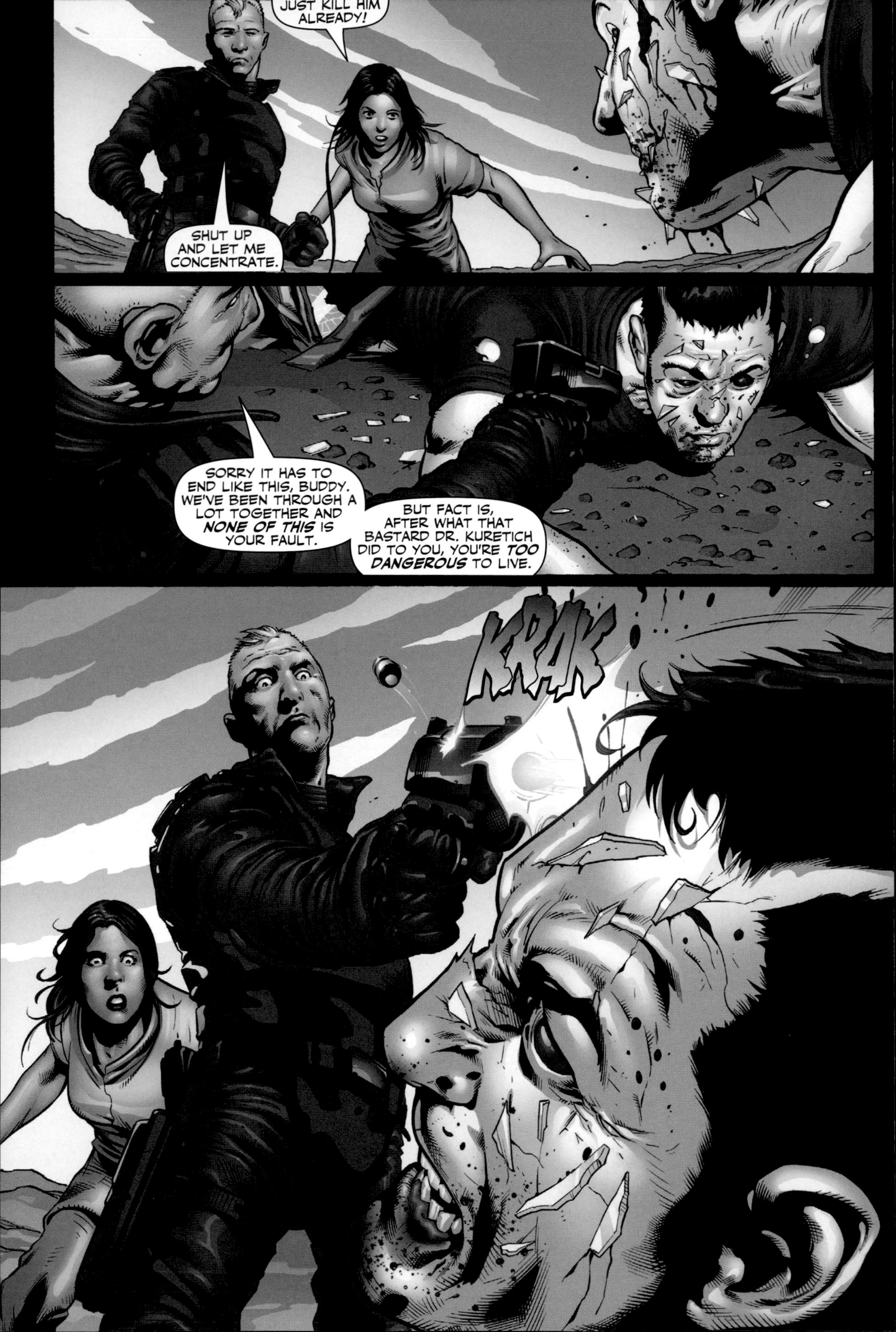
JUST KILL HIM ALREADY!
SHUT UP AND LET ME CONCENTRATE.
SORRY IT HAS TO END LIKE THIS, BUDDY. WE'VE BEEN THROUGH A LOT TOGETHER AND NONE OF THIS IS YOUR FAULT.
BUT FACT IS, AFTER WHAT THAT BASTARD DR. KURETICH DID TO YOU, YOU'RE TOO DANGEROUS TO LIVE.
KRAK

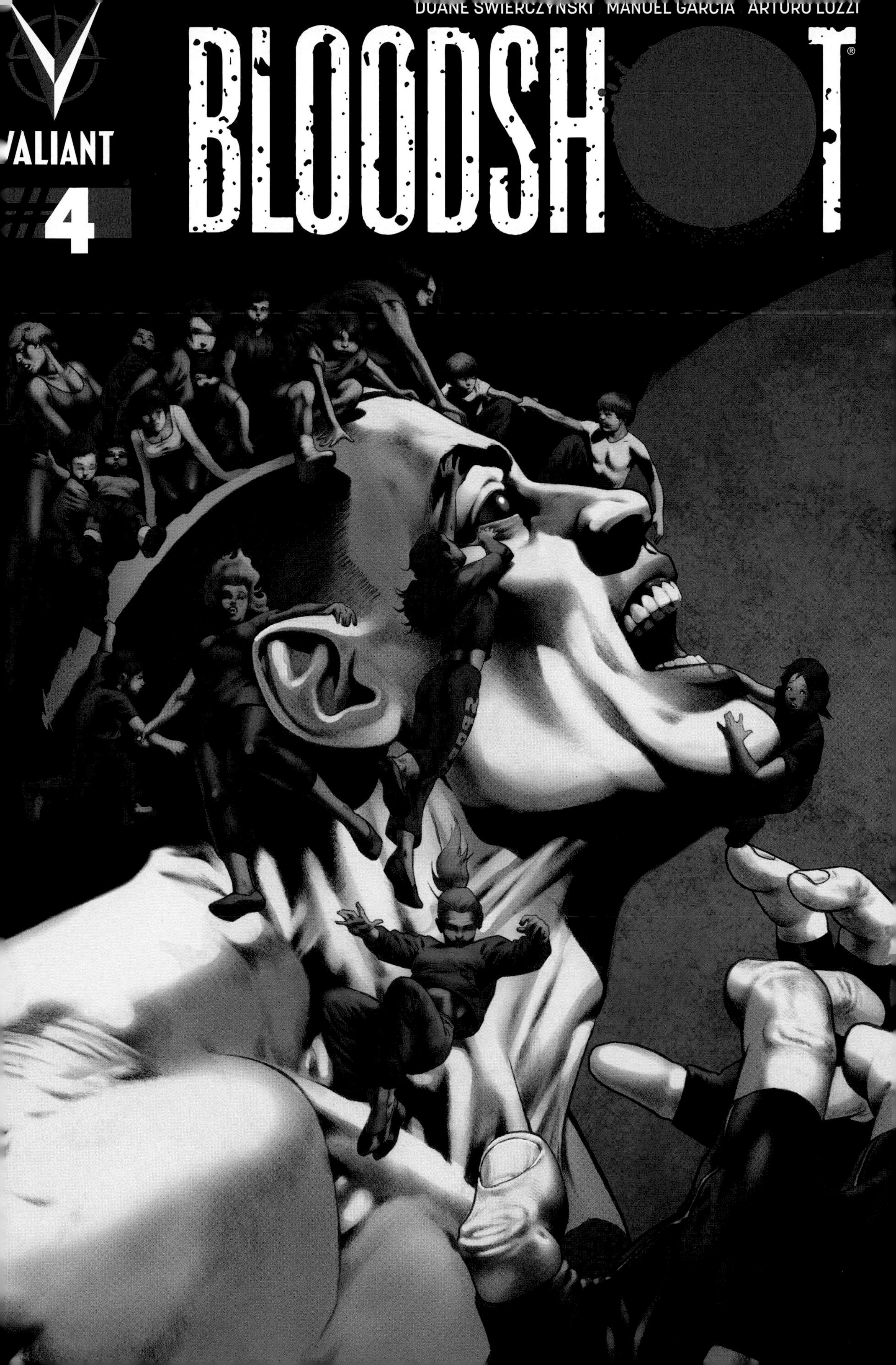
DUANE SWIERCZYNSKI | MANUEL GARCIA | ARTURO LOZZI
BLOODSHOT®
VALIANT
#4

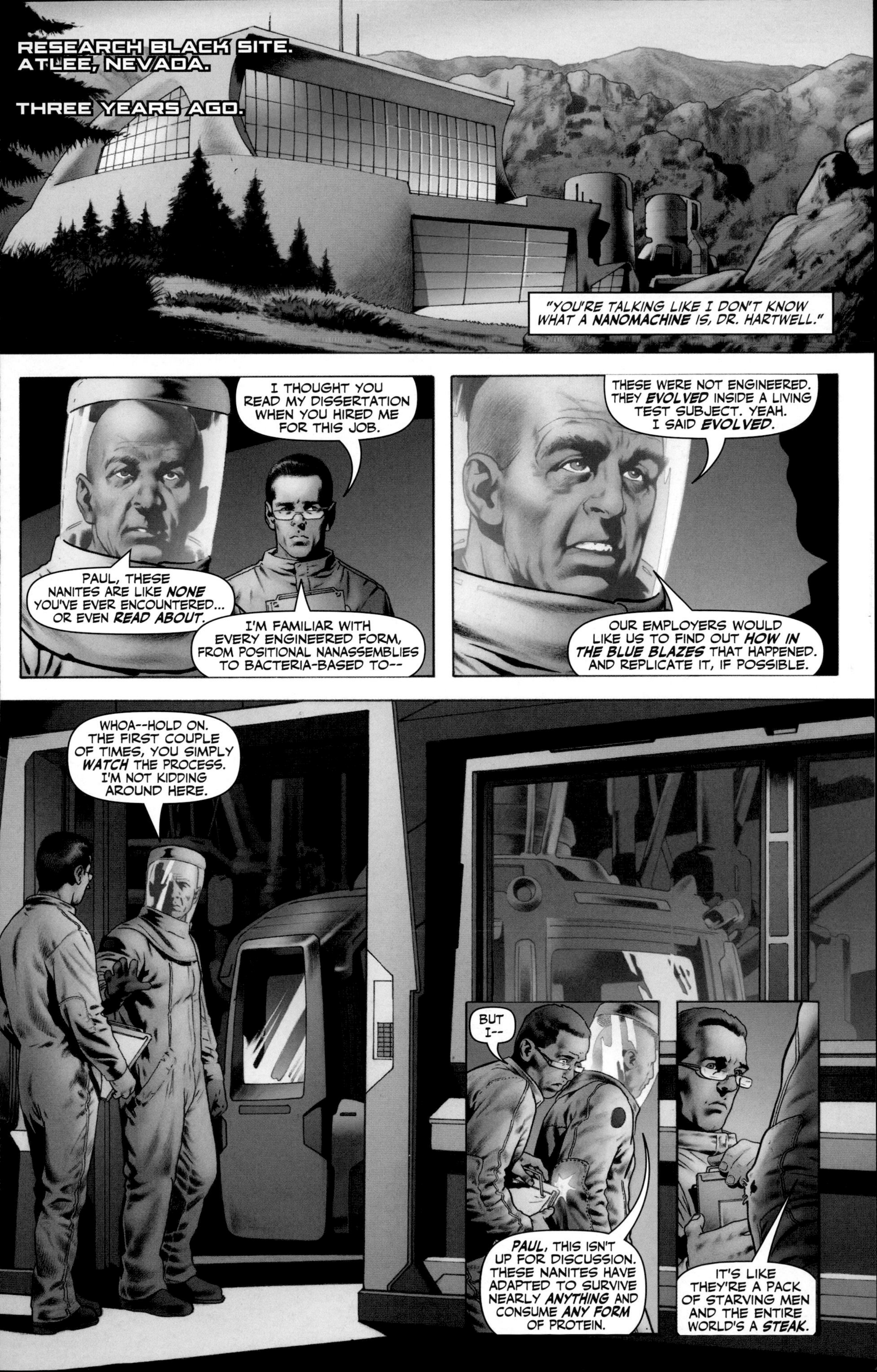
RESEARCH BLACK SITE.
ATLEE, NEVADA.
THREE YEARS AGO.
"YOU'RE TALKING LIKE I DON'T KNOW WHAT A NANOMACHINE IS, DR. HARTWELL."
I THOUGHT YOU READ MY DISSERTATION WHEN YOU HIRED ME FOR THIS JOB.
PAUL, THESE NANITES ARE LIKE NONE YOU'VE EVER ENCOUNTERED... OR EVEN READ ABOUT.
I'M FAMILIAR WITH EVERY ENGINEERED FORM, FROM POSITIONAL NANASSEMBLIES TO BACTERIA-BASED TO--
THESE WERE NOT ENGINEERED. THEY EVOLVED INSIDE A LIVING TEST SUBJECT. YEAH. I SAID EVOLVED.
OUR EMPLOYERS WOULD LIKE US TO FIND OUT HOW IN THE BLUE BLAZES THAT HAPPENED. AND REPLICATE IT, IF POSSIBLE.
WHOA--HOLD ON. THE FIRST COUPLE OF TIMES, YOU SIMPLY WATCH THE PROCESS. I'M NOT KIDDING AROUND HERE.
BUT I--
PAUL, THIS ISN'T UP FOR DISCUSSION. THESE NANITES HAVE ADAPTED TO SURVIVE NEARLY ANYTHING AND CONSUME ANY FORM OF PROTEIN.
IT'S LIKE THEY'RE A PACK OF STARVING MEN AND THE ENTIRE WORLD'S A STEAK.

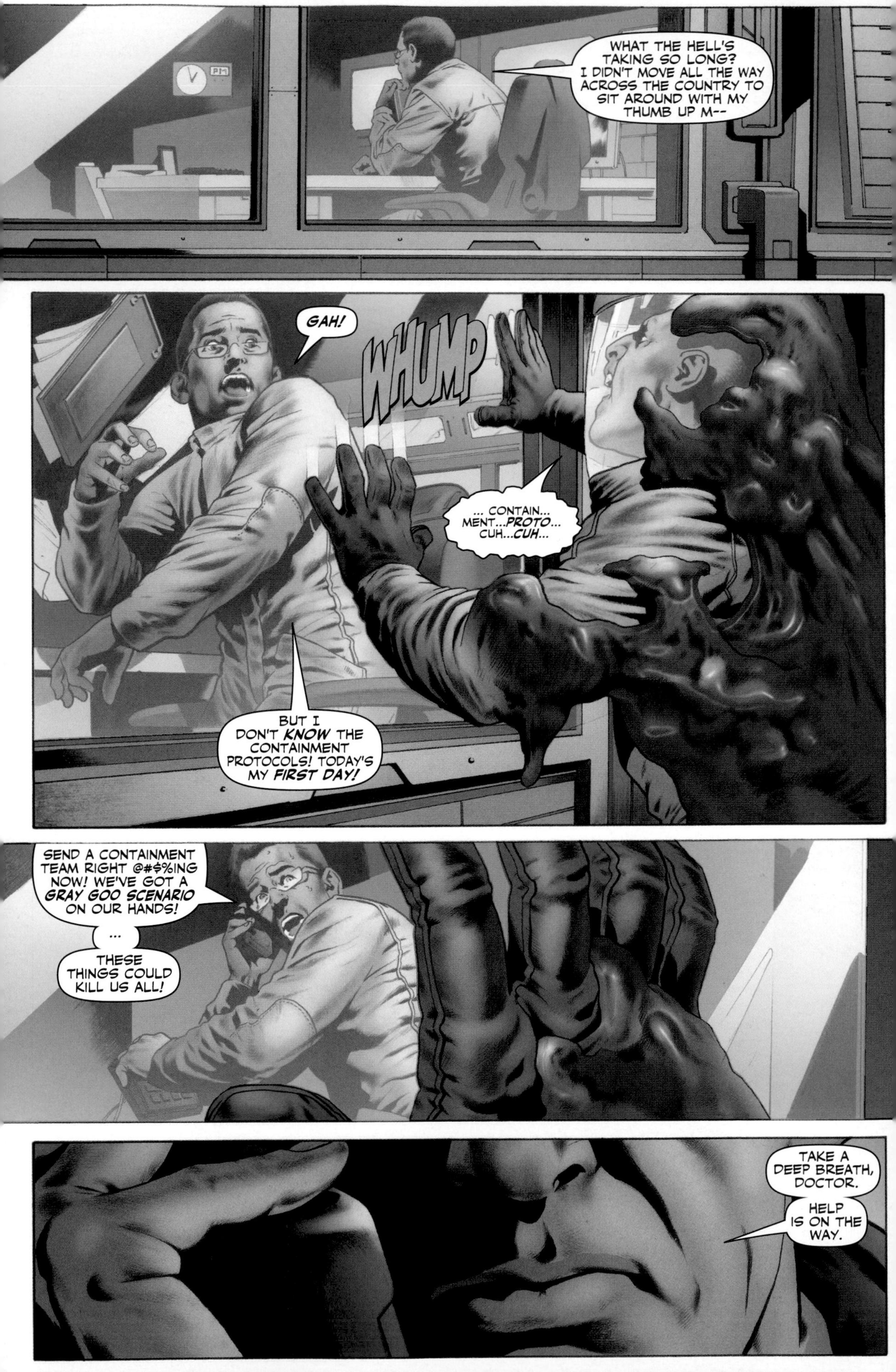

WHAT THE HELL'S TAKING SO LONG? I DIDN'T MOVE ALL THE WAY ACROSS THE COUNTRY TO SIT AROUND WITH MY THUMB UP M--
GAH!
WHUMP
... CONTAIN... MENT...PROTO... CUH...CUH...
BUT I DON'T KNOW THE CONTAINMENT PROTOCOLS! TODAY'S MY FIRST DAY!
SEND A CONTAINMENT TEAM RIGHT @#$%ING NOW! WE'VE GOT A GRAY GOO SCENARIO ON OUR HANDS!
...
THESE THINGS COULD KILL US ALL!
TAKE A DEEP BREATH, DOCTOR.
HELP IS ON THE WAY.

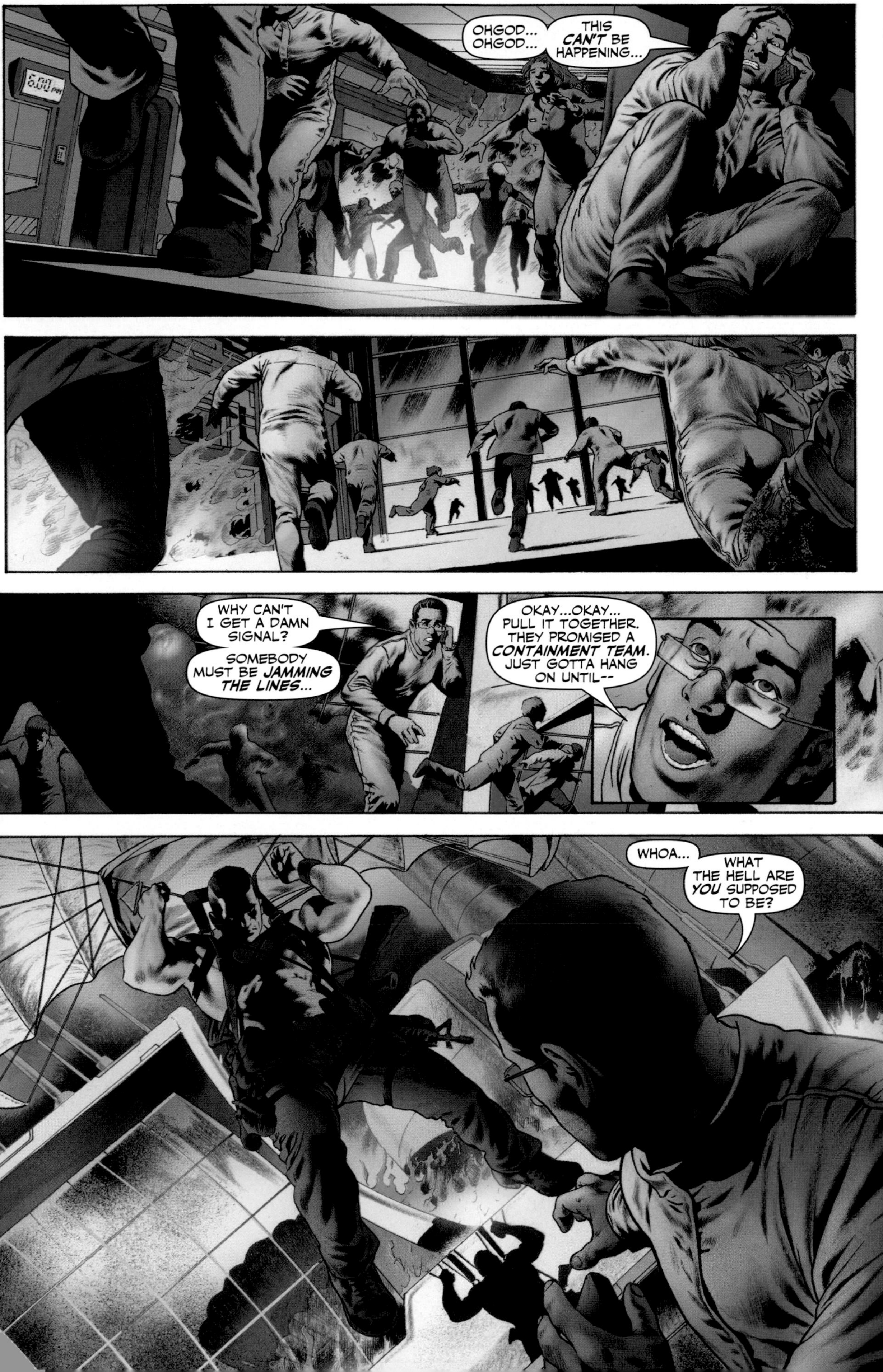
OHGOD... OHGOD...
THIS *CAN'T* BE HAPPENING...
WHY CAN'T I GET A DAMN SIGNAL?
SOMEBODY MUST BE *JAMMING THE LINES*...
OKAY...OKAY... PULL IT TOGETHER. THEY PROMISED A *CONTAINMENT TEAM*. JUST GOTTA HANG ON UNTIL--
WHOA...
WHAT THE HELL ARE *YOU* SUPPOSED TO BE?

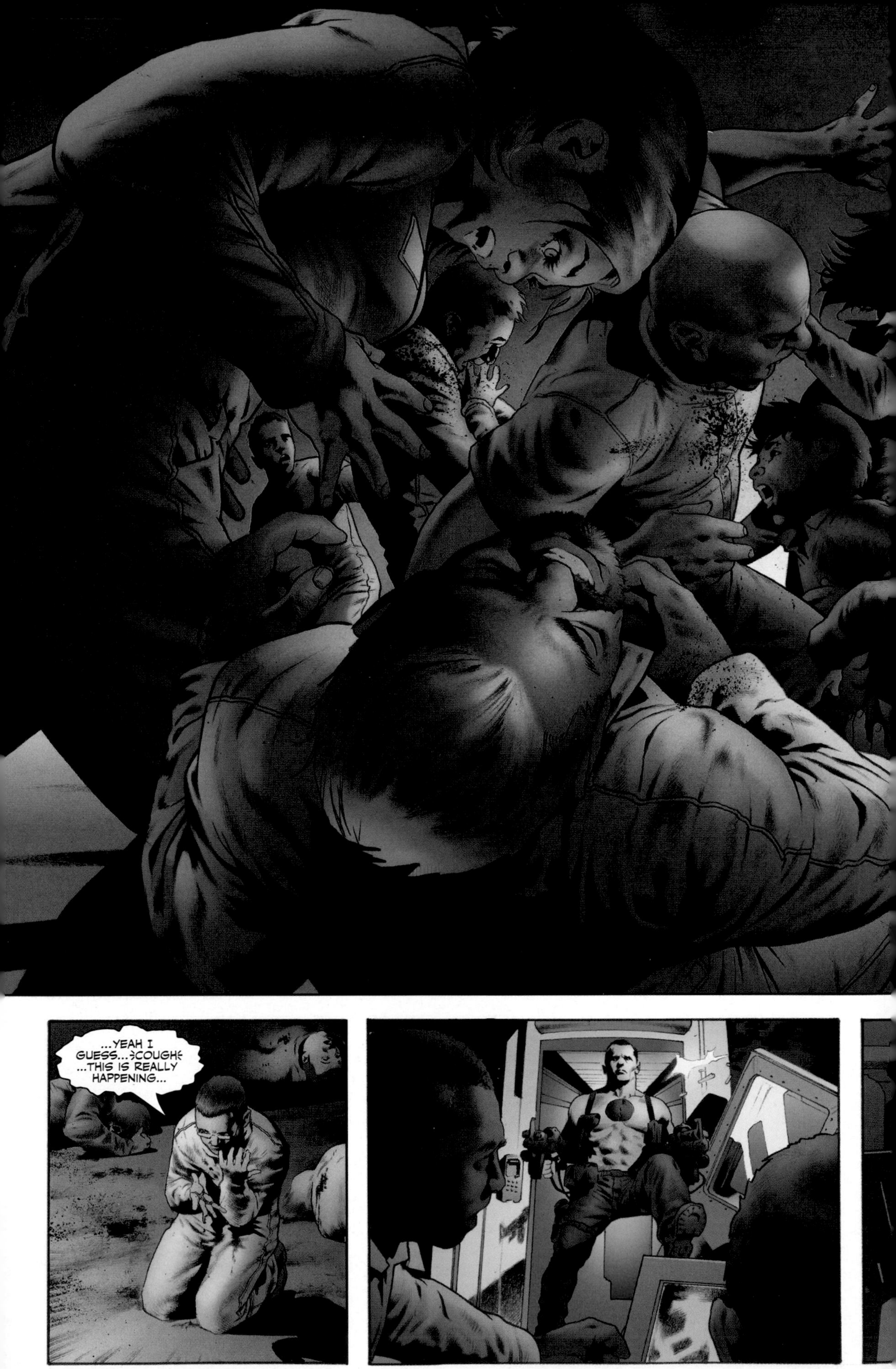
...YEAH I GUESS... COUGH ...THIS IS REALLY HAPPENING...

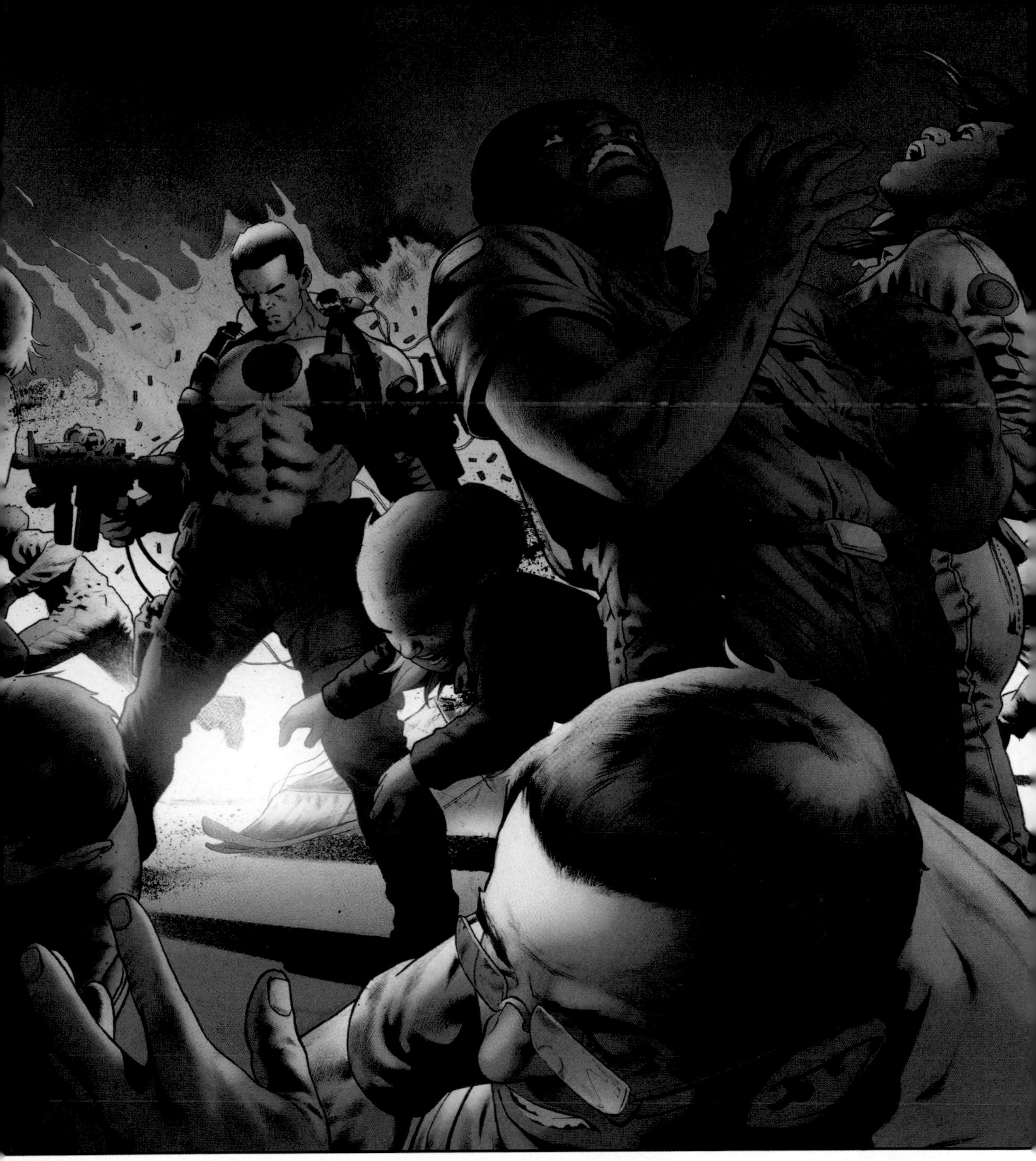

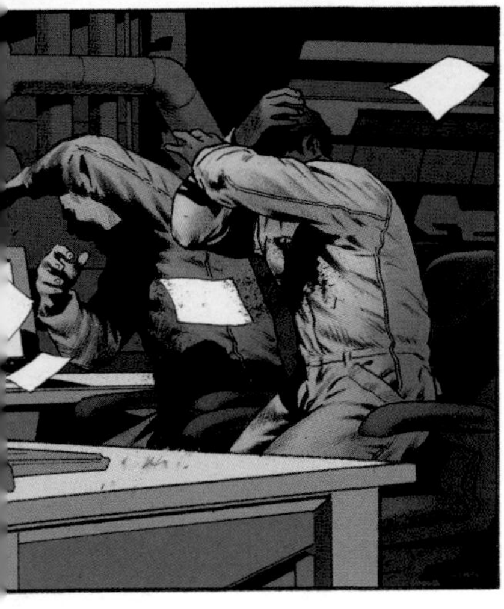

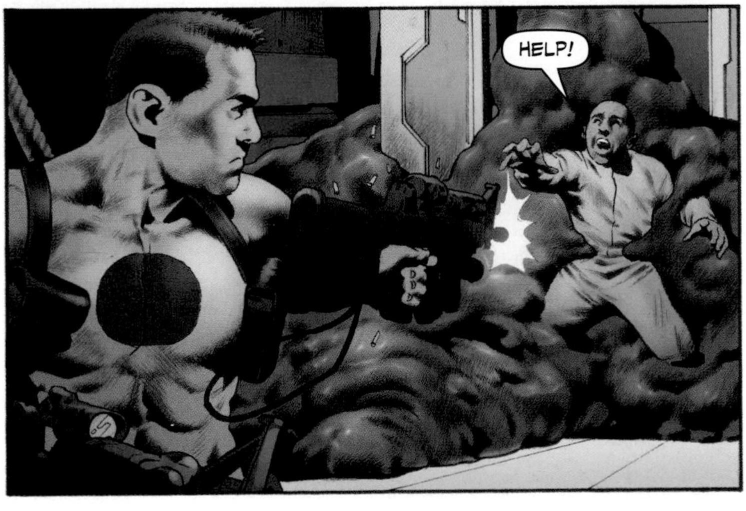
HELP!

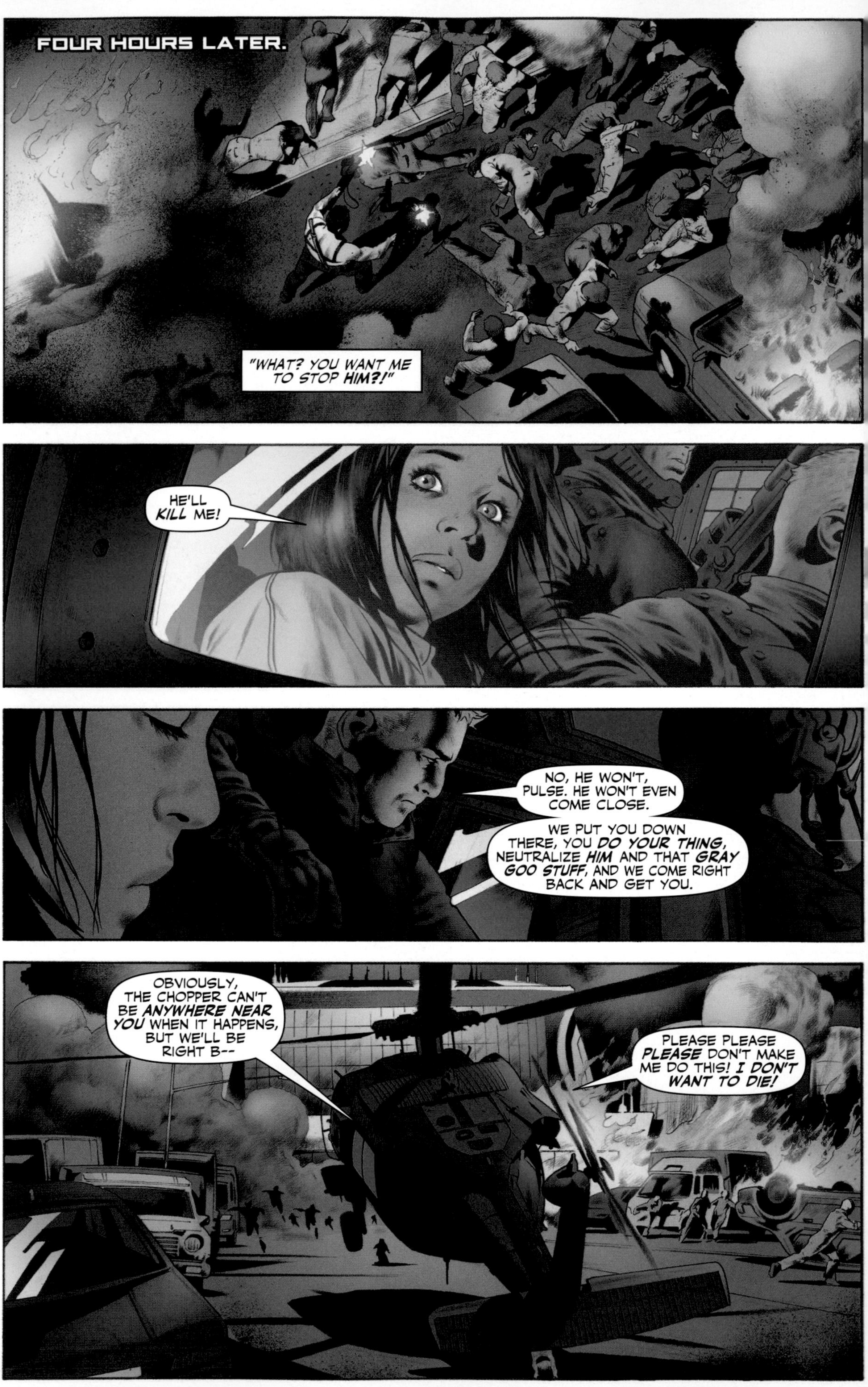
FOUR HOURS LATER.
"WHAT? YOU WANT ME TO STOP HIM?!"
HE'LL KILL ME!
NO, HE WON'T, PULSE. HE WON'T EVEN COME CLOSE.
WE PUT YOU DOWN THERE, YOU DO YOUR THING, NEUTRALIZE HIM AND THAT GRAY GOO STUFF, AND WE COME RIGHT BACK AND GET YOU.
OBVIOUSLY, THE CHOPPER CAN'T BE ANYWHERE NEAR YOU WHEN IT HAPPENS, BUT WE'LL BE RIGHT B--
PLEASE PLEASE PLEASE DON'T MAKE ME DO THIS! I DON'T WANT TO DIE!

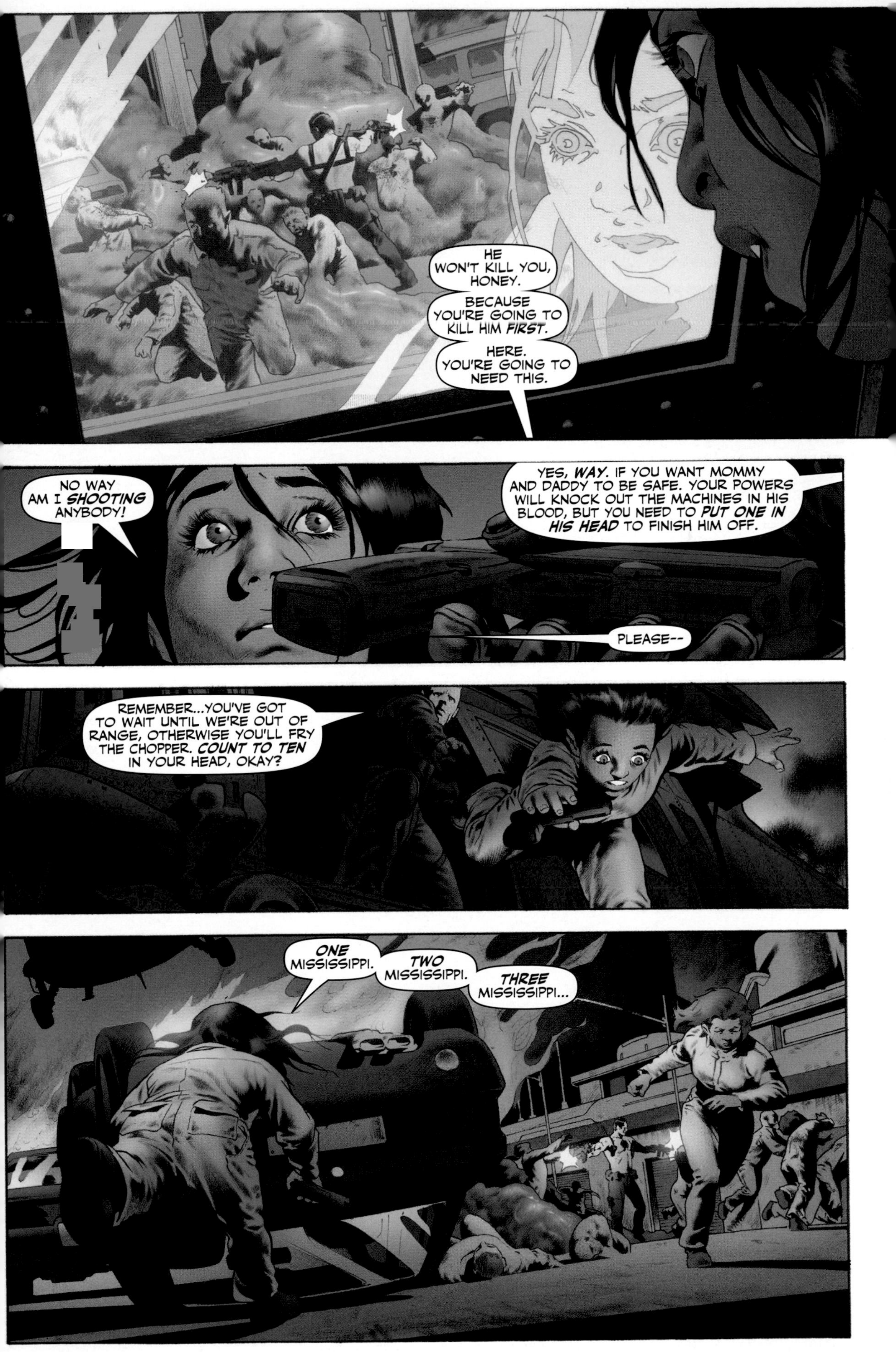
HE WON'T KILL YOU, HONEY.
BECAUSE YOU'RE GOING TO KILL HIM *FIRST*.
HERE. YOU'RE GOING TO NEED THIS.
NO WAY AM I *SHOOTING* ANYBODY!
YES, *WAY*. IF YOU WANT MOMMY AND DADDY TO BE SAFE. YOUR POWERS WILL KNOCK OUT THE MACHINES IN HIS BLOOD, BUT YOU NEED TO *PUT ONE IN HIS HEAD* TO FINISH HIM OFF.
PLEASE--
REMEMBER...YOU'VE GOT TO WAIT UNTIL WE'RE OUT OF RANGE, OTHERWISE YOU'LL FRY THE CHOPPER. *COUNT TO TEN* IN YOUR HEAD, OKAY?
ONE MISSISSIPPI.
TWO MISSISSIPPI.
THREE MISSISSIPPI...

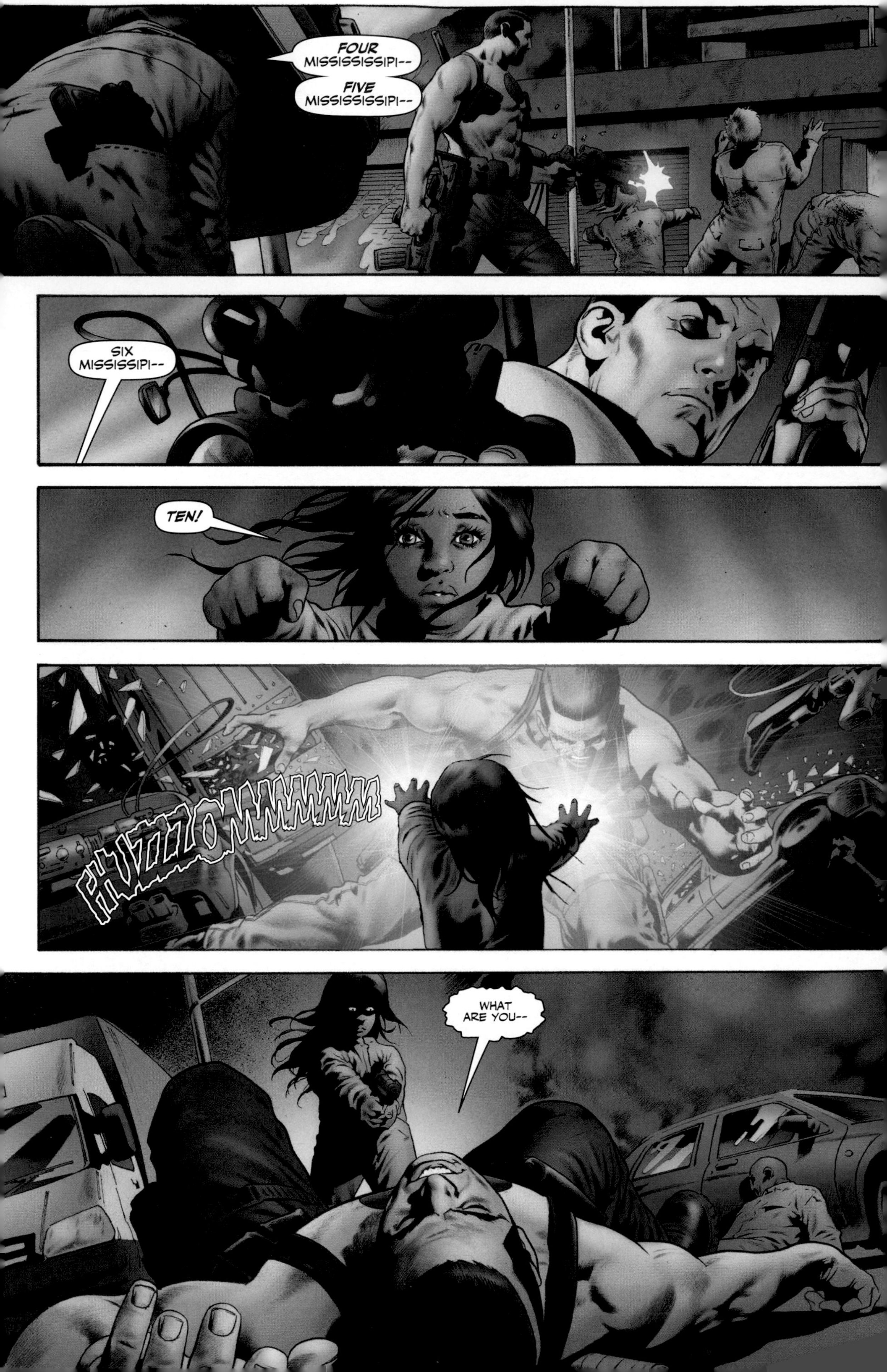
FOUR MISSISSISSIPI--
FIVE MISSISSISSIPI--
SIX MISSISSIPI--
TEN!
CHUZZZOMMMMMM
WHAT ARE YOU--

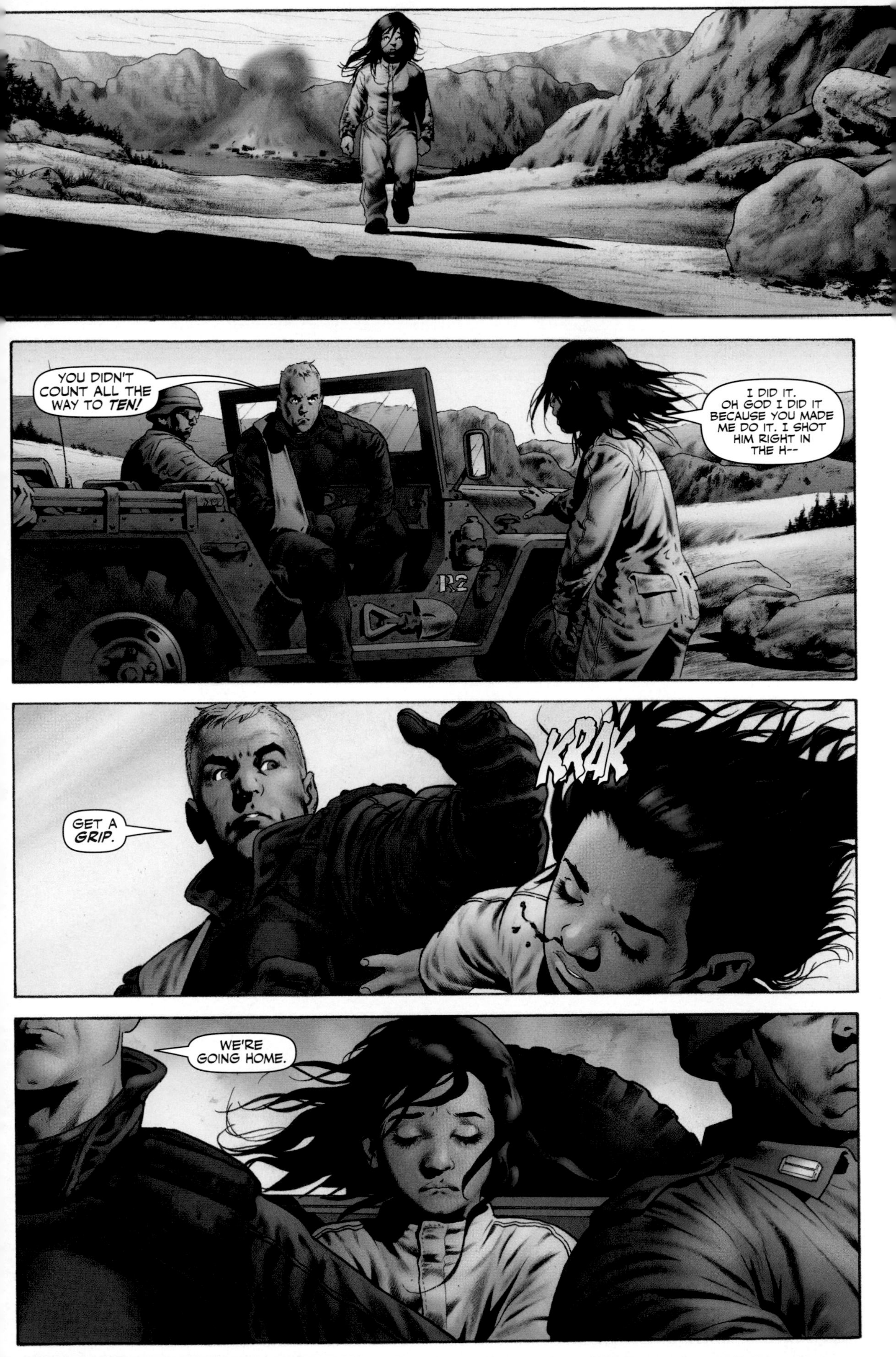
YOU DIDN'T COUNT ALL THE WAY TO TEN!
I DID IT. OH GOD I DID IT BECAUSE YOU MADE ME DO IT. I SHOT HIM RIGHT IN THE H--
KRAK
GET A GRIP.
WE'RE GOING HOME.

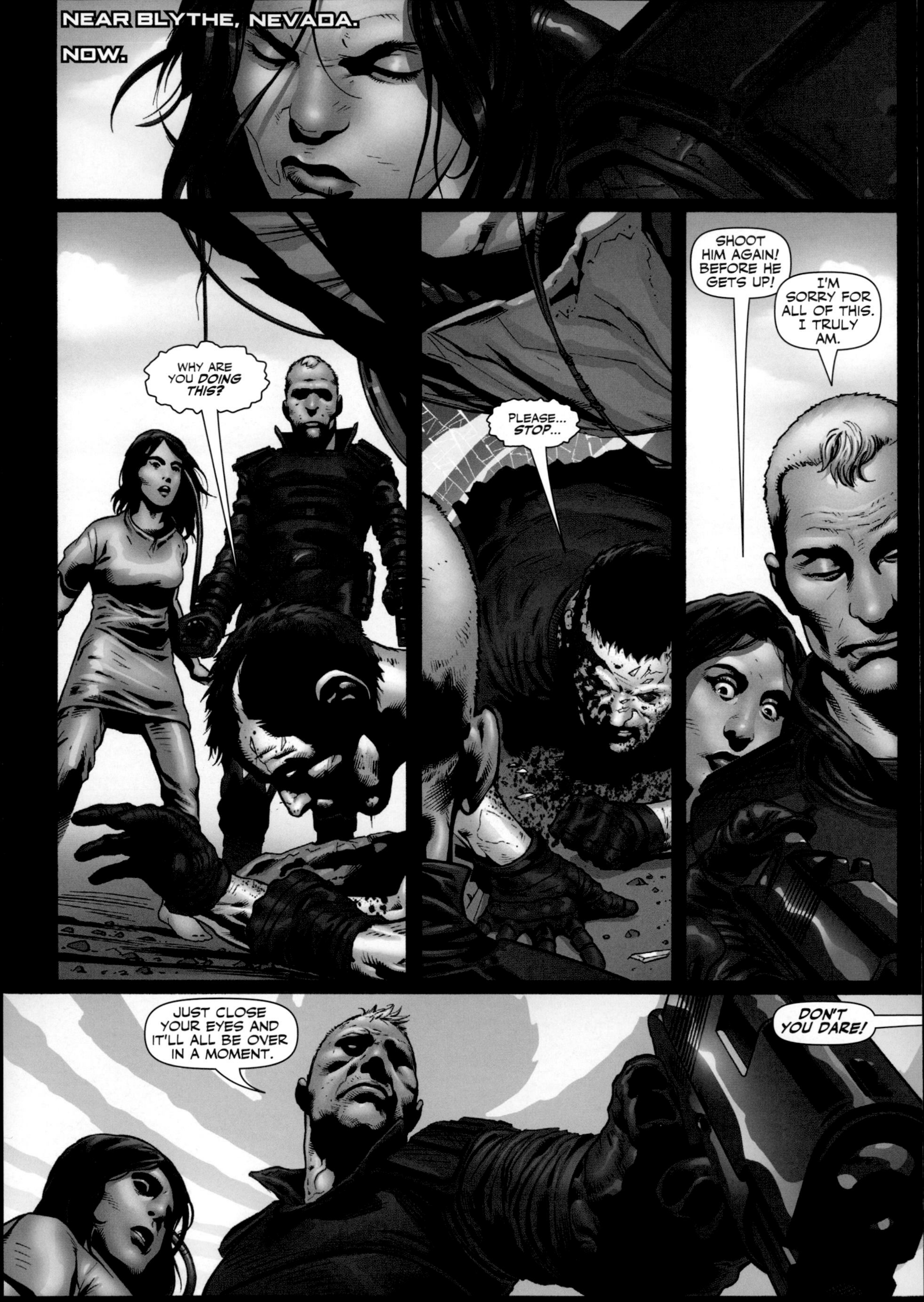
NEAR BLYTHE, NEVADA.
NOW.
WHY ARE YOU DOING THIS?
PLEASE... STOP...
SHOOT HIM AGAIN! BEFORE HE GETS UP!
I'M SORRY FOR ALL OF THIS. I TRULY AM.
JUST CLOSE YOUR EYES AND IT'LL ALL BE OVER IN A MOMENT.
DON'T YOU DARE!

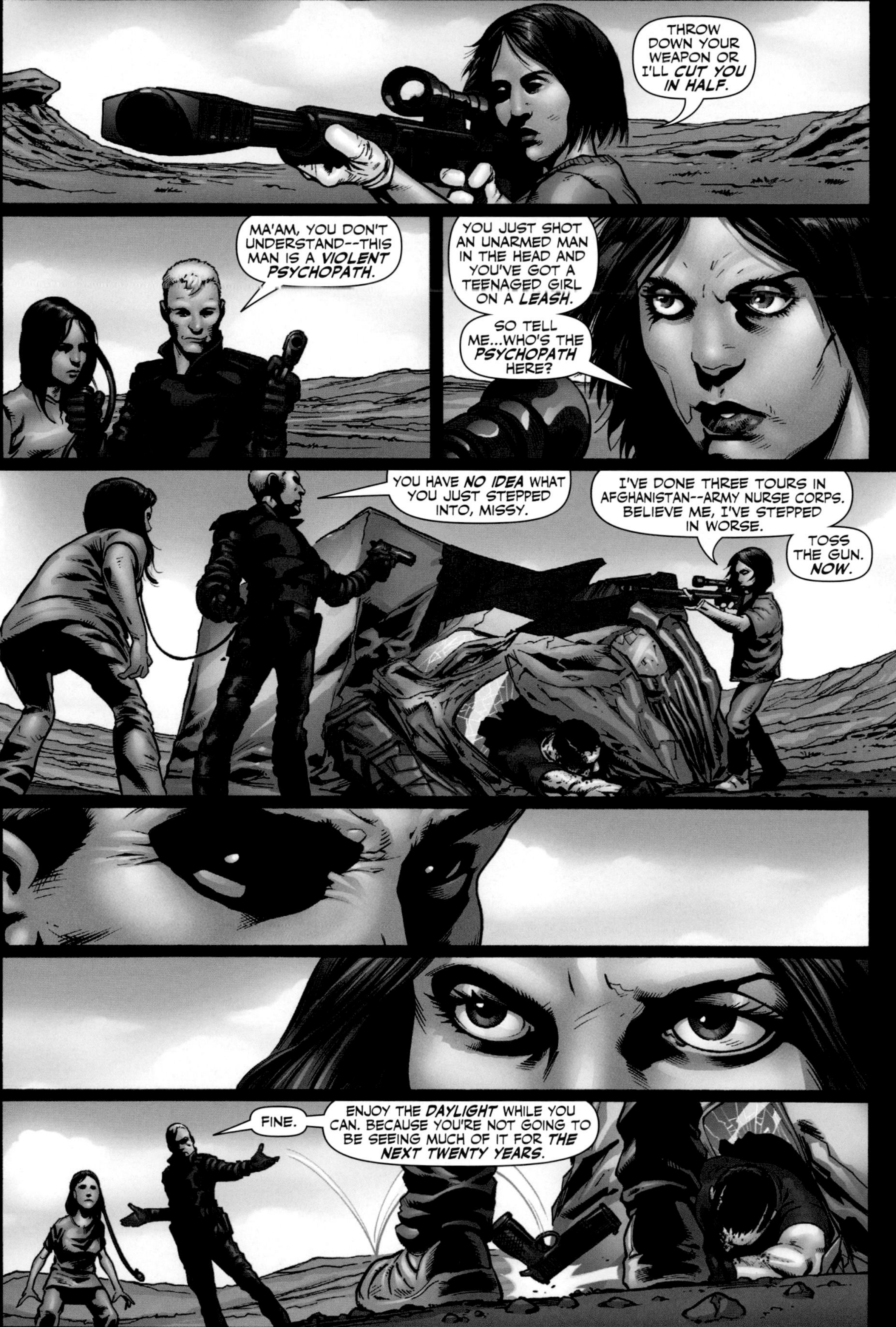
THROW DOWN YOUR WEAPON OR I'LL CUT YOU IN HALF.
MA'AM, YOU DON'T UNDERSTAND--THIS MAN IS A VIOLENT PSYCHOPATH.
YOU JUST SHOT AN UNARMED MAN IN THE HEAD AND YOU'VE GOT A TEENAGED GIRL ON A LEASH.
SO TELL ME...WHO'S THE PSYCHOPATH HERE?
YOU HAVE NO IDEA WHAT YOU JUST STEPPED INTO, MISSY.
I'VE DONE THREE TOURS IN AFGHANISTAN--ARMY NURSE CORPS. BELIEVE ME, I'VE STEPPED IN WORSE.
TOSS THE GUN. NOW.
FINE.
ENJOY THE DAYLIGHT WHILE YOU CAN. BECAUSE YOU'RE NOT GOING TO BE SEEING MUCH OF IT FOR THE NEXT TWENTY YEARS.

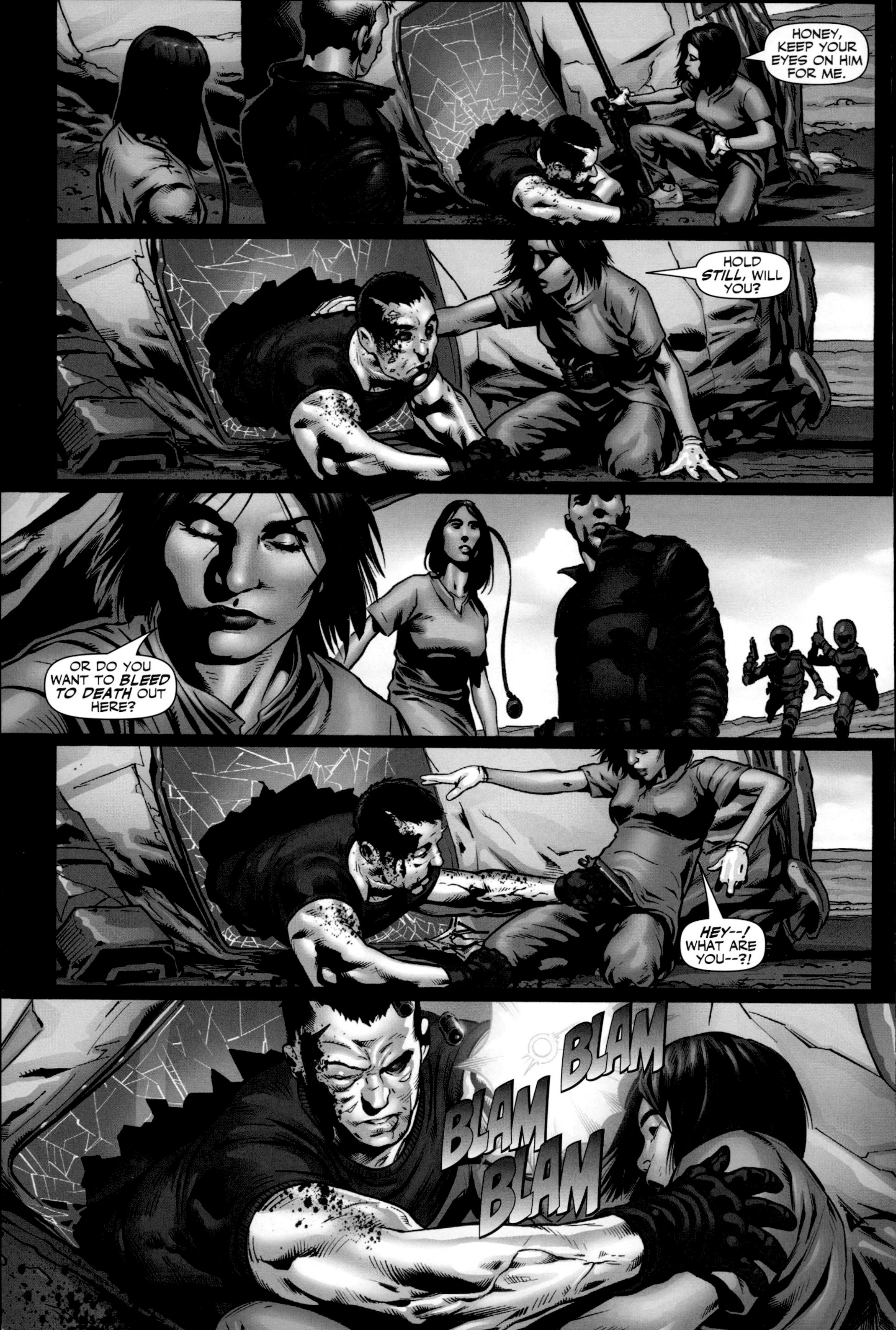
HONEY, KEEP YOUR EYES ON HIM FOR ME.
HOLD *STILL*, WILL YOU?
OR DO YOU WANT TO *BLEED TO DEATH* OUT HERE?
HEY--! WHAT ARE YOU--?!
BLAM
BLAM
BLAM

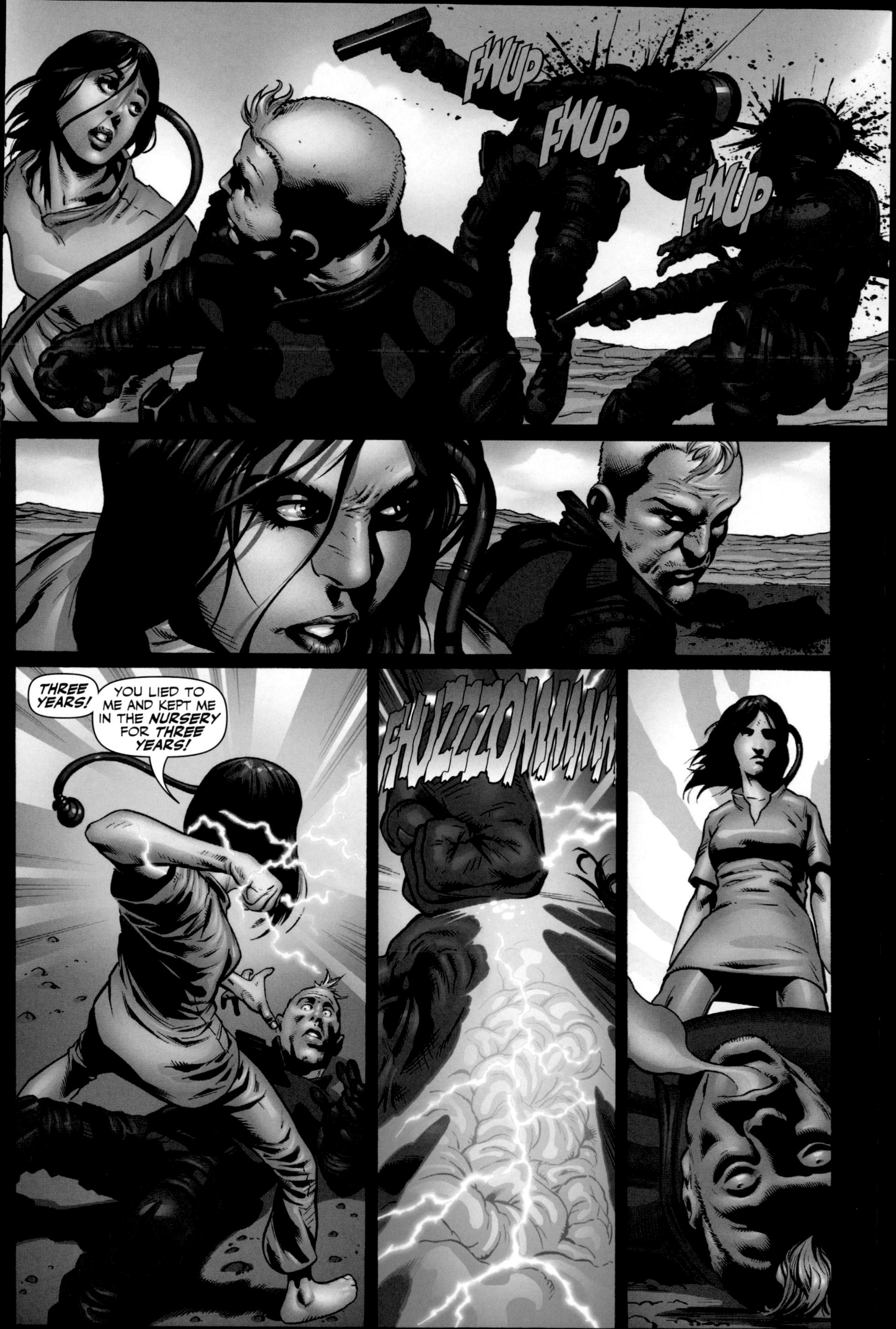
FWUP
FWUP
FWUP
THREE YEARS!
YOU LIED TO ME AND KEPT ME IN THE NURSERY FOR THREE YEARS!
FHUZZZOMMMM

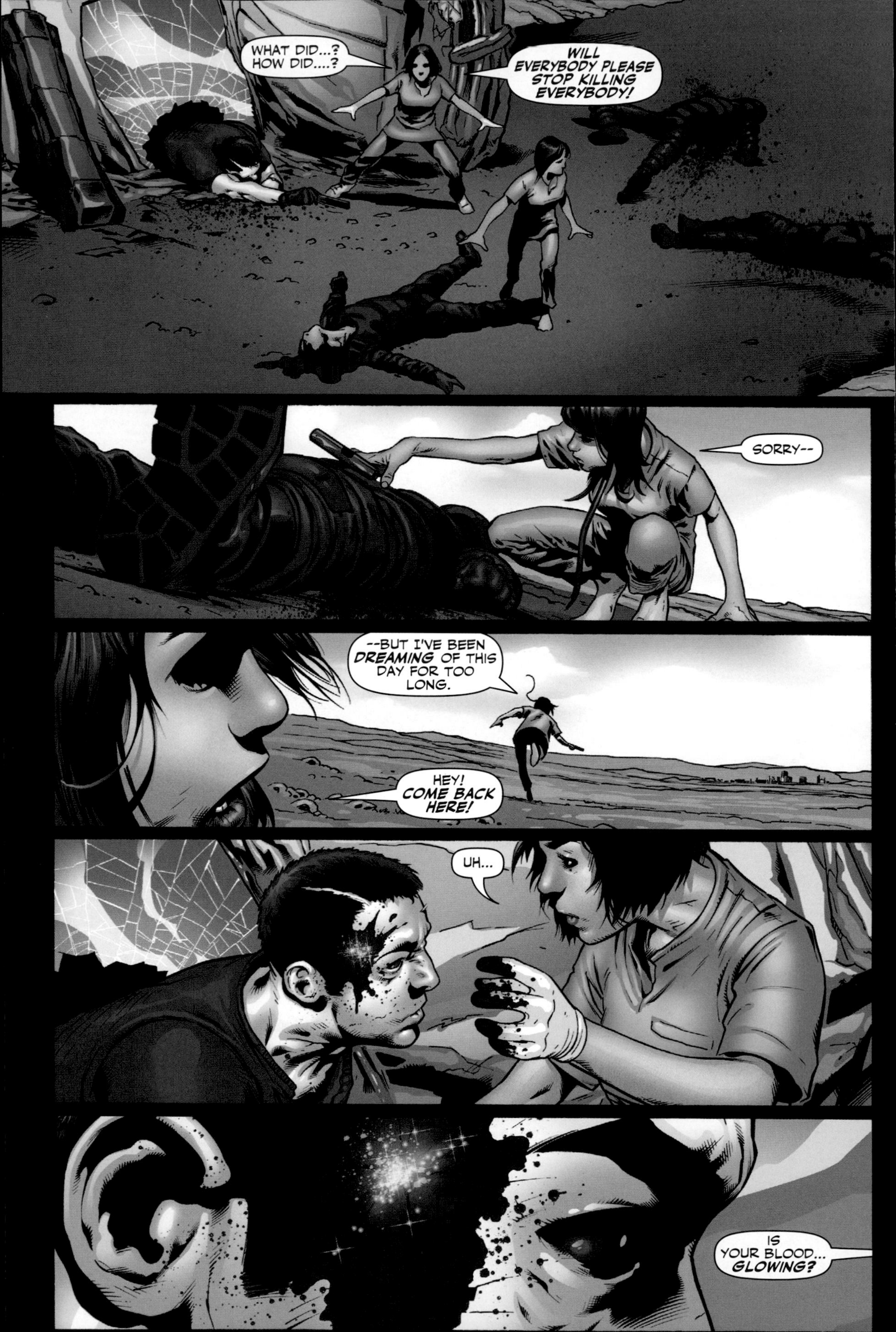
WHAT DID...? HOW DID....?
WILL EVERYBODY PLEASE STOP KILLING EVERYBODY!
SORRY--
--BUT I'VE BEEN DREAMING OF THIS DAY FOR TOO LONG.
HEY! COME BACK HERE!
UH...
IS YOUR BLOOD... GLOWING?

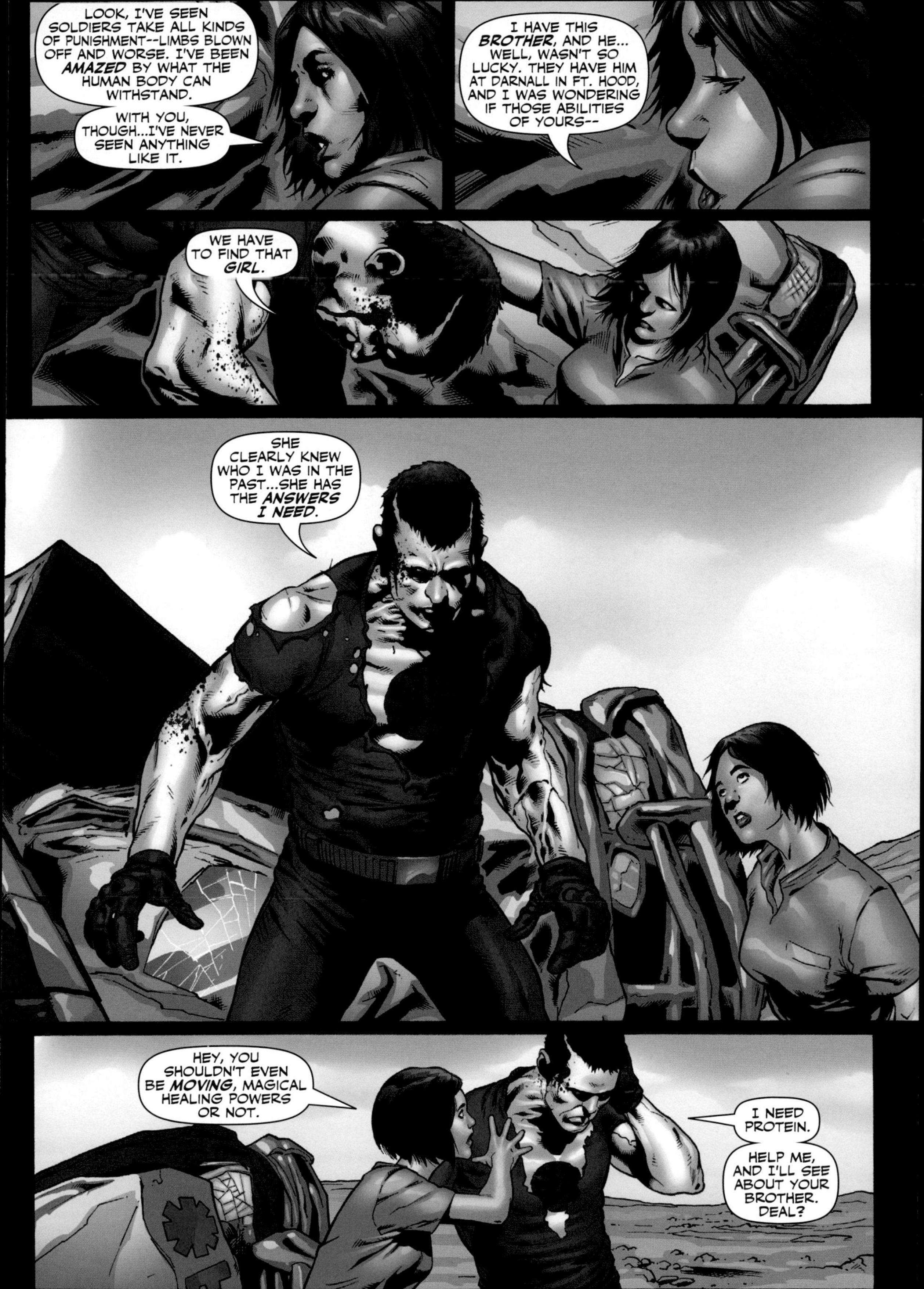
LOOK, I'VE SEEN SOLDIERS TAKE ALL KINDS OF PUNISHMENT--LIMBS BLOWN OFF AND WORSE. I'VE BEEN AMAZED BY WHAT THE HUMAN BODY CAN WITHSTAND.
WITH YOU, THOUGH...I'VE NEVER SEEN ANYTHING LIKE IT.
I HAVE THIS BROTHER, AND HE... WELL, WASN'T SO LUCKY. THEY HAVE HIM AT DARNALL IN FT. HOOD, AND I WAS WONDERING IF THOSE ABILITIES OF YOURS--
WE HAVE TO FIND THAT GIRL.
SHE CLEARLY KNEW WHO I WAS IN THE PAST...SHE HAS THE ANSWERS I NEED.
HEY, YOU SHOULDN'T EVEN BE MOVING, MAGICAL HEALING POWERS OR NOT.
I NEED PROTEIN.
HELP ME, AND I'LL SEE ABOUT YOUR BROTHER. DEAL?

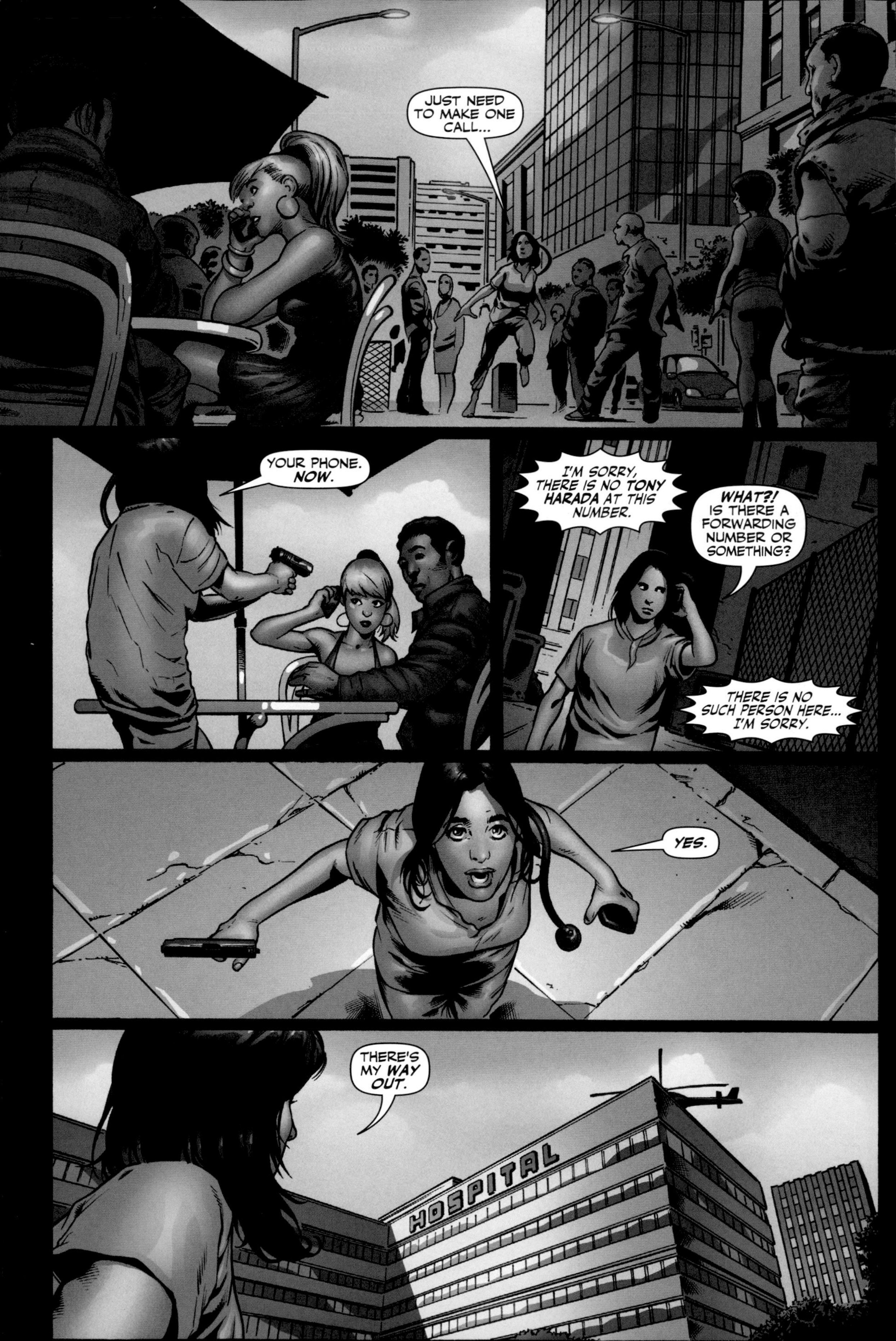
JUST NEED TO MAKE ONE CALL...
YOUR PHONE. NOW.
I'M SORRY, THERE IS NO TONY HARADA AT THIS NUMBER.
WHAT?! IS THERE A FORWARDING NUMBER OR SOMETHING?
THERE IS NO SUCH PERSON HERE... I'M SORRY.
YES.
THERE'S MY WAY OUT.
HOSPITAL

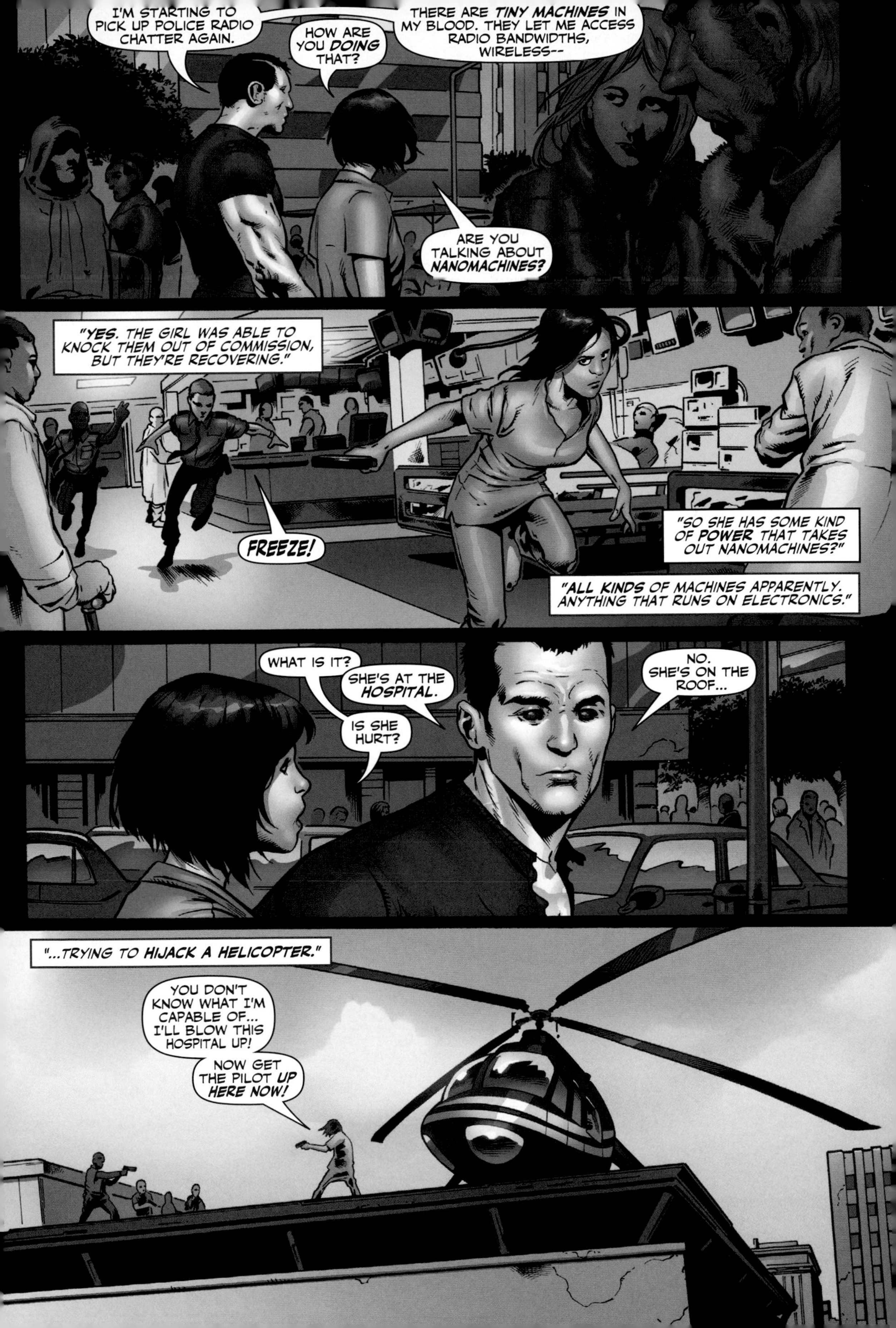
I'M STARTING TO PICK UP POLICE RADIO CHATTER AGAIN.
HOW ARE YOU DOING THAT?
THERE ARE TINY MACHINES IN MY BLOOD. THEY LET ME ACCESS RADIO BANDWIDTHS, WIRELESS--
ARE YOU TALKING ABOUT NANOMACHINES?
"YES. THE GIRL WAS ABLE TO KNOCK THEM OUT OF COMMISSION, BUT THEY'RE RECOVERING."
FREEZE!
"SO SHE HAS SOME KIND OF POWER THAT TAKES OUT NANOMACHINES?"
"ALL KINDS OF MACHINES APPARENTLY. ANYTHING THAT RUNS ON ELECTRONICS."
WHAT IS IT?
SHE'S AT THE HOSPITAL.
IS SHE HURT?
NO. SHE'S ON THE ROOF...
"...TRYING TO HIJACK A HELICOPTER."
YOU DON'T KNOW WHAT I'M CAPABLE OF... I'LL BLOW THIS HOSPITAL UP!
NOW GET THE PILOT UP HERE NOW!

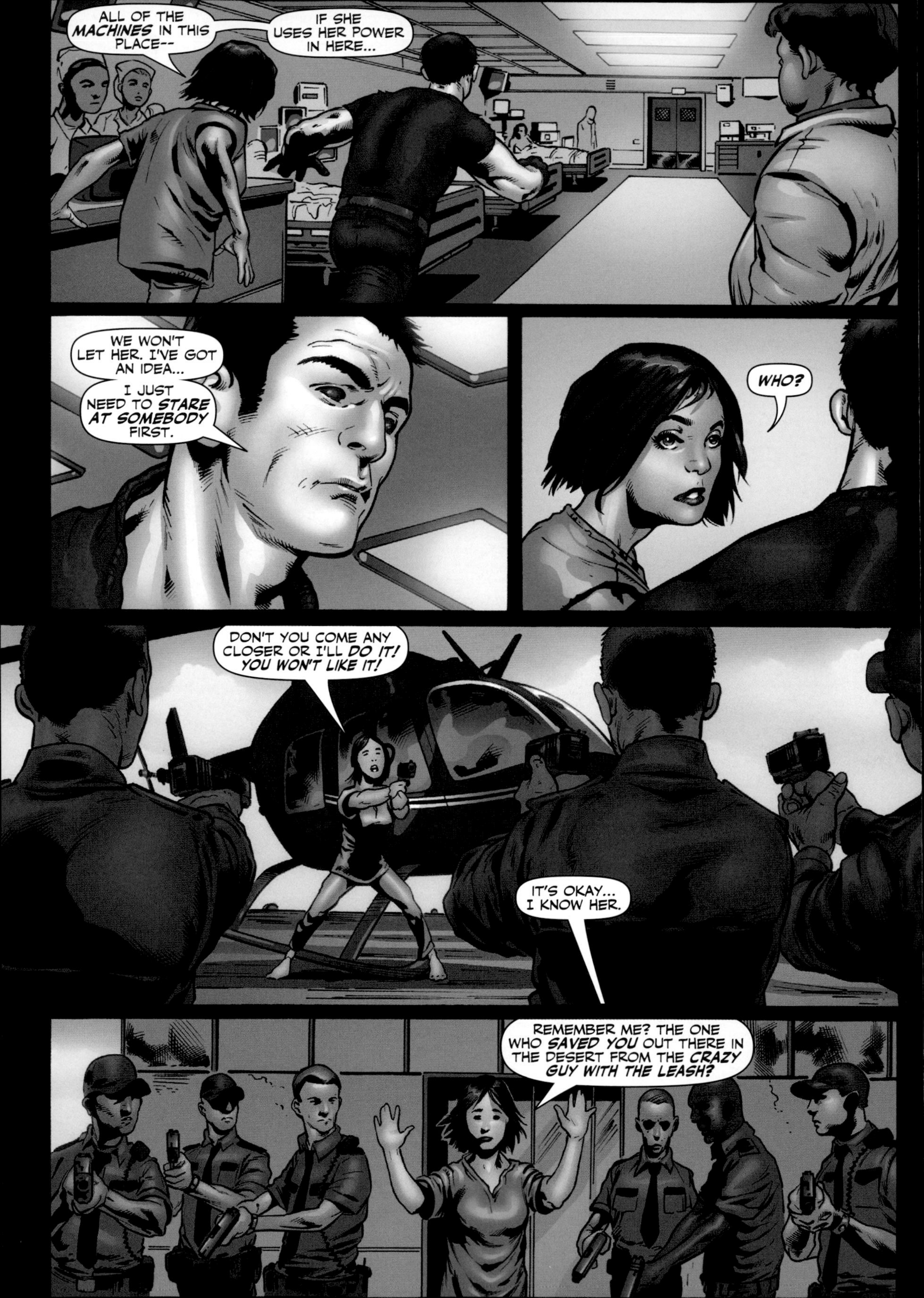
ALL OF THE MACHINES IN THIS PLACE--
IF SHE USES HER POWER IN HERE...
WE WON'T LET HER. I'VE GOT AN IDEA...
I JUST NEED TO STARE AT SOMEBODY FIRST.
WHO?
DON'T YOU COME ANY CLOSER OR I'LL DO IT! YOU WON'T LIKE IT!
IT'S OKAY... I KNOW HER.
REMEMBER ME? THE ONE WHO SAVED YOU OUT THERE IN THE DESERT FROM THE CRAZY GUY WITH THE LEASH?

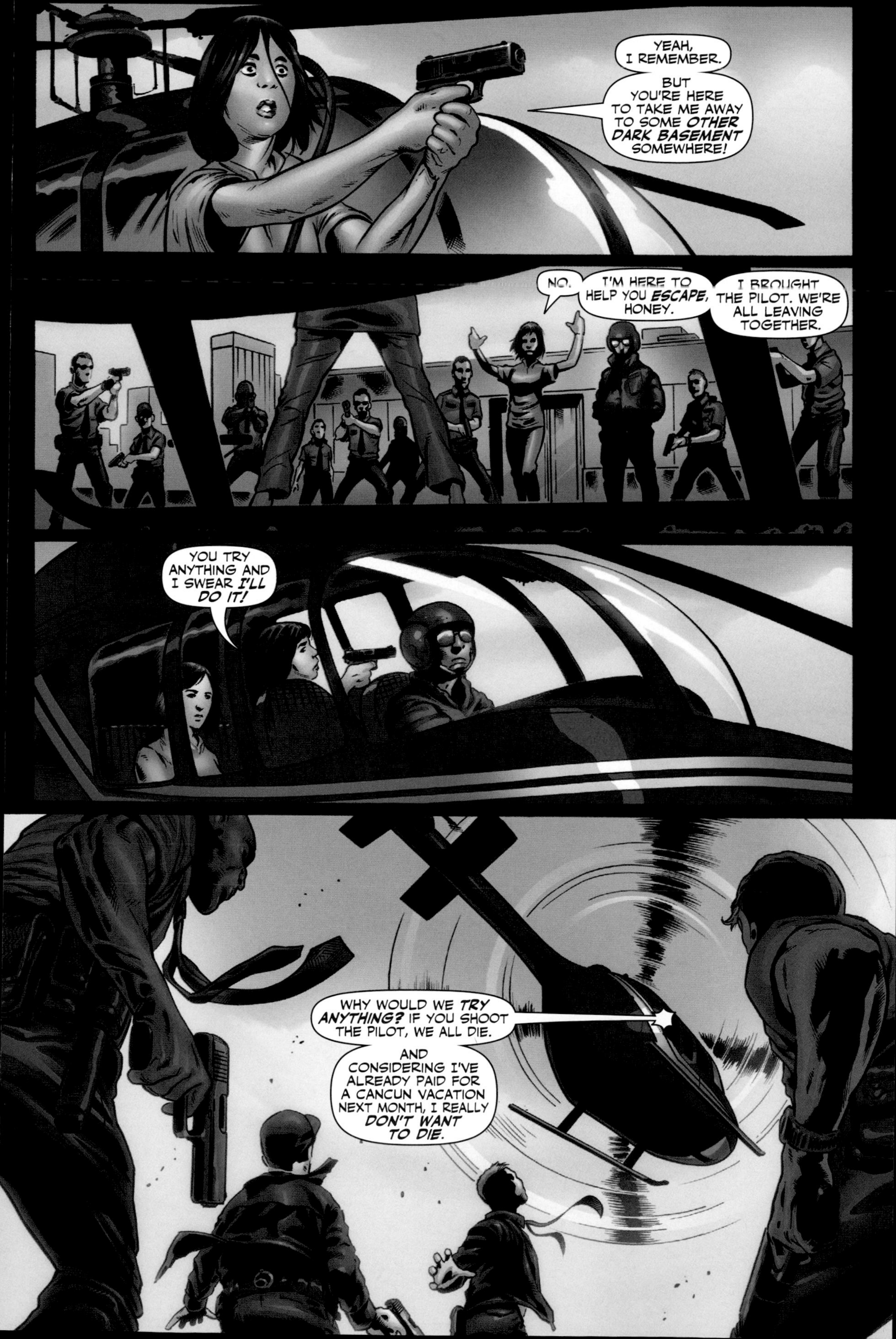
YEAH, I REMEMBER.
BUT YOU'RE HERE TO TAKE ME AWAY TO SOME *OTHER DARK BASEMENT* SOMEWHERE!
NO.
I'M HERE TO HELP YOU *ESCAPE,* HONEY.
I BROUGHT THE PILOT. WE'RE ALL LEAVING TOGETHER.
YOU TRY ANYTHING AND I SWEAR *I'LL DO IT!*
WHY WOULD WE *TRY ANYTHING?* IF YOU SHOOT THE PILOT, WE ALL DIE.
AND CONSIDERING I'VE ALREADY PAID FOR A CANCUN VACATION NEXT MONTH, I REALLY *DON'T WANT TO DIE*.

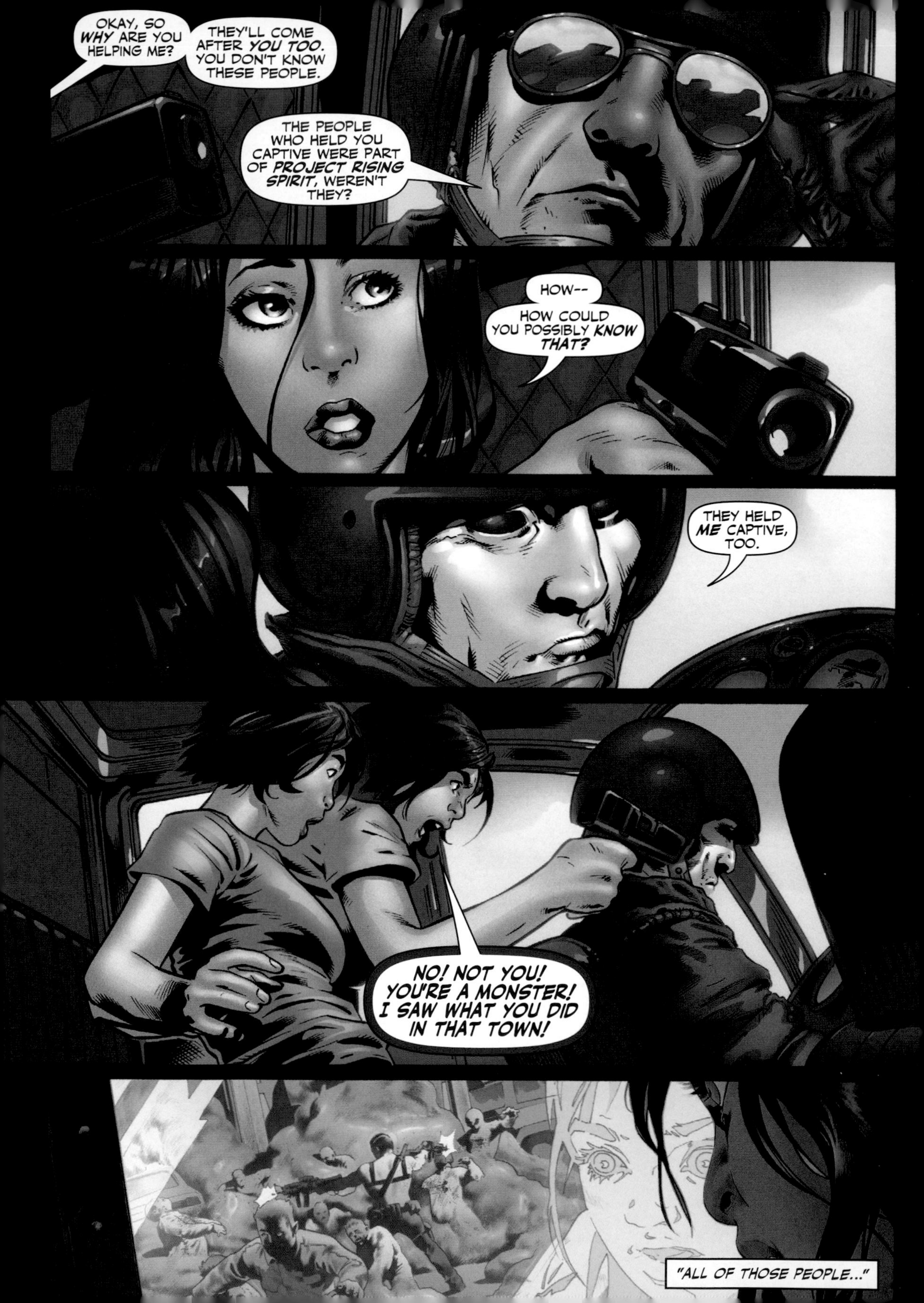
OKAY, SO WHY ARE YOU HELPING ME?
THEY'LL COME AFTER YOU TOO. YOU DON'T KNOW THESE PEOPLE.
THE PEOPLE WHO HELD YOU CAPTIVE WERE PART OF PROJECT RISING SPIRIT, WEREN'T THEY?
HOW--
HOW COULD YOU POSSIBLY KNOW THAT?
THEY HELD ME CAPTIVE, TOO.
NO! NOT YOU! YOU'RE A MONSTER! I SAW WHAT YOU DID IN THAT TOWN!
"ALL OF THOSE PEOPLE..."

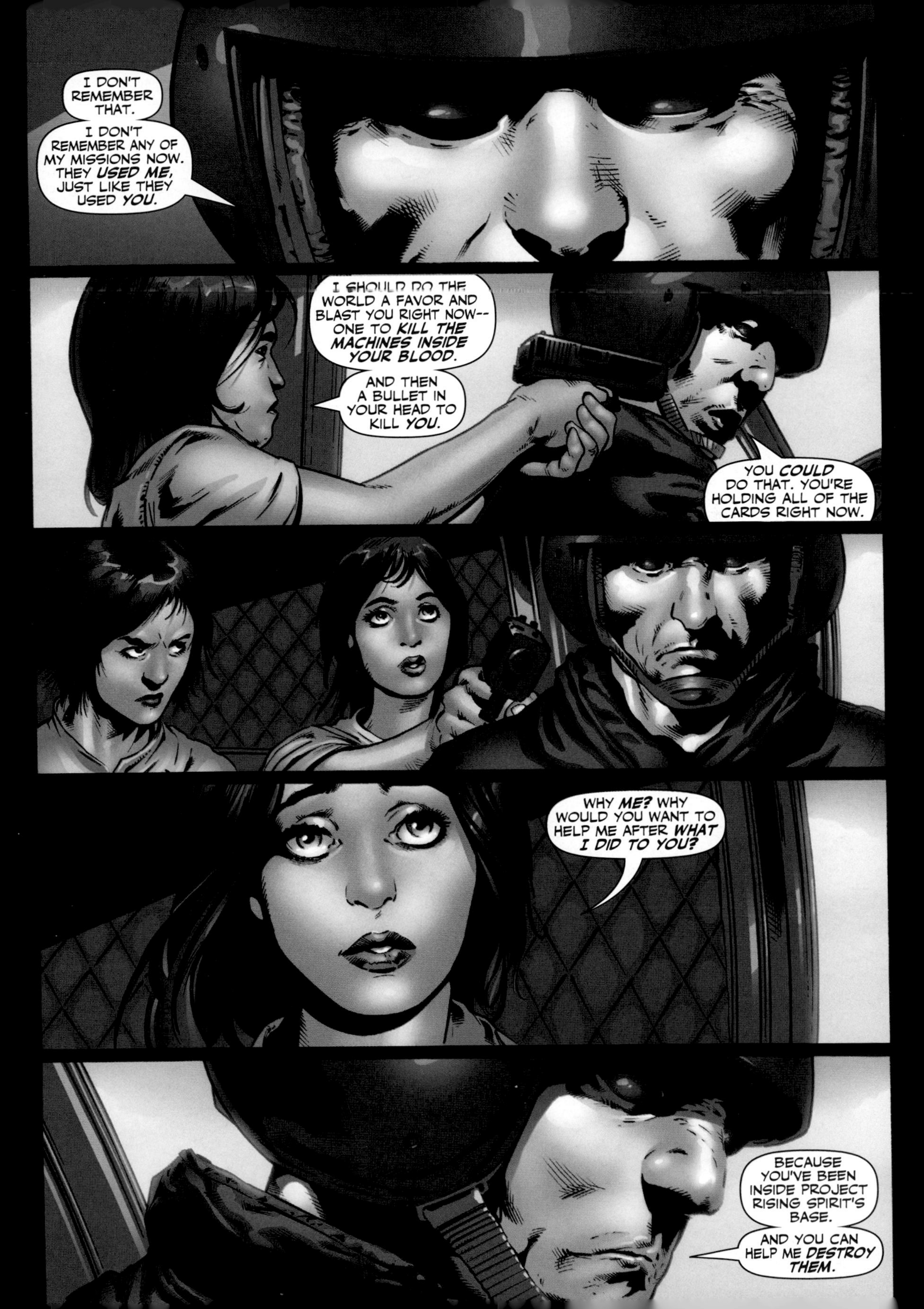
I DON'T REMEMBER THAT.
I DON'T REMEMBER ANY OF MY MISSIONS NOW. THEY USED ME, JUST LIKE THEY USED YOU.
I SHOULD DO THE WORLD A FAVOR AND BLAST YOU RIGHT NOW-- ONE TO KILL THE MACHINES INSIDE YOUR BLOOD.
AND THEN A BULLET IN YOUR HEAD TO KILL YOU.
YOU COULD DO THAT. YOU'RE HOLDING ALL OF THE CARDS RIGHT NOW.
WHY ME? WHY WOULD YOU WANT TO HELP ME AFTER WHAT I DID TO YOU?
BECAUSE YOU'VE BEEN INSIDE PROJECT RISING SPIRIT'S BASE.
AND YOU CAN HELP ME DESTROY THEM.

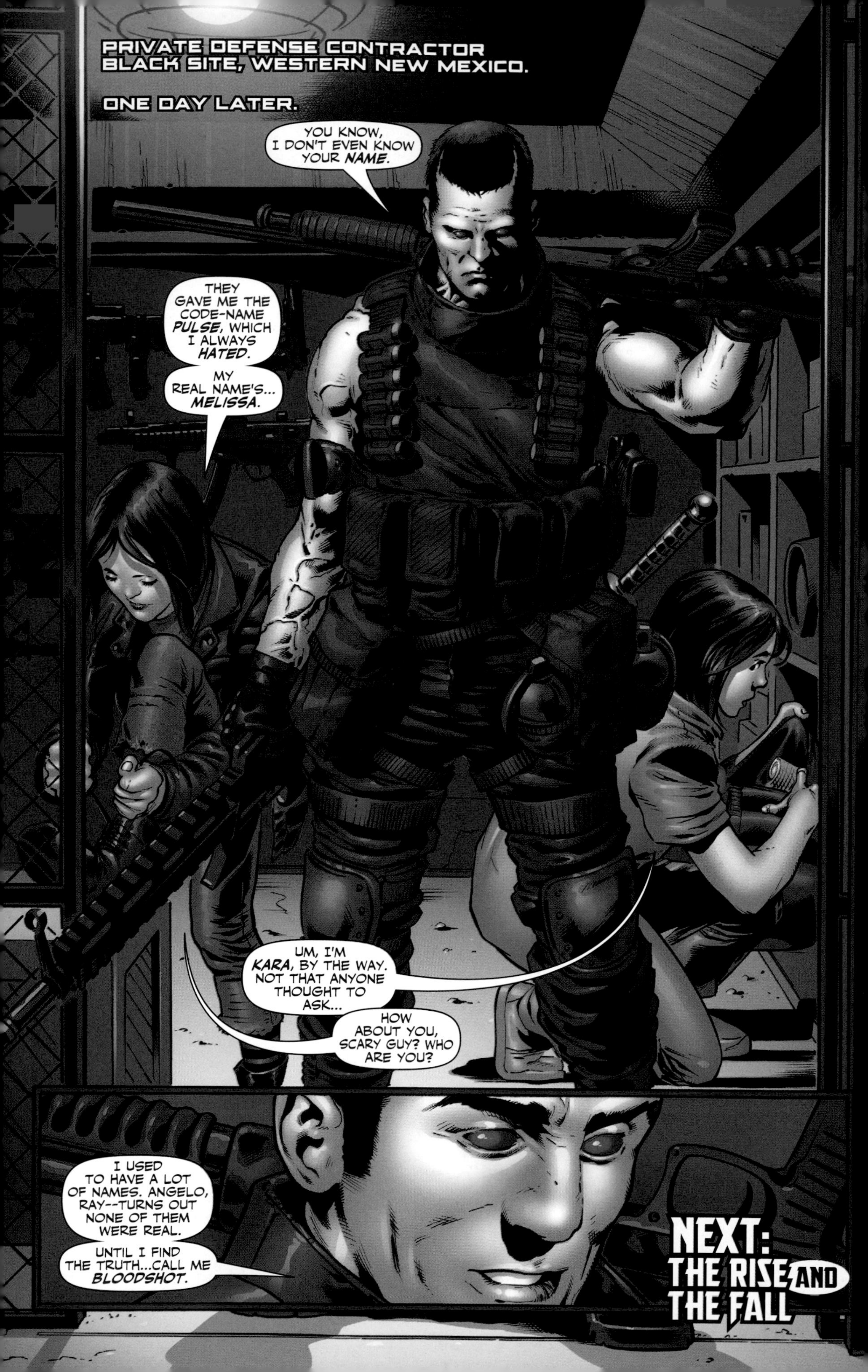
PRIVATE DEFENSE CONTRACTOR BLACK SITE, WESTERN NEW MEXICO.
ONE DAY LATER.
YOU KNOW, I DON'T EVEN KNOW YOUR NAME.
THEY GAVE ME THE CODE-NAME PULSE, WHICH I ALWAYS HATED.
MY REAL NAME'S... MELISSA.
UM, I'M KARA, BY THE WAY. NOT THAT ANYONE THOUGHT TO ASK...
HOW ABOUT YOU, SCARY GUY? WHO ARE YOU?
I USED TO HAVE A LOT OF NAMES. ANGELO, RAY--TURNS OUT NONE OF THEM WERE REAL.
UNTIL I FIND THE TRUTH...CALL ME BLOODSHOT.
NEXT: THE RISE AND THE FALL

GALLERY

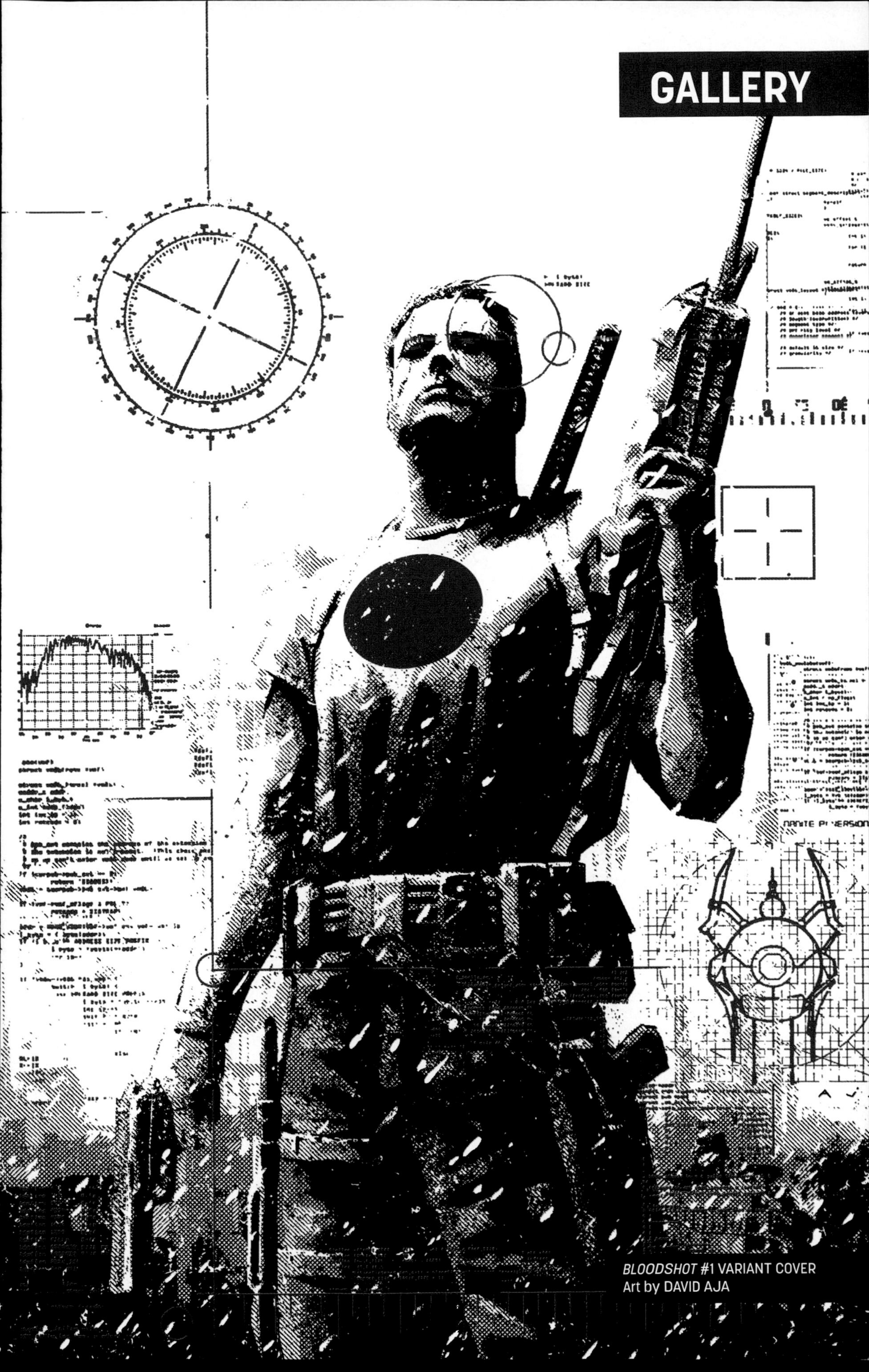

BLOODSHOT #1 VARIANT COVER
Art by DAVID AJA

BLOODSHOT #1 VARIANT COVER
Art by ESAD RIBIC

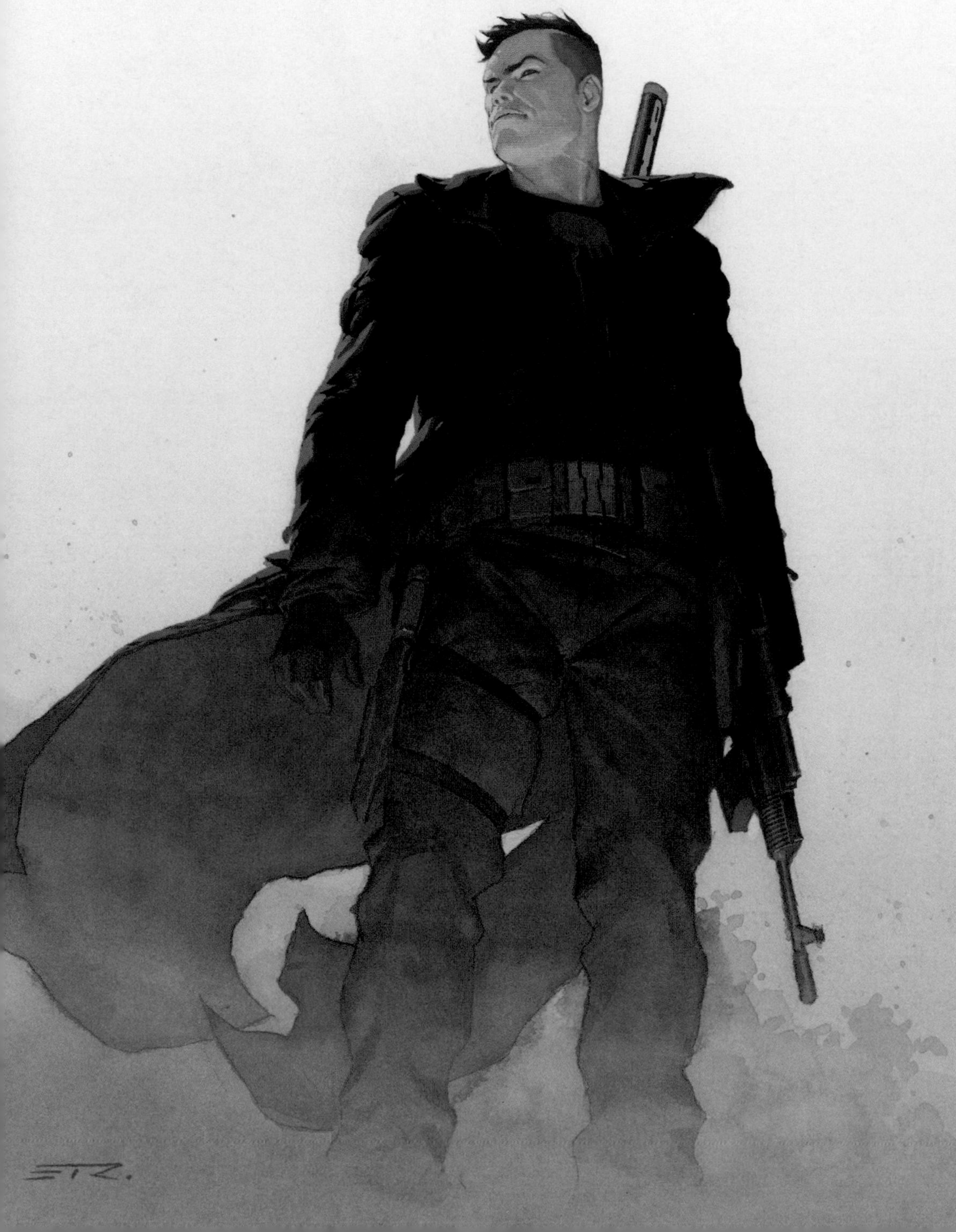

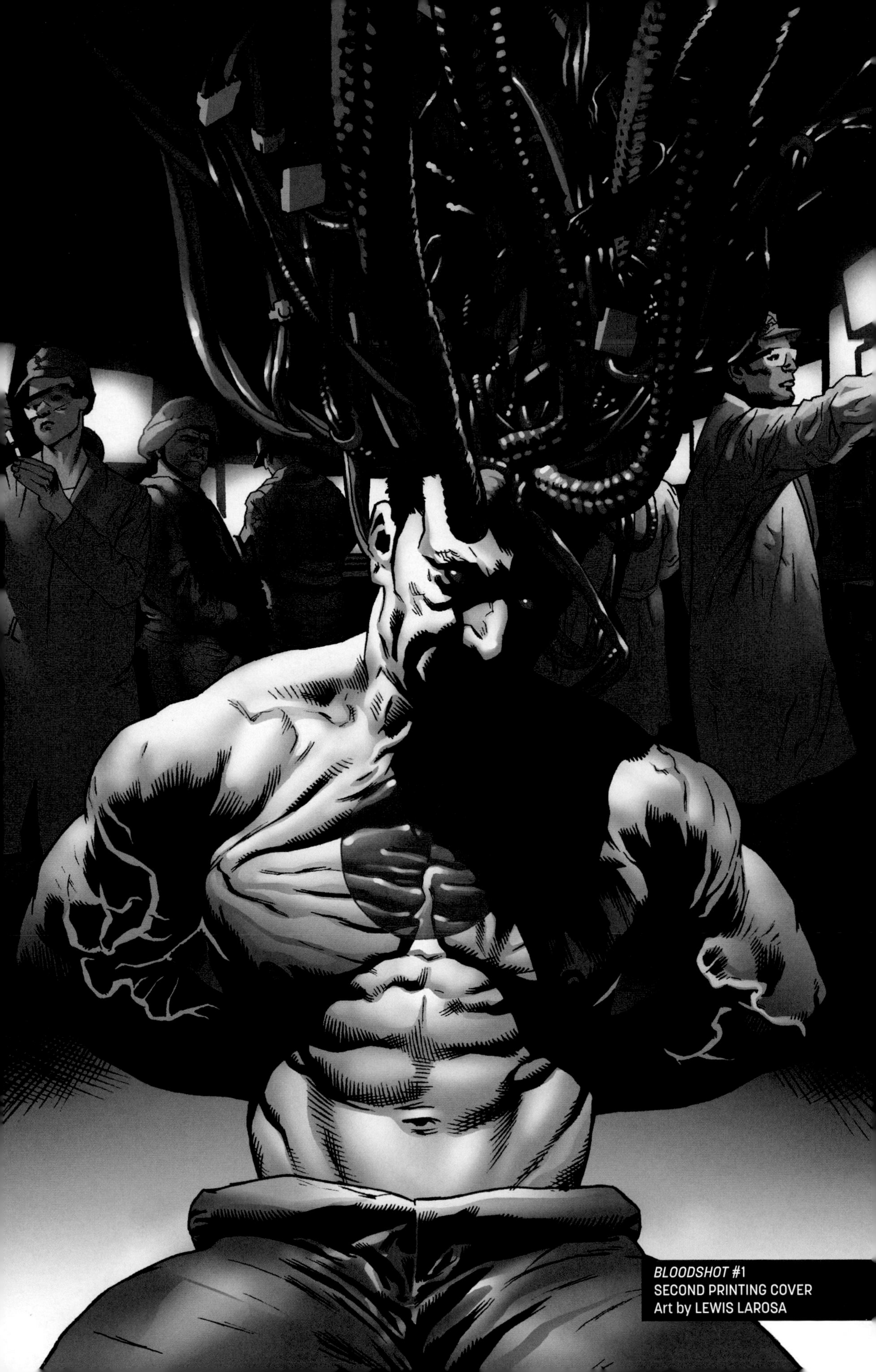

BLOODSHOT #1
SECOND PRINTING COVER
Art by LEWIS LAROSA

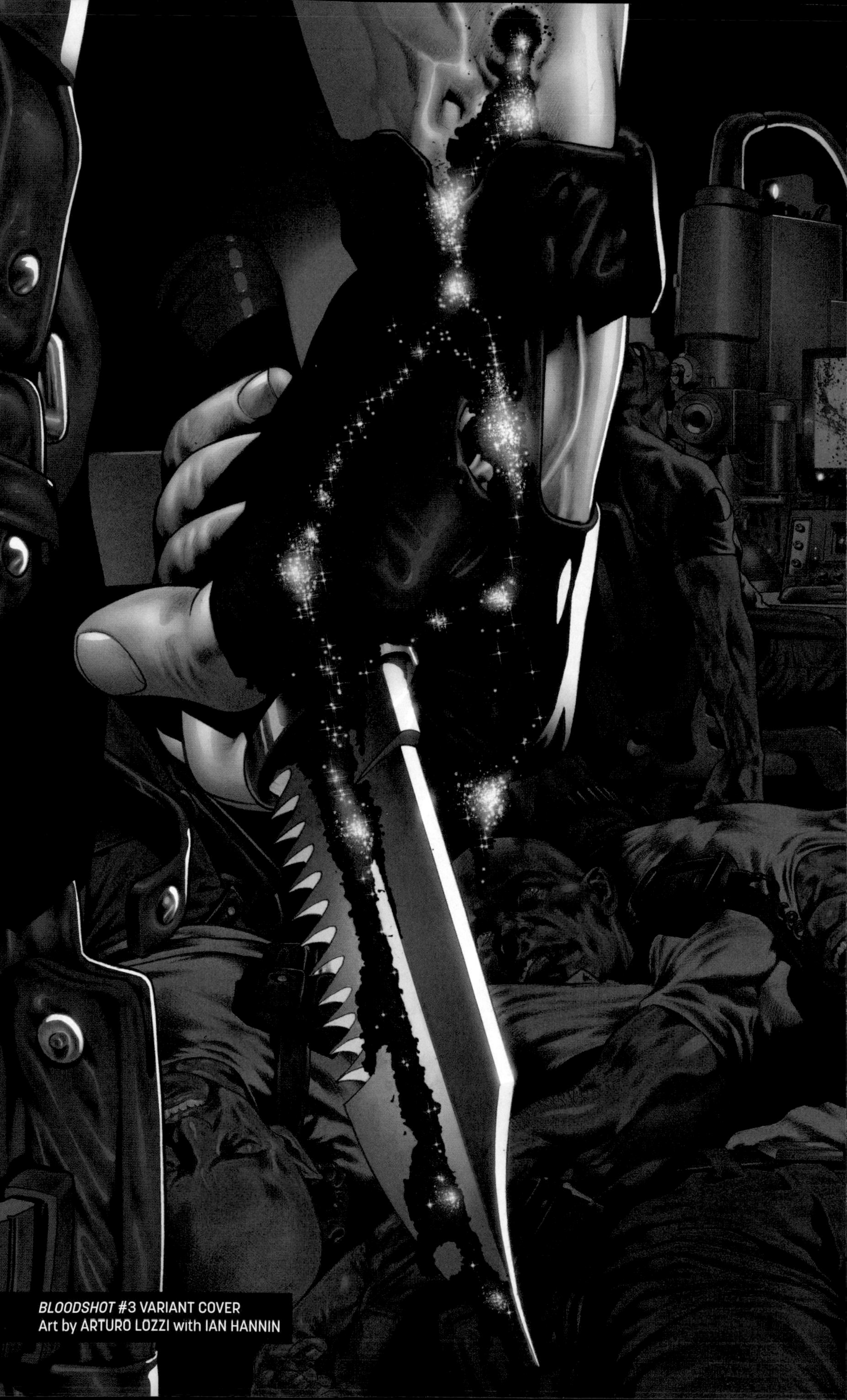

BLOODSHOT #3 VARIANT COVER
Art by ARTURO LOZZI with IAN HANNIN

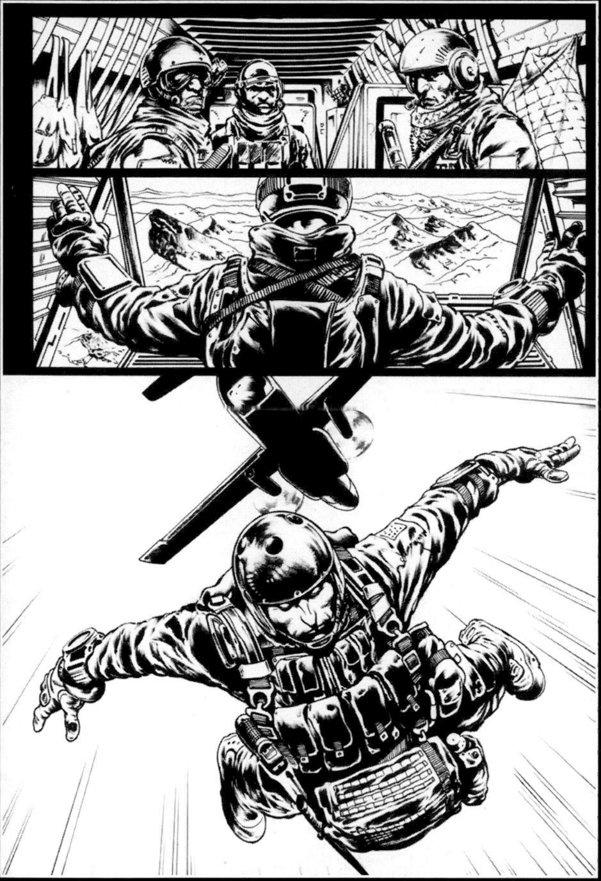

BLOODSHOT #1, p. 5
Pencils by MANUEL GARCIA
Inks by STEFANO GAUDIANO

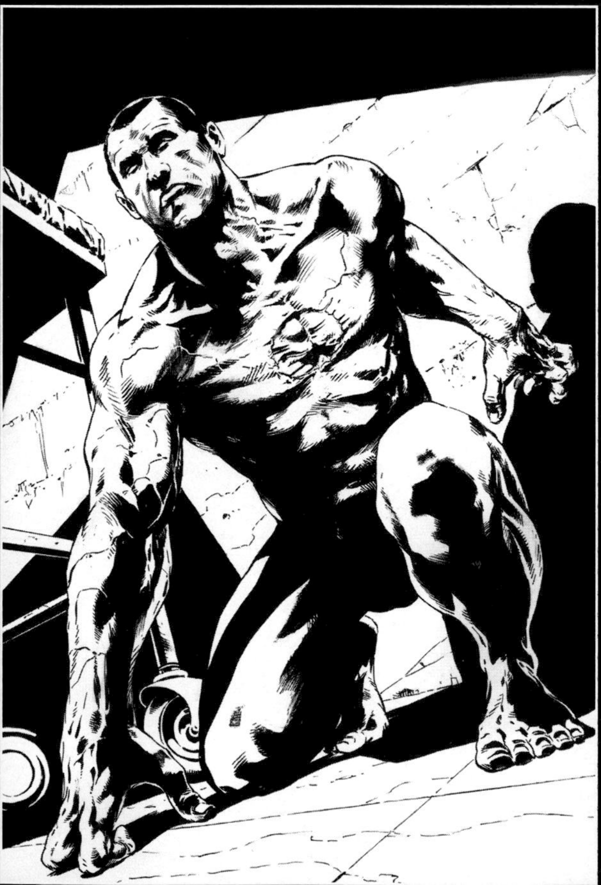

BLOODSHOT #1, p. 10
Pencils by MANUEL GARCIA
Inks by STEFANO GAUDIANO

BLOODSHOT #1, p. 11
Pencils by MANUEL GARCIA
Inks by STEFANO GAUDIANO

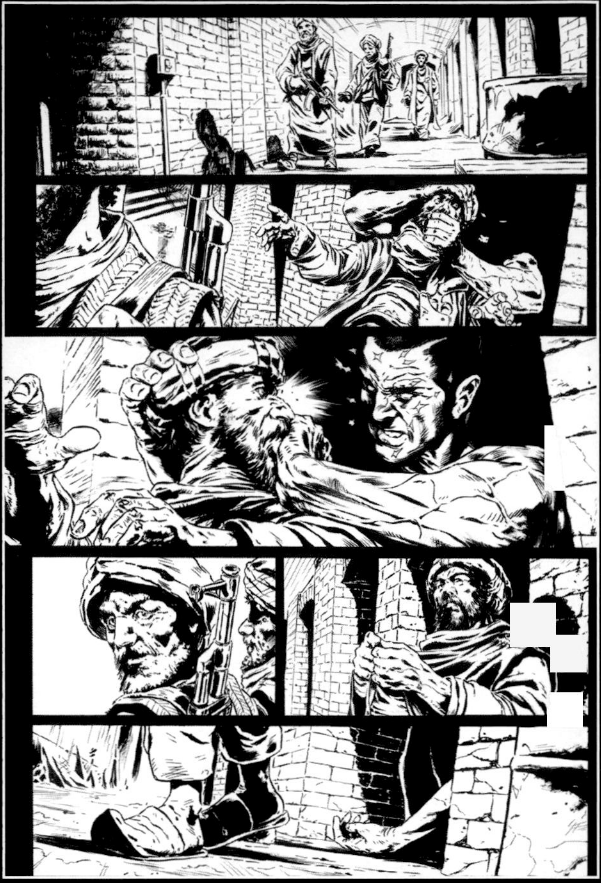

BLOODSHOT #1, p. 18
Pencils by MANUEL GARCIA
Inks by STEFANO GAUDIANO

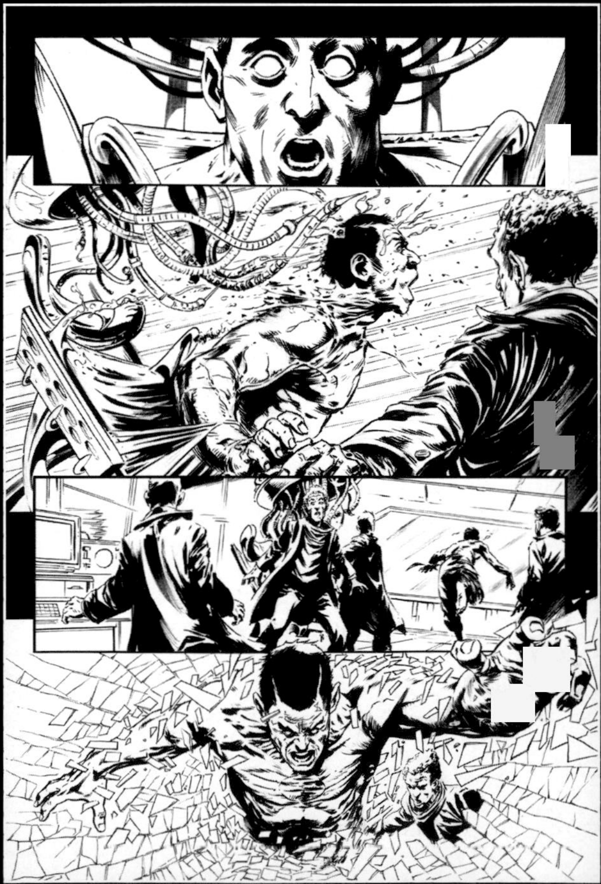

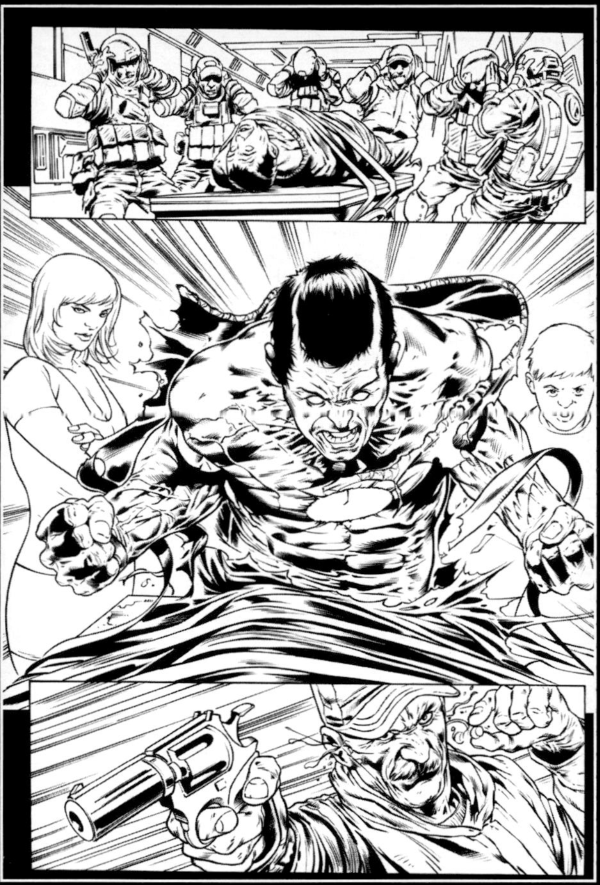

BLOODSHOT #2, p. 5
Pencils by MANUEL GARCIA
Inks by MATT RYAN

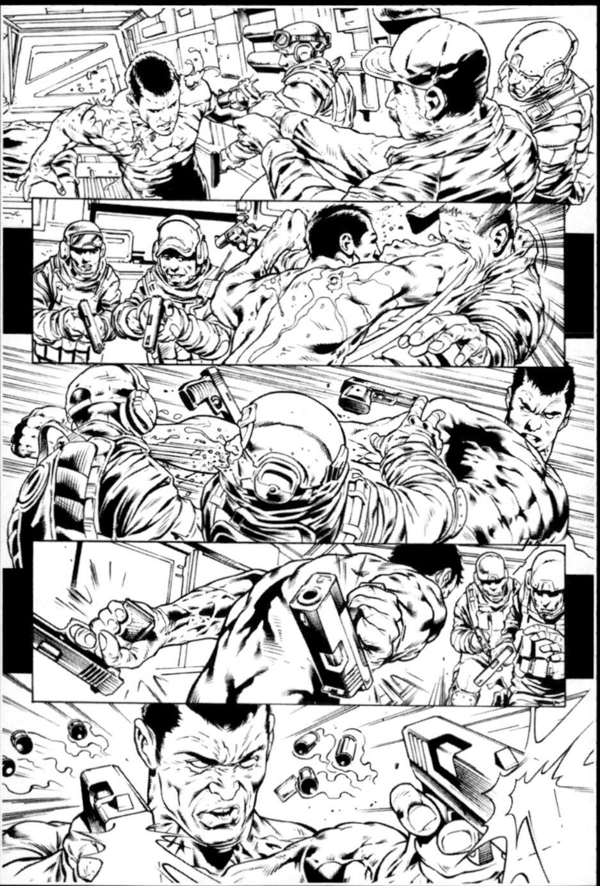

BLOODSHOT #2, p. 6
Pencils by MANUEL GARCIA
Inks by MATT RYAN

BLOODSHOT #2, p. 21
Pencils by MANUEL GARCIA
Inks by MATT RYAN

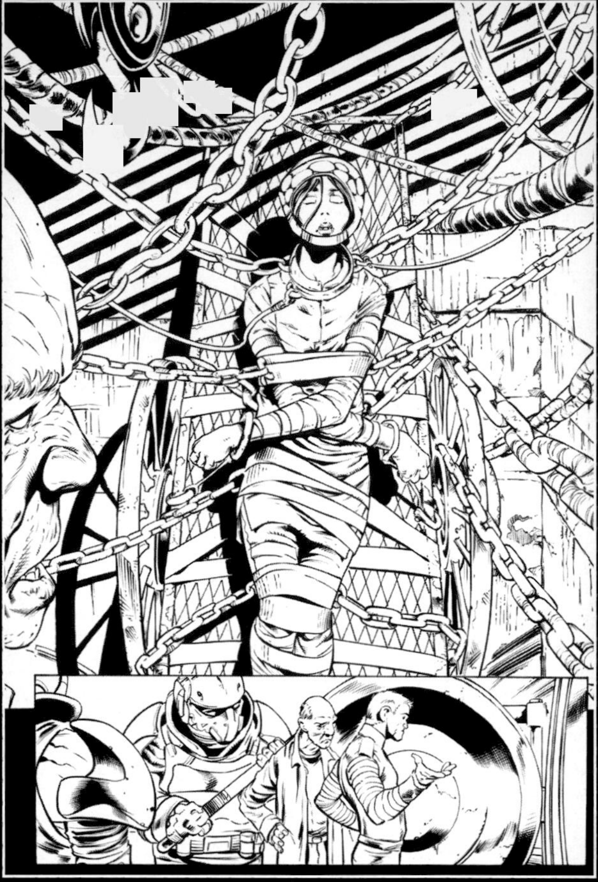

BLOODSHOT #3, p. 6
Pencils by MANUEL GARCIA
Inks by MATT RYAN

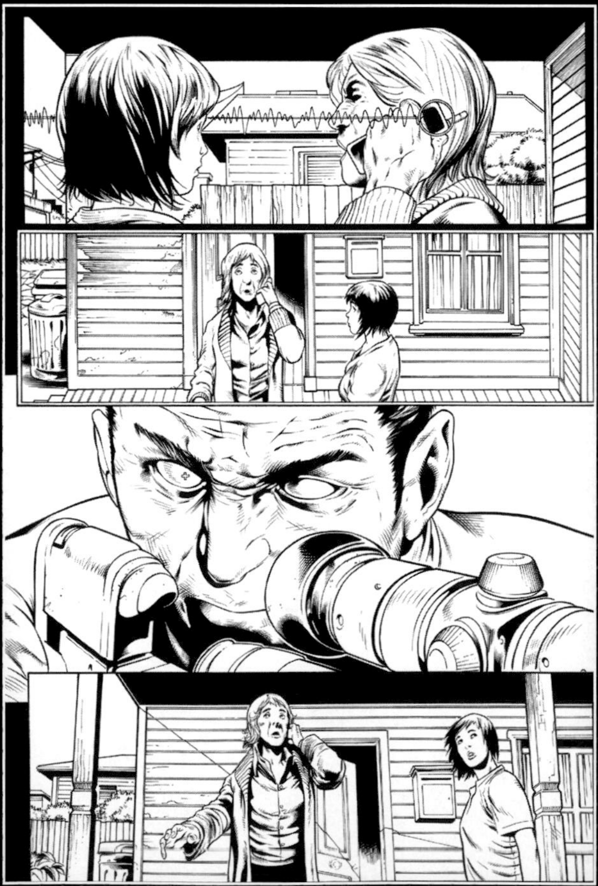

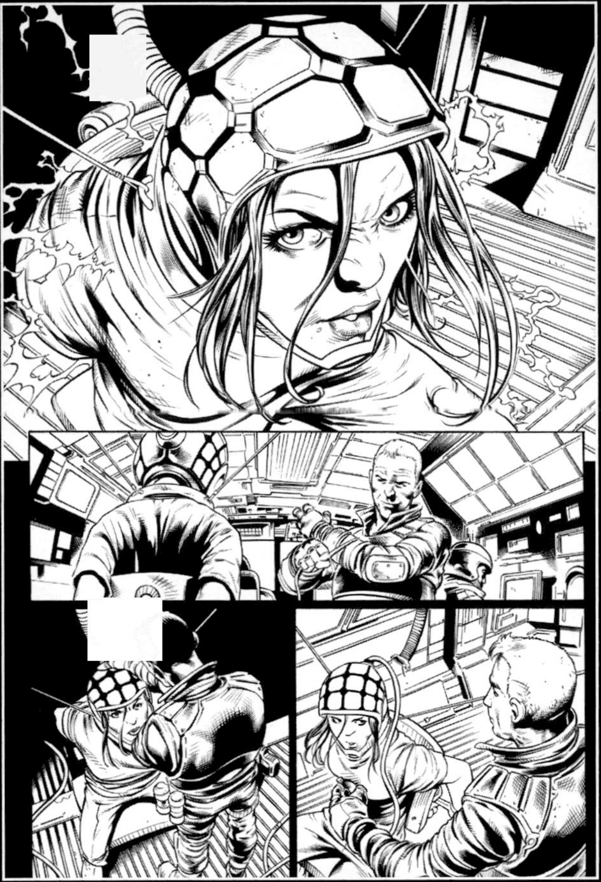

BLOODSHOT #3, p. 15
Pencils by MANUEL GARCIA
Inks by MATT RYAN

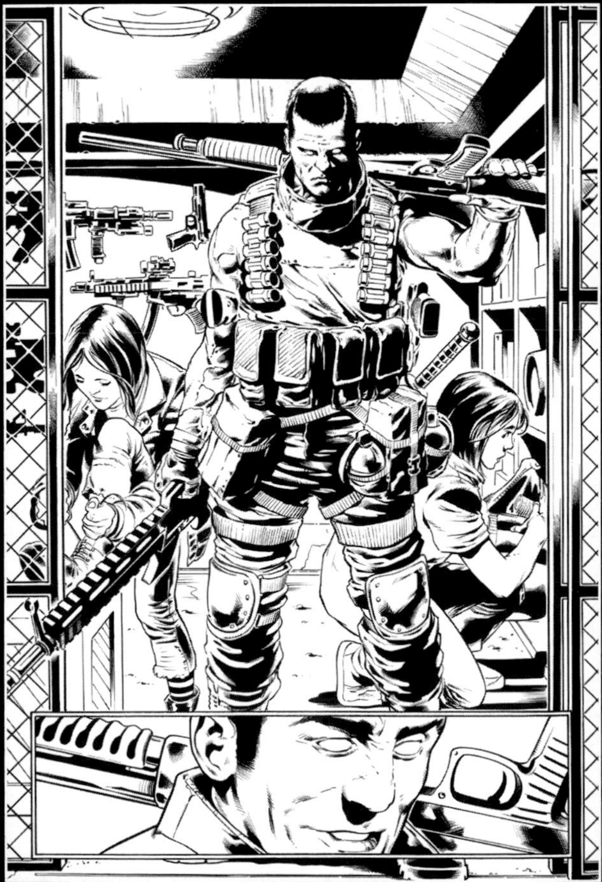

BLOODSHOT #4, p. 22
Pencils by MANUEL GARCIA
Inks by MATT RYAN

EXPLORE THE VALIANT UNIVERSE

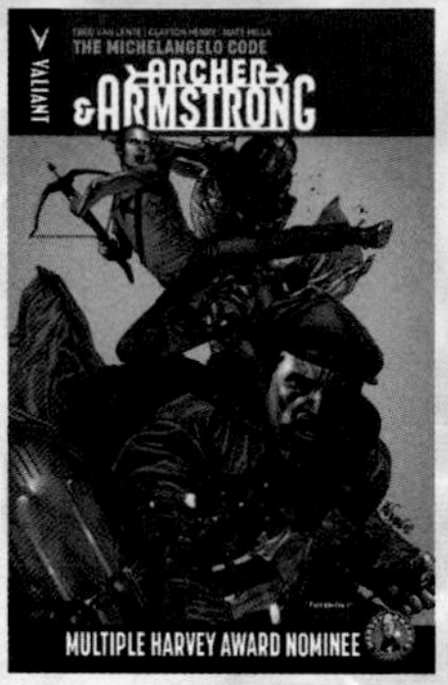
VALIANT
THE MICHELANGELO CODE
ARCHER & ARMSTRONG
MULTIPLE HARVEY AWARD NOMINEE

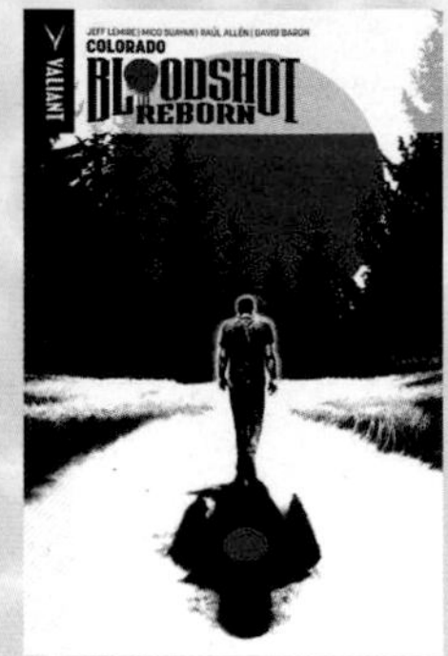
VALIANT
COLORADO
BLOODSHOT REBORN

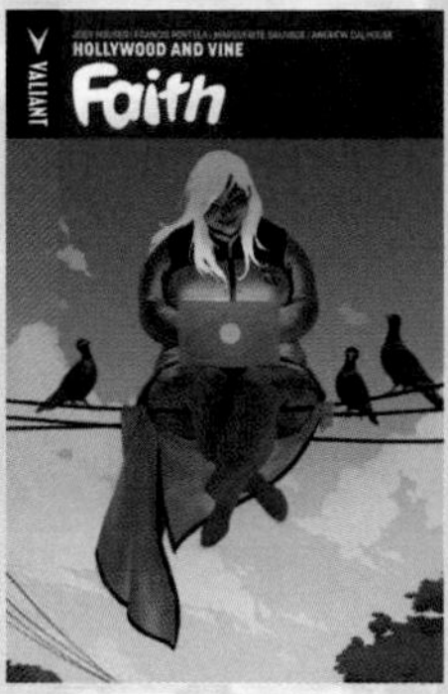
VALIANT
HOLLYWOOD AND VINE
Faith

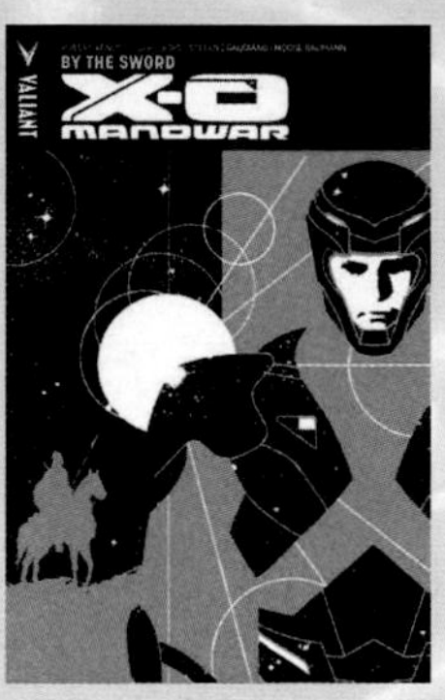
VALIANT
BY THE SWORD
X-O MANOWAR

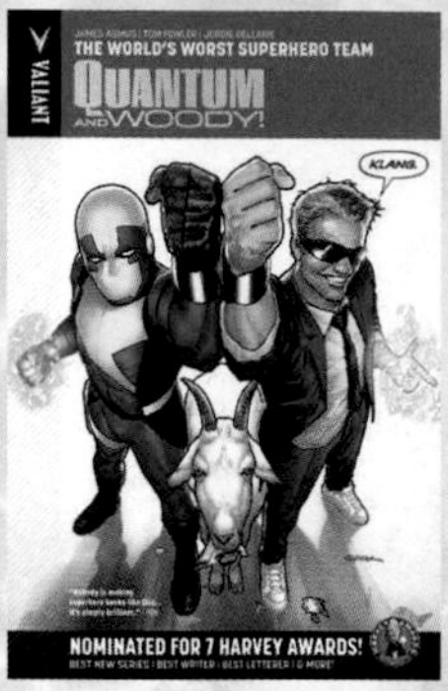
VALIANT
THE WORLD'S WORST SUPERHERO TEAM
QUANTUM AND WOODY!
NOMINATED FOR 7 HARVEY AWARDS!

ARCHER & ARMSTRONG

Volume 1: The Michelangelo Code
ISBN: 9780979640988

Volume 2: Wrath of the Eternal Warrior
ISBN: 9781939346049

Volume 3: Far Faraway
ISBN: 9781939346148

Volume 4: Sect Civil War
ISBN: 9781939346254

Volume 5: Mission: Improbable
ISBN: 9781939346353

Volume 6: American Wasteland
ISBN: 9781939346421

Volume 7: The One Percent and Other Tales
ISBN: 9781939346537

ARMOR HUNTERS

Armor Hunters
ISBN: 9781939346452

Armor Hunters: Bloodshot
ISBN: 9781939346469

Armor Hunters: Harbinger
ISBN: 9781939346506

Unity Vol. 3: Armor Hunters
ISBN: 9781939346445

X-O Manowar Vol. 7: Armor Hunters
ISBN: 9781939346476

BLOODSHOT

Volume 1: Setting the World on Fire
ISBN: 9780979640964

Volume 2: The Rise and the Fall
ISBN: 9781939346032

Volume 3: Harbinger Wars
ISBN: 9781939346124

Volume 4: H.A.R.D. Corps
ISBN: 9781939346193

Volume 5: Get Some!
ISBN: 9781939346315

Volume 6: The Glitch and Other Tales
ISBN: 9781939346711

BLOODSHOT REBORN

Volume 1: Colorado
ISBN: 9781939346674

Volume 2: The Hunt
ISBN: 9781939346827

Volume 3: The Analog Man
ISBN: 9781682151334

BOOK OF DEATH

Book of Death
ISBN: 9781939346971

Book of Death: The Fall of the Valiant Universe
ISBN: 9781939346988

DEAD DROP

ISBN: 9781939346858

THE DEATH-DEFYING DOCTOR MIRAGE

Volume 1
ISBN: 9781939346490

Volume 2: Second Lives
ISBN: 9781682151297

THE DELINQUENTS

ISBN: 9781939346513

DIVINITY

ISBN: 9781939346766

ETERNAL WARRIOR

Volume 1: Sword of the Wild
ISBN: 9781939346209

Volume 2: Eternal Emperor
ISBN: 9781939346292

Volume 3: Days of Steel
ISBN: 9781939346742

WRATH OF THE ETERNAL WARRIOR

Volume 1: Risen
ISBN: 9781682151235

FAITH

Volume 1: Hollywood and Vine
ISBN: 9781682151211

HARBINGER

Volume 1: Omega Rising
ISBN: 9780979640957

Volume 2: Renegades
ISBN: 9781939346025

Volume 3: Harbinger Wars
ISBN: 9781939346117

Volume 4: Perfect Day
ISBN: 9781939346155

Volume 5: Death of a Renegade
ISBN: 9781939346339

Volume 6: Omegas
ISBN: 9781939346384

HARBINGER WARS

Harbinger Wars
ISBN: 9781939346094

Bloodshot Vol. 3: Harbinger Wars
ISBN: 9781939346124

Harbinger Vol. 3: Harbinger Wars
ISBN: 9781939346117

EXPLORE THE VALIANT UNIVERSE

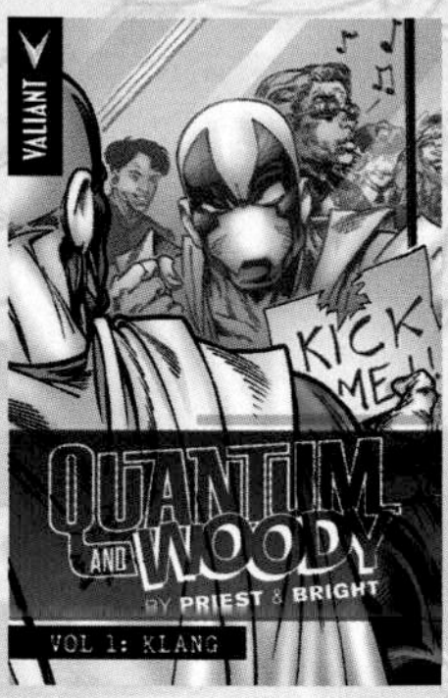
VALIANT
KICK ME!!
QUANTUM AND WOODY
BY PRIEST & BRIGHT
VOL 1: KLANG

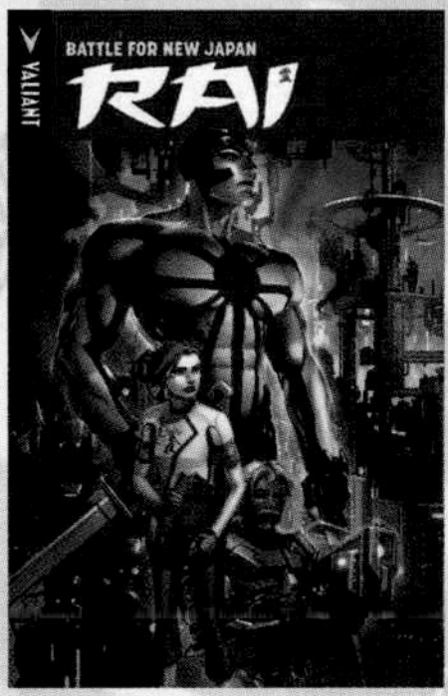
VALIANT
BATTLE FOR NEW JAPAN
RAI

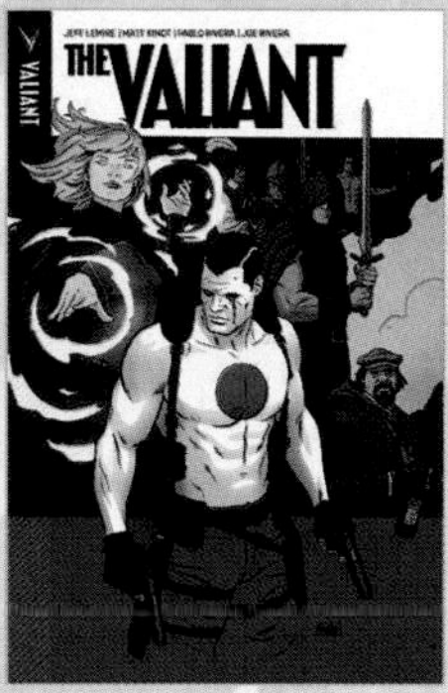
VALIANT
THE VALIANT

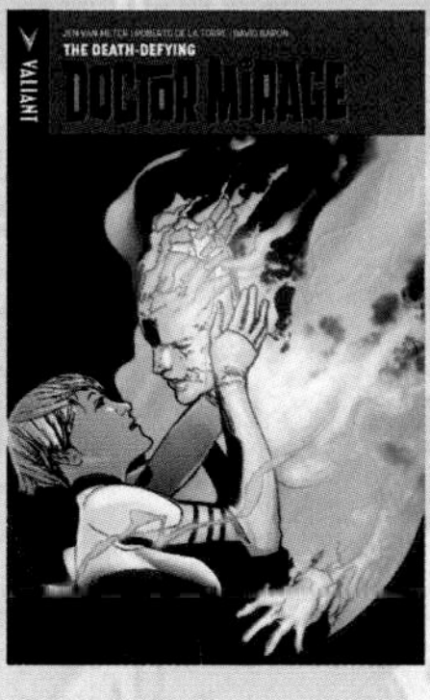
VALIANT
THE DEATH-DEFYING
DOCTOR MIRAGE

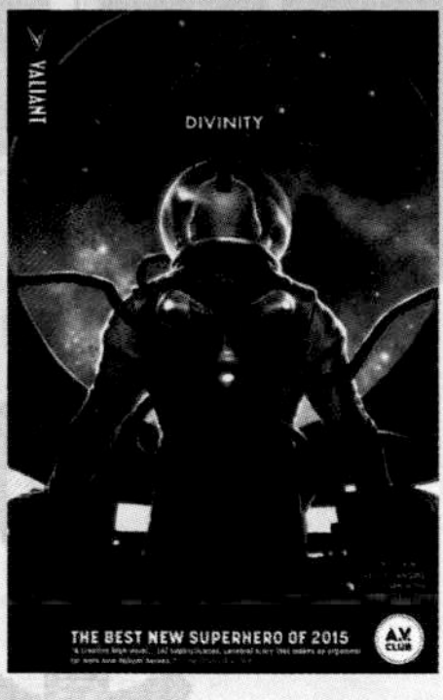
VALIANT
DIVINITY
THE BEST NEW SUPERHERO OF 2015

IMPERIUM

Volume 1: Collecting Monsters
ISBN: 9781939346759

Volume 2: Broken Angels
ISBN: 9781939346896

Volume 3: The Vine Imperative
ISBN: 9781682151112

NINJAK

Volume 1: Weaponeer
ISBN: 9781939346667

Volume 2: The Shadow Wars
ISBN: 9781939346940

Volume 3: Operation: Deadside
ISBN: 9781682151259

QUANTUM AND WOODY

Volume 1: The World's Worst Superhero Team
ISBN: 9781939346186

Volume 2: In Security
ISBN: 9781939346230

Volume 3: Crooked Pasts, Present Tense
ISBN: 9781939346391

Volume 4: Quantum and Woody Must Die!
ISBN: 9781939346629

QUANTUM AND WOODY BY PRIEST & BRIGHT

Volume 1: Klang
ISBN: 9781939346780

Volume 2: Switch
ISBN: 9781939346803

Volume 3: And So...
ISBN: 9781939346865

Volume 4: Q2 - The Return
ISBN: 9781682151099

RAI

Volume 1: Welcome to New Japan
ISBN: 9781939346414

Volume 2: Battle for New Japan
ISBN: 9781939346612

Volume 3: The Orphan
ISBN: 9781939346841

SHADOWMAN

Volume 1: Birth Rites
ISBN: 9781939346001

Volume 2: Darque Reckoning
ISBN: 9781939346056

Volume 3: Deadside Blues
ISBN: 9781939346162

Volume 4: Fear, Blood, And Shadows
ISBN: 9781939346278

Volume 5: End Times
ISBN: 9781939346377

IVAR, TIMEWALKER

Volume 1: Making History
ISBN: 9781939346636

Volume 2: Breaking History
ISBN: 9781939346834

Volume 3: Ending History
ISBN: 9781939346995

UNITY

Volume 1: To Kill a King
ISBN: 9781939346261

Volume 2: Trapped by Webnet
ISBN: 9781939346346

Volume 3: Armor Hunters
ISBN: 9781939346445

Volume 4: The United
ISBN: 9781939346544

Volume 5: Homefront
ISBN: 9781939346797

Volume 6: The War-Monger
ISBN: 9781939346902

Volume 7: Revenge of the Armor Hunters
ISBN: 9781682151136

THE VALIANT

ISBN: 9781939346605

VALIANT ZEROES AND ORIGINS

ISBN: 9781939346582

X-O MANOWAR

Volume 1: By the Sword
ISBN: 9780979640940

Volume 2: Enter Ninjak
ISBN: 9780979640995

Volume 3: Planet Death
ISBN: 9781939346087

Volume 4: Homecoming
ISBN: 9781939346179

Volume 5: At War With Unity
ISBN: 9781939346247

Volume 6: Prelude to Armor Hunters
ISBN: 9781939346407

Volume 7: Armor Hunters
ISBN: 9781939346476

Volume 8: Enter: Armorines
ISBN: 9781939346551

Volume 9: Dead Hand
ISBN: 9781939346650

Volume 10: Exodus
ISBN: 9781939346933

Volume 11: The Kill List
ISBN: 9781682151273

EXPLORE THE VALIANT UNIVERSE

VALIANT
HARBINGER
DELUXE EDITION 2

VALIANT
ARMOR HUNTERS
DELUXE EDITION

VALIANT
JIM SHOOTER : DAVID LAPHAM
CHILDREN OF THE EIGHTH DAY
HARBINGER
VALIANT MASTERS
L8-AGIN

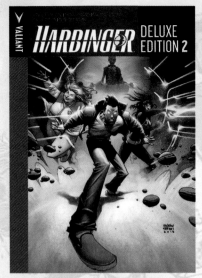

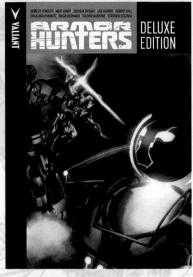

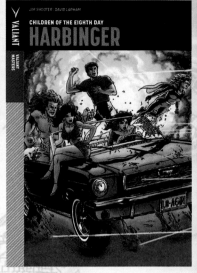

Omnibuses

Archer & Armstrong: The Complete Classic Omnibus
ISBN: 9781939346872
Collecting ARCHER & ARMSTRONG (1992) #0-26, ETERNAL WARRIOR (1992) #25 along with ARCHER & ARMSTRONG: THE FORMATION OF THE SECT.

Quantum and Woody: The Complete Classic Omnibus
ISBN: 9781939346360
Collecting QUANTUM AND WOODY (1997) #0, 1-21 and #32, THE GOAT: H.A.E.D.U.S. #1, and X-O MANOWAR (1996) #16

X-O Manowar Classic Omnibus Vol. 1
ISBN: 9781939346308
Collecting X-O MANOWAR (1992) #0-30, ARMORINES #0, X-O DATABASE #1, as well as material from SECRETS OF THE VALIANT UNIVERSE #1

Deluxe Editions

Archer & Armstrong Deluxe Edition Book 1
ISBN: 9781939346223
Collecting ARCHER & ARMSTRONG #0-13

Archer & Armstrong Deluxe Edition Book 2
ISBN: 9781939346957
Collecting ARCHER & ARMSTRONG #14-25, ARCHER & ARMSTRONG: ARCHER #0 and BLOODSHOT AND H.A.R.D. CORPS #20-21.

Armor Hunters Deluxe Edition
ISBN: 9781939346728
Collecting Armor Hunters #1-4, Armor Hunters: Aftermath #1, Armor Hunters: Bloodshot #1-3, Armor Hunters: Harbinger #1-3, Unity #8-11, and X-O MANOWAR #23-29

Bloodshot Deluxe Edition Book 1
ISBN: 9781939346216
Collecting BLOODSHOT #1-13

Bloodshot Deluxe Edition Book 2
ISBN: 9781939346810
Collecting BLOODSHOT AND H.A.R.D. CORPS #14-23, BLOODSHOT #24-25, BLOODSHOT #0, BLOODSHOT AND H.A.R.D. CORPS: H.A.R.D. CORPS #0, along with ARCHER & ARMSTRONG #18-19

Book of Death Deluxe Edition
ISBN: 9781682151150
Collecting BOOK OF DEATH #1-4, BOOK OF DEATH: THE FALL OF BLOODSHOT #1, BOOK OF DEATH: THE FALL OF NINJAK #1, BOOK OF DEATH: THE FALL OF HARBINGER #1, and BOOK OF DEATH: THE FALL OF X-O MANOWAR #1.

Divinity Deluxe Edition
ISBN: 97819393460993
Collecting DIVNITY #1-4

Harbinger Deluxe Edition Book 1
ISBN: 9781939346131
Collecting HARBINGER #0-14

Harbinger Deluxe Edition Book 2
ISBN: 9781939346773
Collecting HARBINGER #15-25, HARBINGER: OMEGAS #1-3, and HARBINGER: BLEEDING MONK #0

Harbinger Wars Deluxe Edition
ISBN: 9781939346322
Collecting HARBINGER WARS #1-4, HARBINGER #11-14, and BLOODSHOT #10-13

Ivar, Timewalker Deluxe Edition Book 1
ISBN: 9781682151198
Collecting IVAR, TIMEWALKER #1-12

Quantum and Woody Deluxe Edition Book 1
ISBN: 9781939346681
Collecting QUANTUM AND WOODY #1-12 and QUANTUM AND WOODY: THE GOAT #0

Q2: The Return of Quantum and Woody Deluxe Edition
ISBN: 9781939346568
Collecting Q2: THE RETURN OF QUANTUM AND WOODY #1-5

Rai Deluxe Edition Book 1
ISBN: 9781682151174
Collecting RAI #1-12, along with material from RAI #1 PLUS EDITION and RAI #5 PLUS EDITION

Shadowman Deluxe Edition Book 1
ISBN: 9781939346438
Collecting SHADOWMAN #0-10

Shadowman Deluxe Edition Book 2
ISBN: 9781682151075
Collecting SHADOWMAN #11-16, SHADOWMAN #13X, SHADOWMAN: END TIMES #1-3 and PUNK MAMBO #0

Unity Deluxe Edition Book 1
ISBN: 9781939346575
Collecting UNITY #0-14

The Valiant Deluxe Edition
ISBN: 97819393460986
Collecting THE VALIANT #1-4

X-O Manowar Deluxe Edition Book 1
ISBN: 9781939346100
Collecting X-O MANOWAR #1-14

X-O Manowar Deluxe Edition Book 2
ISBN: 9781939346520
Collecting X-O MANOWAR #15-22, and UNITY #1-4

X-O Manowar Deluxe Edition Book 3
ISBN: 9781682151310
Collecting X-O MANOWAR #23-29 and ARMOR HUNTERS #1-4.

Valiant Masters

Bloodshot Vol. 1 - Blood of the Machine
ISBN: 9780979640933

H.A.R.D. Corps Vol. 1 - Search and Destroy
ISBN: 9781939346285

Harbinger Vol. 1 - Children of the Eighth Day
ISBN: 9781939346483

Ninjak Vol. 1 - Black Water
ISBN: 9780979640971

Rai Vol. 1 - From Honor to Strength
ISBN: 9781939346070

Shadowman Vol. 1 - Spirits Within
ISBN: 9781939346018

BLOODSHOT READING ORDER

DUANE SWIERCZYNSKI | MANUEL GARCIA | ARTURO LOZZI
SETTING THE WORLD ON FIRE
BLOODSHOT
VALIANT

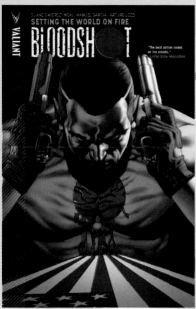

Bloodshot Vol. 1: Setting the World on Fire

THE RISE AND THE FALL
BLOODSHOT
VALIANT

Bloodshot Vol. 2:
The Rise and the Fall

HARBINGER WARS
BLOODSHOT
VALIANT

Bloodshot Vol. 3:
Harbinger Wars

HARBINGER
WARS

Harbinger Wars
(OPTIONAL)

H.A.R.D. CORPS
BLOODSHOT
VALIANT

Bloodshot Vol. 4:
H.A.R.D. Corps

Archer & Armstrong Vol. 5:
Mission: Improbable
(OPTIONAL)

GET SOME!
BLOODSHOT
VALIANT

Bloodshot Vol. 5:
Get Some!

BLOODSHOT

Armor Hunters:
Bloodshot
(OPTIONAL)

THE GLITCH AND OTHER TALES
BLOODSHOT
VALIANT

Bloodshot Vol. 6: The
Glitch and Other Tales

THE VALIANT

The Valiant
(OPTIONAL)

COLORADO
BLOODSHOT
REBORN
VALIANT

Bloodshot Reborn Vol. 1:
Colorado

THE HUNT
BLOODSHOT
REBORN
VALIANT

Bloodshot Reborn Vol. 2:
The Hunt

THE ANALOG MAN
BLOODSHOT
REBORN
VALIANT

Bloodshot Reborn Vol. 3:
The Analog Man

**"Absolutely amazing...
You won't be disappointed."**
– IGN

**"The best action comic
on the stands."**
– Comic Book Resources

An action packed and unpredictable odyssey
from New York Times best-selling writers
DUANE SWIERCZYNSKI
and **JOSHUA DYSART**
With acclaimed artists
**MANUEL GARCIA, LEWIS LAROSA,
EMANUELA LUPACCHINO,** and more!

BLOODSHOT

VOLUME TWO: THE RISE AND THE FALL

ASSAULT ON PROJECT RISING SPIRIT!

Bloodshot is finally free of the memories that have haunted him since his awakening – but now even greater mysteries remain. Who was he before he was transformed into a walking weapon of mass destruction? And does he have a real family out there somewhere? Unfortunately, the only man with the answers is the former mastermind of Project Rising Spirit, the quasi-governmental science division that created him – and he's just struck a devil's bargain with Bloodshot. "Destroy your creators and I'll reveal everything." Well, almost everything...

BLOODSHOT VOL. 2: THE RISE AND THE FALL

Collecting **BLOODSHOT #5-9** by acclaimed writer Duane Swierczynski (*Birds of Prey*) and artists Manuel Garcia (*Black Widow*), Arturo Lozzi (*Immortal Weapons*), and Matthew Clark (*Avenging Spider-Man*), Bloodshot's brutal, bullet-riddled tour of duty through the Valiant Universe continues right here in the second shock-inducing volume of the series that Complex calls "hard and heavy with each issue."

TRADE PAPERBACK
ISBN. 978-1-939346-03-2

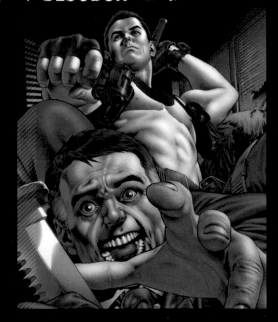

DUANE SWIERCZYNSKI | MANUEL GARCIA | ARTURO LOZZI | MATTHEW CLARK

THE RISE AND THE FALL

BLOODSH T